CONVERSATIONS WITH CASALS

Prades: The morning walk with "Follet"

CONVERSATIONS

WITH

CASALS

J. MA. CORREDOR

Translated from the French by
ANDRÉ MANGEOT

With an Introduction by
PABLO CASALS

And an appreciation by
THOMAS MANN

Illustrated

New York
E. P. DUTTON & CO., INC.

INTRODUCTION BY PABLO CASALS

Prades, 28th April, 1954.

Dear friend,

I have just read the manuscript of the friendly conversations we had together, and I congratulate you most sincerely on the diligence and faithfulness with which you have gathered them together.

I am astonished at the proportions your work has assumed! While we talked, I had not realized that our conversations would stretch into a long book. But you were evidently bent on collecting all my memories, on comparing my opinions with those of other musicians, and on exactly determining my moral position in relation to the failures of our times. How much patience and good-will you have shown!

Reading your book has awakened many thoughts in my mind which it would perhaps be out of place to record here: you would have to start a new chapter—discussions on our discussions—and where would that lead us? On the whole, I think it better to leave the reader to his own reactions and judgments. Our talks were free from mental reservations of any kind, and it would be useless to overload this letter of introduction with them.

I quite foresee that some of my views on music are liable to cause controversy, even impassioned controversy. To every man his convictions. Every point of view is worthy of respect, so long as it is sincere and genuine. I should add only that I remain faithful to the human values of music, and that for me art and life remain inseparable. As a student, I used to be fascinated by drops of dew on a wild flower, and felt that here, for any artist, was source of inspiration and inexhaustible matter for reflection. Even now, each morning, before renewing contact with Bach's immortal message, I open my window and in contemplating the symphony of colours on the peak of Canigou I feel the same need to adore. I thank Providence that years and disillusions have never blunted my natural power to wonder.

I am well aware that the attitude I have adopted in recent years has been the object of much comment, some of it revealing, to a more or less justified extent, a lack of knowledge of the facts. It may be that your book will help to dispel some of these misunderstandings. I sincerely hope it will. I see you mention the crisis through which I passed when I was 16, which led me to the edge of the abyss. At heart, I haven't changed. I still feel free estranged from injustice and brutality; I still have the same need to protest against any attack on the dignity of man. The only difference, alas, is that whereas injustice and brutality have spread more and more widely since my young days, the desire to protest is becoming steadily more and more blunted. How sad a sight it is—this guilty and deplorable indifference of our times!

My dear friend, once more let me congratulate you, and also assure you of all my affection,

Yours,
PABLO CASALS.

A LETTER FROM THOMAS MANN

Sir,

My opinion of Pablo Casals? I have no opinion, only profound respect and joyful admiration for a man whose art, for all its impetuousness, is allied to a rigid refusal to compromise with wrong, with anything that is morally squalid or offensive to justice—and this in a way which ennobles and broadens our understanding of the artist, placing him out of reach of our irony and setting an example, in our corrupt times, of proud incorruptible integrity. Here is no hint of escapism, no neutral attitudes to human problems. No trace either of that tendency, so common in the precious little world of artists, to prostitute oneself by admitting that "He who pays the piper calls the tune".

A fantastic talent, sought after and assured of overwhelming success all over the world, offered fortunes to harness itself to business arrangements, but laying down its own conditions, which have nothing to do with either money or success.

This great creative artist will set foot in no country where liberty and right are not respected. Nor will he go to those countries which call themselves free, but make opportunist deals with injustice. He withholds his genius from a world which, though steeped in wrong, would still like the aesthetic pleasure of hearing him—notably from Spain, the land of his birth. He no longer accepts invitations or leaves the village near the Franco-Spanish frontier which he has chosen as his refuge—Prades. This name, almost unknown till linked with his, has become universally known as a symbol of art devoid of all compromise—of the unbreakable union of art and morality.

A victorious union, for the hermit's mountain retreat has become the shrine of pious pilgrims from all over the world. Yes, the world crowds to the man who withdrew from the world, and the Prades Festivals have grown quite as much from the magnetism of a great character as from the musical enthusiasm which, in these circumstances, also inevitably becomes a protest against the rule of wrong.

iii

What a triumph. What a reassuring satisfaction. The human race, in its frailty, has always needed men to save its honour. This artist is one of them, one of those who come to the rescue of humanity's honour. I am happy to place on record that for me, as for thousands of others, his existence is a source of joy.

(Translated from French.)

Erlenbach-Zürich, March 1954.

CONTENTS

LIST OF ILLUSTRATIONS

PREFACE

This small room, which serves the dual purpose of bedroom and study in a pretty little house in Prades, is very well known to me. For several years I have spent most Sunday afternoons there, going with various friends to visit Maestro Pau Casals.

Our illustrious fellow-countryman would welcome us with unvarying warmth and friendliness, sitting in his patriarchal armchair in front of a table covered with books and papers—and, of course, pipes and tobacco.

More and more papers, on the table, on an old piano, sometimes on chairs and sometimes on the bed, which is occupied at night by the Master and in the daytime by his 'cello. Why all these papers? Simply because this artist, who is known all over the world, conceives it his moral obligation to answer all letters—and goodness only knows how many he gets!

For many years he has made a point not only of answering every letter, but also of writing the answers in his own hand. One day I begged him to let me help, because this preoccupation with a mounting volume of correspondence seemed to me a sad waste of his time and energy. Casals showed his appreciation of my offer by his acceptance of it.

From then onwards I would spend a few hours once or twice every week in this little room, open in summer to birdsong from neighbouring gardens and in winter to the sound of the tramontana sweeping down from the snow-topped Canigou. While I was taking the great man's instructions as to how to deal with some—only some—of his mail, I found it impossible not to question him about his memories and opinions, and he would talk with that simplicity and charm so well known to his friends. It occurred to me then to take notes also of his answers to my questions, with the idea of arranging them and later on incorporating them in a book. When told of my project Casals whole-heartedly agreed to it, a token of confidence for which I am profoundly grateful, and which I hope my work will have justified.

So much for the origins of this book. From what has been said above it follows that my task can be summed up in the one word "fidelity" (so great is the responsibility that I could not think of showing the manuscript to a publisher without Casals having first seen it); fidelity in collecting the material and in arranging it without distortion of content or style, that is to say, directly and informally. Readers must not be surprised, therefore, if I seem not to allow Casals to digress at length, if I sometimes confine myself only to his negations or affirmations, or if in transcribing his words I include those spontaneous remarks and colloquialisms which would be out of place in a lecture but which make a conversation more vivid. My aim is that anyone reading these pages should share as much as is possible in the intimate atmosphere of their origins.

It is not for me to talk of the position Pau[1] Casals occupies in the world of music. Since that October day in 1899 when Charles Lamoureux "dubbed" him "Knight of the Order of the Violoncello, now and hereafter", his art and his sincerity have been sung from every roof-top. The comments below are reproduced in virtue of their authors' standing.

Eugène Ysaye: Casals is truly sensitive and profound, a musician in the deepest sense of the word. Not a single detail is neglected, everything is defined with delicacy, knowledge and discrimination. In him action is the direct outcome of thought and is true, vibrant and deeply moving.

Fritz Kreisler: The monarch of the bow.

Wilhelm Furtwängler: Those who have never heard Pablo Casals have no idea how a string instrument can sound. This is a unique synthesis of material and spiritual beauty.

Alfred Cortot: He is not only the greatest musical interpreter of his own generation, he is also its most finished spiritual representative, enhancing with an uncompromising nobility of character the miraculous privilege of those gifts of perception which enabled him from the first, with the seal of his contemporaries' wondering respect, to penetrate the deepest secrets of his art and to communicate with incomparable eloquence and sensibility the most sublime expressions of great minds.

Jacques Thibaud: One of the purest talents in music, Pablo Casals will always have my deepest admiration and dearest affection.

[1] "Pau" is the Catalan version of the Castilian "Pablo".

Auguste Mangeot (1909): Of all musical interpreters Casals is assuredly the only one in the world who is not argued about.

Sir Donald Tovey: The greatest musician I have known since Joachim.

Isaac Stern: All my life I shall treasure the musical stimulus of these concerts I have given with you and the days I have spent near you.

Diran Alexanian: Casals has revealed the quintessence of the violoncello as no-one has yet been able to do. He has become the model with which everything is compared.

We would like to take this opportunity of expressing our gratitude for the opinions reproduced below, which were sent direct by the people concerned.

Albert Schweitzer: You ask me my opinion of Casals? He is a great musician in all he does: a 'cellist without equal, an extraordinary conductor and a composer with something to say. I have been profoundly impressed by all I have heard of his work; but he is a musician of this stature because he is also a great man. As I write to you I feel a profound regret at not having been able to come to Prades during the last few years, to be with him and to get to know him still better. Fortunately, I had some splendid days with him in Edinburgh, when we were both guests of Tovey.

Albert Einstein: It is certainly unnecessary to await my voice in acclaiming Pablo Casals as a very great artist, since all who are qualified to speak are unanimous on this subject. What I particularly admire in him is the firm stand he has taken, not only against the oppressors of his countrymen, but also against those opportunists who are always ready to compromise with the Devil. He perceives very clearly that the world is in greater peril from those who tolerate or encourage evil than from those who actually commit it.

Vincent Auriol: This summer I shall go to Prades in order to applaud Pablo Casals and celebrate with all his admirers his art and his humanity, which are equally so great. Having renounced the glory which still awaits him through the world, he prefers to watch from the doors of his native land, in his solitude and with his dreams and his art! What a magnificent example of nobility, dignity, and human pride!

Bruno Walter: I am sure that a collection of your talks with Pablo Casals will be read with the very greatest interest by all who have been affected by the mastery of this great man. It is hardly possible to estimate the value of Casals' influence on our time. Not only has he given to present-day violoncellists priceless and lasting enlightenment on the unlimited possibilities of their instrument, but the whole existence of this great musician, from the ethical as well as the artistic point of view, is a source of inspiration and encouragement to all those who aspire to humanity's highest achievements.

Yehudi Menuhin: The image which is evoked in my mind by the great master Pablo Casals is that of a jeweller. His art and his nature show qualities characteristic of his vocation. An almost microscopic searching into the depths of detail, an unshakeable patience, a sense of belonging to a land, to a tradition, to a concept, to a way of living which is deeply rooted, almost botanical, a calm persistence bordering on stubbornness, like the resistance of plants against the cruelties of Nature; all these things testify to the presence, in this world of small men and faint hearts, of a being whose simplicity, grandeur and integrity restore our faith in human nature.

Eugène Ormandy: Pablo Casals, in my opinion, is not only the greatest 'cellist, he is probably the greatest musician alive today.

Ernest Ansermet: About Casals the 'cellist there is nothing left to say. He has left his mark on all 'cellists of our time, that is to say he is the "norm", and all other comment is superfluous. But, it seems to me that the value of his musical personality, in this age of over-rational, over-sophisticated music-making, lies in a nature so sound, so certain and so rich that it always reveals the truth of the music, dissolving the difficulties which so many others seem to find.

Sir John Barbirolli: I can do no better than to condense my opinion of the Maestro Pablo Casals into one phrase—"Great artist, great man, great friend."

Maestro Casals, after all our efforts to gather and faithfully record your words, there arises this question: how to convey to the reader, by means of the written word, the generosity and sweetness of your soul? Someone has said that it is always dangerous to know a great man at close quarters. At the moment of deciding to publish these talks we can vouch for the fact that at the end of each visit we admired and loved you more than ever.

Solitary and glorious in a little house in a little town, you are able to pass on to those who know you that which appears increasingly outmoded— the love of man—and that which is denied this sombre epoch—hope. . . .

After each visit, as you stretched out your hand and said good-bye with your beautiful smile, we were strengthened in our conviction that you are one of the great men of whom Romain Rolland speaks, one who knows how to remain human.

I

Childhood

If I remember rightly, Maestro, you were born in 1876.

Yes, on December 29th, 1876. I was born in Vendrell, a little Catalan town some seventy kilometres west of Barcelona, to which I have always been attached by bonds of the deepest affection.

Shall we talk of your parents' influence?

This was considerable, maybe decisive. My father was the church organist at Vendrell, and quite a remarkable musician in a quiet way. It was he who awoke in me the love of music through his lessons and his example. It was the example of a man who, without departing for a moment from modesty, was nevertheless a true and pure artist.

And your mother? I always heard you talk of her with great veneration.

Oh, my mother was a very exceptional woman! What I owe to her energy, her genuine understanding and her deep humanity! Right through her life she was my guardian angel.

Are your earliest recollections connected with your native town?

Rather with the Hermitage of Sant Salvador, five kilometres from Vendrell. From there come my earliest recollections, my awakening to conscious life, so to speak: rays of light filtering through the window-pane caught my virgin imagination with their iridescent reflections.

When I was small my mother would take us, my brothers and myself, for short spells to the hermitage, which was very near the coast. It was rapture to me to contemplate the luminous tonalities and unceasing flow of the sea. I stayed for hours, resting my elbows on the windows watching this spectacle, always changing, yet always the same. Neither have I forgotten the appearance of the hermit called *El Pau de la Centa* (his wife was called *Vicenta*), an old seadog who would take my hand and lead me to the shore to teach me swimming. This cottage at Sant Salvador was the only luxury we could afford, as our family had very modest means and expenses had to be calculated carefully.

Wherever I have found myself in the course of my travels, this hermitage and the shores of Sant Salvador, as well as the little town of Vendrell, have exercised the same powerful attraction, whose spell evokes the wonder world of childhood. It was there, at Sant Salvador, that in 1912 I built my house, that house which, alas, I have not seen for so long.

Did your musical vocation begin very early?

In my case it is, perhaps, beside the point to talk of vocation, since from my earliest days music was for me a natural element, an activity as natural as breathing, if you like. I certainly sang in tune before I could speak clearly. Thanks to my father I learned to combine sounds at the same time that I expressed myself in words.

This paternal instruction proved to be excellent, then?

Excellent in every way. Only think, that when I was seven I could do any transposition. Besides, it was not only the teaching: how could I describe this musical atmosphere which cradled my early dreams— I was bathed in it the whole time! I remember when I was two or three, sitting on the floor and resting my head against the piano to hear better what my father was playing. I was transported. I also remember that when my brother Artur[1] and I were very young, my father ordered us to stand behind the piano (and I must own here that my brother had a better ear than mine!). We had to name the notes of anything he played at random.

How long was it before you performed in public?

Well, if you can call it a *début*, I was five when I was admitted as a second soprano to the church choir. It was on April 27th, the saint's day of Notre Dame de Montserrat, patron of Catalonia. From that day I went to all the offices and got used to singing plainsong. I shall never forget the first Christmas night. The night before, my mother sent me to bed early, as I had to get up in time to sing at *la misa del gall* (Mass of the Cock), High Mass at five in the morning, since Vendrell did not have a midnight Mass. I could not sleep and wriggled about in bed. I could not understand the atmosphere of mystery by which I was surrounded, but I felt that some extraordinary thing was about to happen. At five o'clock, walking in the dark streets, I was struck by the quiet concentration of the people walking to the church in the starry night.

There was this great silence, instead of the merrymaking on other feast days. And suddenly I saw all the lights through the open doors of

---

[1] *Casals' parents had eleven children: nine boys and two girls. The only surviving three are Pablo, the eldest, Lluis and Enric.*

the church. My father played the organ and I sang—I sang with all my heart. . . .

In after years I witnessed many Christmastides in capitals of Europe and America (some of them indeed full of melancholy), but this first one at Vendrell, with its luminous enchantment, has not died in my memory.

What about instruments?

In those days I was very curious about any new instruments I saw, and I was irresistibly attracted by them. I first learned to play the piano. And when I was eight years old I took part in a concert given in Vendrell as a solo violinist.

Is it true that when you played the violin the village children said you looked like a blind man, and this teasing made you give up the violin?

You can imagine that in a village like Vendrell, in those days, the only violinists the kids had seen were beggars. So they could not think otherwise. But it was really after I heard a 'cello for the first time that I was so impressed that I put the violin away.

At what age did you begin playing the organ?

As soon as I could reach the pedals. I used to sit next to my father when he was playing in church, and kept on asking him to teach me. I used to climb down, trying to reach the pedals with my feet, but my father just told me to realize I was still too small to do it!

But, of course, when my legs got long enough my father initiated me into all the wonders of an organ. (It was an old instrument, made at the same period as the one Bach played when in Leipzig.) I was soon able to take my father's place if he was ill. A nice anecdote comes back to my mind . . . just opposite the church was the shoemaker, who used to work out of doors when the weather permitted. He was a fervent admirer of my father's playing. One day, as I came out of the church, the shoemaker told me with an ecstatic air how he loved listening to my father. "My father is ill today, it was I who was playing." He would not believe his ears and called his wife and said to her, "It was not Carlets[1] who was playing today, but Paulito."[2] They kissed me and offered me some *carquinvolis* (dry biscuits) and *vi bo* (sweet wine).

What about your compositions?

I also started writing early. It was my father's real passion, and I think if he had had a more complete and developed technique, he

[1] *Catalan for Charles.*
[2] *Diminutive of Paul.*

would have occupied an honourable place amongst our good composers. His songs and some small pieces still have an attractive charm and freshness. I must have been about seven when, before Christmas, a Catholic centre we belonged to had the idea of putting on *Els Pastorets* (The Adoration of the Shepherds). We had the text and my father agreed to set to music some special episodes. But, as he was overworked, he asked me to help him. I began to write—and you must realize that my father was not surprised to see a boy of seven diligently writing notes and musicial signs on the stave. I think he thought it was quite natural.

The show was a success (I took the part of a devil who used all sorts of stratagems to stop the shepherds arriving at Bethlehem). And you can guess my emotion on hearing my first melodies at Vendrell, and in some other villages nearby, many years after the time I am speaking of! As a matter of fact I had a letter from Colombia some three years ago saying: "I am so and so . . . I remember the music of *Els Pastorets*. As I am not a musician, I whistled it for a composer who took it down and I am sending it to you." What a souvenir. . . .

Were these tunes written for the Nativity of Our Lord your first composition?

To tell the truth it was my second. My first *opus* (to use the word with ironic indulgence) had been a Mazurka. I took it to my godfather, who paid me with dry figs and a ten-sous' coin.

When you spoke to me of the folk tunes you used to hear as a child, you said something about those of the grallers?

Yes, these unforgettable messengers of our festivities. In the morning people were awakened by the sound of these instruments, which announced a holiday. The *gralls* is an old instrument played with a reed, probably of Arab origin. It was very popular round Vendrell. It produces a diatonic scale and if the player is clever he can make it produce semi-tones. Once I met a *graller* who had come to ask my father for some new dance tunes. As my father was absent I asked him to play a scale as I wished to imitate it. He agreed, looking at me with a sceptical smile, but after I had tried to play the scale four or five times, I started playing all the tunes of his repertoire which I knew by heart. One day I'll play you some of these tunes on the piano.

(The walls of the room where we sit are almost covered with photographs: evocations of the past, souvenirs of every sort. Amongst them there is one which shows the pyramide humaine, *a strange sight for*

those who are not Catalan. Men stand on each other's shoulders in circles, making seven tiers, their heads bent with the effort.)
The Castells *(castles)* . . .

This is another moving recollection. As you know, this is not a gymnast's "turn". It is a traditional game for us. We practise playing it when quite small: our fathers teach us to stand on their shoulders. This *entente* is an admirable thing, what with the concentration and the respect of each player for the combined effort necessary to make a success of building the "tower".

Your childhood was during the quiet period of the Restoration, after all the troubled times which had marked the 19th century in Spain till 1874. Did your parents or your friends support the Carlistes *or the* Progressistes *who had fought each other so fiercely?*

Oh, my father was an ardent liberal, and followed the federal republicanism of Pi y Margall. He had risked his life in 1874—the year he got married—when the *Carlistes* came into Vendrell.

Am I right in saying that your father initiated you into the cult of Bach?

Not exactly. He had shown me certain aspects of great music and in fact made me play *The Well-Tempered Clavier*, which I consider the foundation of all music. But, really, he admired the Beethoven sonatas and the piano music of Chopin most.

You seem to have been a very good boy, Maestro.

There you are mistaken. I was mischievous and, for my age, had a remarkable strength. One of my "performances" which made the village talk was when I descended a hilly street on a cycle that my old friend Matines had made for me. (He was an extraordinary person. Would you believe it, he threw himself from the roof of his house, wearing wings he had made himself!) On my first attempt at riding I met a stone on the road and fell so violently that I fractured my skull. But I got up, mounted the cycle again and this time could ride successfully.

Another time I was playing *gendarmes et voleurs* (a sort of glorified version of hide-and-seek) near the station. I thought of running away through the barrier where a plank was missing, but I got caught by one big nail which was supporting it. I could not move and as I desperately tried to free myself, the nail went into my head. Do you know what I thought of? To lie down on my back in the middle of the village square so that the sun would dry the blood! My father happened to walk that way; imagine his feelings, he thought I was dead.

Hooligan also?

No. I never fought with others unless it was a case of injustice; an older boy using his strength to impose his will on a weaker one. Then I would intervene.

Already you disliked violence?

Yes, but this violence did not frighten me and I often intervened in order to separate the combatants. I remember what happened to the "bad boy" of the village. He was called *El Pep fuster* (Joseph the Carpenter). He frightened all the other boys and he was fond of imposing his will in a high-handed way. One day, when I could not stand it any longer, I threw myself upon him and after a hard fight I got the upper hand, although he was three or four years older than I. Strange things can happen. I had lost trace of my old enemy for a long time when in 1938 I found myself playing in Buenos Aires. At the hotel I was handed some visiting cards, one of which said "I am Joseph, the carpenter". What a surprise! The former rascal had become a man full of kindness, even a sort of lay saint!

And what about your treatment for hydrophobia at the Barcelona Hospital? You showed great courage.

I had taken to heart my father's exhortation, "Say to yourself that men don't cry."

The Pasteur serum saved your life?

I was only ten years old and the Pasteur discovery had only been applied a very short time. A mad dog had bitten my leg and my parents thought I had no chance of survival. I was hastily transported to Barcelona, where I entered a ward in the hospital. I saw an old man who had arrived too late and who was dying in delirious screams. As they started treating me I stuffed my mouth with a handkerchief (I remembered my father's words to me, "men don't cry"). I had to endure sixty-four injections of boiling serum. In those days the treatment was ghastly.

I suppose you attended the communal school in Vendrell?

Of course. My family could not afford to send me anywhere else, and it was only when I got to Madrid that the Count de Morphy took my education seriously in hand.

How many inhabitants had Vendrell?

About five thousand. The village only grew fairly recently. The population was mostly composed of peasants (the majority cultivated vines), artisans, shopkeepers and a few landlords. I used to stand for hours outside the sheds of carpenters, coopers, smiths, wheelwrights.

. . . All my life I have found great pleasure in talking to those people, most of them have such personalities and seem to bring to their work the same care and perseverance that one should to any creation.

When did the violoncello appear?

You may have seen those curious musicians who go from one village to another. One day there came to Vendrell a group of these strolling players, who called themselves *Los Tres Bemoles* (The Three Flats). They were made up to look like clowns and were loaded with guitars, mandolines and some very queer instruments (some of them were simply kitchen utensils arranged with curious gadgets). One of the players was performing on a sort of bent broom, which might have suggested a violoncello.

I sat down in the front row of the audience, looking, listening, full of wonder. A few days later my father, finding me so insistent, built me an instrument of the same kind. But it was a great improvement on the one I had heard, as he used a pumpkin as a sounding-board. It was my first 'cello. . . .

It sounded rather well . . . It was exhibited in the *Exposition Internationale de Barcelone* in 1929. I keep it in my house at Sant Salvador, in a glass case, like a real treasure.

What about the real one?

When I was eleven the Catholic centre organised some chamber music concerts. It was then that I heard a real 'cello for the first time. And it was played by Josep Garcia of Barçelona, who was later to be my teacher. I was fascinated.

Was this impression stronger than you had when you heard other instruments?

Yes. My impression was quite extraordinary. The same evening I said to my father, "I would very much like to learn to play a violoncello." Soon after, he bought me one. My fate, I seem to remember, was decided then. My father thought that music would not earn me a living and that I ought to find a profession. In his opinion that was a necessity, and he had already asked the carpenter of Vendrell to take me as an apprentice. As a matter of fact, our circumstances were so modest that any extra income, however small, would have been very welcome. But my mother did not agree and just said: "Since he has heard this instrument our son has shown such enthusiasm for it that he must have lessons from a teacher. Here, in Vendrell, he is going to waste his time as there is no teacher. He must go to Barcelona, and I shall take him there." My father thought that all these schemes did not make sense, and attributed them to what he called my mother's *folie des grandeurs*. They argued with such bitterness that it pained me terribly and I felt very guilty.

I suppose that if your mother had not shown so much energy and foresight you would have become a carpenter?

Quite possibly. Perhaps I would have followed in my father's footsteps. His musical feeling was equal to his modesty. He was the parish organist, as you know. He also gave elementary singing lessons, taught the piano, and played for dances at the *festes majors* (village festivity). He never complained of his lot and when he played, even when it was just for dancing, he put into his playing all the dreams and aspirations of his soul. Beauty was his aim. It looked as if I was going to do the same. And, actually, that is what I did do during my years in Barcelona. I went from village to village in the summer trying my best to extract all the music there might have been out of waltzes and rigodons.

During those years, were you vaguely thinking of becoming a great artist?

No, not in the slightest. Neither then nor later. It was not in accordance with my character. Sometimes my mother said to me, "You ought to be an organist or a violinist." I thought she was right and realized that if I showed promise, it was certainly for some musical activity—and that was all.

How old were you when you went to Barcelona?

I was eleven and a half. My mother came with me and installed me with some distant relations with the idea that I should attend the violoncello and composition classes at the *École Municipale de Musique de Barcelone*. I have never forgotten this departure, and first journey. I was very sad at leaving the countryside where I had been brought up, the background of my happy, carefree childhood.

However, you never lost contact with the village of your birth.

No. Even before I built my house at Sant Salvador, I went back to Vendrell every year. For twenty-one years, when I had finished the music season in America, I always took the first boat to come home.

How do you account for your constant attachment to your native soil, after you became an artist of world-wide reputation?

It seems to me quite a natural thing, and there is nothing to explain. Do you remember the words of our dear Maragall with which I finished my speech at the *Jeux Floraux de la Langue Catalane*, at the palace of the Majorcan kings at Perpignan? *"It is on the firm soil of our native land that we must place our feet in order to take flight to Heaven."*

Do believe me, no attachment to *terra firma* can spoil our spiritual heritage; and what a solace it is to be able to see again the landscapes we were familiar with in childhood!

It is very painful for me now, not to be able to go to Vendrell and my house.

But it seems that your childhood of so long ago is still very much alive.

I am glad to say that through my long journeys in Europe and America, and even in this village of Prades, the child I was at Vendrell has never left me.

We remember Charles Péguy's saying: "All is accomplished by the time we are twelve years old."

II

The Years of Apprenticeship

What of your studies at the Municipal School of Music in Barcelona?

I studied harmony and counterpoint with Rodoreda and the 'cello with Josep Garcia. At that time. I was mainly interested in composition.

I believe there's a story about some harmony exercise. . . .

Yes, I had to do a figured bass. I felt so terribly frightened on the first day that I just did not understand a thing my teacher explained to me: even less did I understand the task that was set to us for the next day. I got home in a very nervous state and in tears, and told my mother all about it. I was feeling desperate and I thought the best thing to do was to write something of my own on the figured bass our teacher had given us. When I produced it the next day at the class, my teacher looked at it, seemed to laugh and cry at the same time, and ended by embracing me.

What about your 'cello studies?

My teacher was a very gifted 'cellist; he had good fingers, not too thin or too thick, which helps for fingering. Bearing in mind the technique and style of 'cello playing at that period, one could say he was an excellent 'cellist. Nevertheless, even at the first lesson I was very disturbed by all sorts of queer and conventional things which seemed absurd to me. Although I followed the classes quite diligently, I started revising his instructions, and as soon as I got home I created a technique of my own. When the others noticed my way of playing they used to say: "What are you doing? You will catch it for this." But that did not stop me. I wanted to get rid of all the unnecessary conventions and stiffness, which, to my mind, did not help to solve the real problems.

It sounds incredible: you were elaborating a new technique of the 'cello when you were twelve—a technique which in later years was to spread all over the world!

Why incredible? Don't you think that even a child can observe and think what he likes of his teacher and notice what may be wrong

24

in his teaching? We were taught to play with a stiff arm and obliged to keep a book under the armpit! What rhyme or reason is there in such an idea? I have always advocated complete freedom in the movement of the right arm, including the elbow (this new theory caused a *furore* among the traditionalists). This free action makes the whole bow technique stronger and easier.

I also undertook to revise the method of fingering and the action of the left hand, keeping to my "natural" line of approach and observation of life and nature, which can always teach us anything, if we are prepared to observe with patience and humility.

These researches and thinking on technique that I started then still continue: and they will for as long as I have the strength to do so.

Were you very homesick when you first went to Barcelona?

Yes. I arrived there when they were pulling down the buildings of the Great Exhibition of 1888. My mother installed me with some near relations who came from Vendrell. She returned home after a few days, but the following year came to stay for good. My hosts were very good people, and kind to me. Benet, the man, a carpenter, was a sort of modern Don Quixote, quite a unique character. He used to disappear in the evenings, apparently to go to "dangerous" cafés in the low quarters of Barcelona. His idea was to curb the activities of a lot of toughs he found there. He would come home with knives and pistols he had snatched from them, and kept these trophies in drawers—the only weapon he used was an ash stick! One evening he came home with a wound—he had been knifed! But he just told us it was nothing, and the next evening his comment when he returned, rather pleased with himself, was, "That chap of yesterday and I are now quits!"

Tell me, I believe you played in public quite early in Barcelona?

I could not help it. I had to keep studying and making a living at the same time. Nine months after my arrival in the capital of Catalonia, I got an engagement from the proprietor of the Café Tost in the suburb of Garcia. I belonged to a trio, and as you may well imagine, our repertoire consisted of marches, waltzes and well-known operatic airs! Also some medleys. However, soon after I began, I managed to persuade them to have a classical programme once a week.

In the summer I joined some bands which took part in the *festes majors* of Catalonia. It was very hard work. The heat, the travelling in old horse buses, the inns, the crowds, the dances which always lasted till dawn. The amount of waltzes, "Americaines", mazurkas, "*chotis*" (schottisches), rigodons and lancers I played during these tours! But, as I told you before, I took this playing very seriously. I had a growing conviction that big occasions and big works were not the *only* important things in life. If we give ourselves devotedly to the small daily tasks we shall see miracles every day! At the end of these dances, peasants and fishermen applauded me and shouted—and I could read in their looks that they could see beyond the immediate and passing pleasure of the dancing. A sort of mutual understanding was established between us, a homage, as it were, to the miraculous language of art! And when, later in my life, I found myself playing in very different circumstances, in big concert halls where serious audiences listen, it seemed to me that my artistic nature had not changed.

Can you remember any musical occasions which left their mark on you in those days?

Monsieur Tost, the proprietor of the café, sometimes came with me to concerts or operatic representations. I can remember how deeply impressed I was once, to see and hear Richard Strauss conducting some of his works. It was a period when Brahms and Wagner were revealed to me. A choral society, which later became the *Orfeo Gracieno*, used to meet above the Café Tost: they had made me an honorary member of their society and I treasure the diploma they presented to me on that occasion, as it was my first distinction! A great Wagner enthusiast called Fluvia, who came regularly to the *Orfeo*, was the first to introduce me to the *Tetralogy*. He sent me scores of *Lohengrin*, *Parsifal* and *Tristan*, which we read together with great excitement. Having "discovered" Wagner and Brahms, I came to Strauss, who became for me another source of exaltation—a youthful emotion that has never left me.

M. Tost and I also went to hear Sarasate together.

What impression did the celebrated virtuoso make on you?

That of a breathtaking spectacle, like a star *danseuse* of dazzling agility.

I suppose M. Tost felt very proud of you?

Yes. He was a good sort. But he did not like to see me arriving late at his café, since the concert was supposed to begin at nine o'clock sharp, and I often forgot the time simply because I used to get lost in daydreams, looking over the gardens of the old *Théâtre Lyrique* opposite. Music, all sorts of books I read, the meaning of life, were all problems to me and kept my mind in a state of perpetual conflict. Once I arrived really very late at the café. Tost was waiting for me at the door looking very cross. He put his hand in his pocket and produced a watch. As he handed it to me he said, "Here you are, and I hope you will learn to be on time!" It was my first watch. . . .

And when did you first discover the Bach Suites?

This was the great event of my life: my father, who had already bought me a full-size 'cello, came to see me once a week. We used to go to the different music shops in Barcelona in search of scores of serious music for the weekly concerts of classical music, given at the Café Tost where I played solos. One day, quite by chance, I came across the *Six Suites* of Bach in one of these music shops. I was thirteen then. I wondered what could be hidden there, what mystery lay behind the words: *Six Suites for 'Cello Solo.* I did not even know they existed, neither did my teacher, and no one had ever spoken to me about them. It was the great revelation of my life. I felt immediately that it was something of exceptional importance. On the way home I hugged my treasure! I started playing them in a wonderful state of excitement, and it was only after twelve years' practice of them that I made up my mind to play them in public.

Before I did, neither violinists or violoncellists had ever played a Suite in its entirety: one or the other would play a Saraband, a Gavotte or an Allemande. But my intention was to play them *in extenso*: the Prelude, followed by five dance movements bearing the names by which they were called in the period, doing all the repeats shown so as to keep the coherence and inner structure of each movement. In those days these compositions were thought of as cold and academic works. How could anyone think of Bach as "cold", when these Suites seem to shine with the most glittering kind of poetry! As I got on with the study of the Suites I discovered a new world of space and beauty— and I can say now that the feelings I experienced were among the purest and most intense of my artistic life.

Did you give any recitals in those days?

Well, I gave my first concert in the *Théâtre des Nouveautés* in Barcelona. I remember how agitated I was when, with my father who joined me for this great occasion, I went to the Hall by tram. My head was going round, fear gripped me fast and I said, as I got up: "What am I going to do? I cannot remember the beginning of the composition I am going to play!" My father, wishing to calm me, said, "Don't worry, all will go well."

Nerves and stagefright before playing have never left me throughout the whole of my career. Can you realize that at each of the thousands of concerts I played at, I felt as bad as I did on that first occasion!

Do tell us about Albeniz's visit?

It was in the days of the Café Tost. The Barcelona people were coming in great numbers to hear *"el nen"* (the child). *I* was *"el nen"*.

Once when Albeniz was in Barcelona with his two friends, Arbos the violinist and Rubio the 'cellist, with whom he had formed a well-known trio, he had heard about the playing of "the child", so he came to the café and was so pleased with my playing that he wanted to take me to London with him. But my mother would not hear of it and said I had to work and get much better before thinking of this. But he gave me a letter of introduction to the Count de Morphy, an illustrious patron of music, who had been tutor and private secretary to King Alphonso XII. He was at that time private adviser to Doña Maria Cristina, the Queen Regent. My mother kept this letter very carefully for three years, just waiting for the opportune moment to use it!

In fact these three years in Barcelona, when you divided your time between composition and 'cello playing, must have been peaceful and profitable?

The last year was *not* peaceful. Far from it.

I read in Emil Ludwig's book that he seemed to sense what he calls "a Wertherian sentimentality" marking your adolescence.[1]

Yes, in a broad sense, perhaps that is true, if it implies an excessively emotional nature, overflowing sensitivity. I have told you before that my parents' ideas about my future were very different. My greatest wish was to get them to agree with each other about this. But how could I do it? Fortunately, when I was sixteen and the crisis was at its height, my mother backed me up with incredible tact and understanding. But my father could not understand me and did not realise how near I was to a fatal crisis.

Was it an ordinary phase one goes through in the course of adolescence?

It was much more serious than that. I had come to the conclusion that suicide was the only way out, and that idea pursued me for months on end. I felt at loggerheads with a world where there was no justice, selfishness was rampant and charity non-existent. When I

---

[1] Emil Ludwig, *Galerie de Portraits*, translated from the German by Pierre Nelon. (*Librairie Fayard*, Paris.)

saw people walking peacefully in the streets, or going to their occupations, I thought: "How stupid they are to enjoy this miserable life!" I was desperately searching for a door through which I could find peace of mind.

So I went through a period of religious mysticism. Coming out of the *École Municipale de Musique*, through the Rue Fernando, I would walk inside the Sant Jaume church and look for a dark corner where I could pray and meditate in peace—and, often, as soon as I got out of the church I hurried back again, more anguished than ever. I felt that here was my only hope of salvation. Obviously when I got home my face showed my mother all the painful anxiety of my mind. "What is the matter?" she would say, and I, "Oh, it's nothing." I was too fond of her to tell her of my obsession with suicide. But I could not get rid of it.

Nietzsche said: "It is folly and perdition for a young mind to go about in a sea of doubt without guide or compass."

Anything you like; but it was not metaphysical problems that made me so wretched: it was a mental revulsion in the face of a horrible world. My religious fervour did not do any good. I used to notice so many signs of "officialdom" in the Church, and nothing to appease my ardour and exaltation. I tried the socialist doctrines and read Marx and Engels, but I was not long deceived. Marxist ideology foretold a world too good to be true. My critical mind could not accept this. I had only to look about me to see what men were like, and I sadly realized that nothing would change them—that they would never become "brothers".

It was the period when the anarchists began their crimes in Barcelona— the 1st May 1890 was marked by some violent incidents.

For my part I could not possibly understand why these people thought they would improve humanity by spilling blood. I always instinctively hated violence.

There are some people who go through religious phases cyclically. With me they did not recur, although I think I possess an essentially religious mind. All religions have admirable ways of preaching fraternity, and elevating the moral sense of the human race, giving us hope and consolation. As far as I am concerned, and since my youthful religious crises, I have kept up a sort of personal and intimate dialogue between my conscience and the Divinity.

Ludwig also speaks of the pessimism which surrounded the tribulations of your adolescence.

Yes, that is true: there is so much injustice in this world of ours, and it seems so difficult to try to raise the moral standard of men, that it is easy to feel pessimistic. A permanent sorrow seems to occupy my inner self (although it seldom comes to the surface) and it has increased again during these last few years of threats and disasters.

Did this crisis of pessimism, of which Ludwig speaks, last very long?

It lasted over a year, but passed slowly when I was in Madrid. All this painful period, of which I have just spoken, remains permanently in my mind. I have always tried to act according to what I consider my duty. Injustice is so abhorrent to me that on many occasions I have not hesitated to act like a Don Quixote!

It was in 1894 that you went to Madrid?

Yes. I was seventeen, and had just finished my studies at the Municipal School of Music. My father was very cheerful when he showed my diplomas to his friends in Vendrell.

I believe you snatched all the first prizes?

Yes. When I played for the piano and 'cello exams the audience seemed to fill up the hall and I could see the members of the jury listening with tears in their eyes!

My mother thought there was not much more I could learn in Barcelona and that the time was ripe for her to use Albeniz's letter to the Count de Morphy.

She came with me to Madrid, and since she did not like to leave my two younger brothers behind, there were four travellers leaving Barcelona.

How did the Count receive you?

Wonderfully. My mother gave him Albeniz's letter and I, a packet containing some of my compositions. He wanted to hear me play my pieces. He was so pleased that he arranged for me to play to the *Infanta* Isabel, the sister of the dead King Alphonso XII, who had a reputation for knowing a lot about music. I shall never forget this occasion at the Royal Palace with my mother and my small brothers. As I was playing, Enric, who was a baby in arms, wanted his dinner, and in his own way provided a noisy accompaniment to my playing; so my mother fed him there and then to stop him crying.

So my *début* in the Royal suite did not lack in atmosphere and colour! After this the Count talked about me to the Queen Regent and she received me very kindly; and so I came to know the Queen Doña Maria Cristina who, from that moment, became a second mother to me. She organized a concert at the Palace where I appeared as 'cellist and composer. With the violinists Arbos and Bordas, and also a viola player (whose name I have forgotten), I played the 'cello part in my first string quartet, a work the Count de Morphy was interested in.

Then the Queen granted you a scholarship?

Yes. We rented a small place, a kind of garret. Our neighbours were fine specimens of the Madrid people, so alert and charming: there were a few *cigarières* (women who make cigars), a hall porter at the Palace, very proud of his uniform and madly adored by his wife, and a shoemaker who had two mentally deficient children. There were four doors opening on the same landing. What a landing! People coming in and out, shouting, singing, and quarrelling, night and day! But in spite of all the noise I spent long hours there practising the 'cello or composing. When, in 1935, the Municipality of Madrid gave me the title of *Hijo adoptive* (honorary citizen) of the town, I mentioned this with great emotion in my speech of thanks.

All these good neighbours you had sound as if they belonged to the Verbena de la Paloma. . . .

Certainly; do you know that I went to the first performance of this famous "*Zarzuela*" with the Count de Morphy. The author, Tomas Breton, was my composition teacher in Madrid and Jesus de Monasterio my teacher in chamber music.

You always speak of Monasterio with great admiration.

Yes, admiration and gratitude: I often say that he was the greatest teacher one could have had. I was very lucky to have him at such a crucial period of my musical development. All my personal tendencies, and my artistic doubts, found in his well-tried convictions an admirable anchorage, which had a wonderfully stimulating effect on the growth of my convictions. For instance, I had almost created a personal mania for good intonation (which was neglected in those days) and also for what I may describe as "musical accentuation". As Monasterio felt just the same on these two points, he encouraged me no end and made me persevere in that direction. So that all my suggestions and aspirations, still in an embryonic state, met in him the best understanding, so vital to me for their completion. Also Monasterio never thought of music as a social amusement or as an excuse for showing off. He was the kind who evoked devotion because his art and teaching were guided by a sense of greatness and nobility.

Did you take notes during his classes?

Yes, or more exactly I wrote my personal reactions and thoughts of what he said. My mother had advised me to do that. This diary, which occupied about one page a day, was kept until my first tour in the United States in 1901 . . . and now I have mislaid them all![1]

And what about the Count de Morphy?

Ah! I can still see him. He was a great gentleman, very simple, very human. From the moment I came to Madrid he seemed to "adopt" me, and showed me an affection that I can only describe as paternal. (Since he had no male child he used to say he had two children— Alphonso XII and me!) He made himself responsible for my education just as he had been the preceptor of the King Alphonso—and every morning at his home he gave me lessons on general culture. The Countess, who had been a pupil of Liszt, and his daughter were also very good to me. She gave me my first lessons in German.[2]

The text-books we used were the same ones Alphonso XII had, and I could read the annotations he wrote himself in the margins of the books.

Have you kept these books?

Unfortunately, no. Often the Count took me to his library and said, "Pablito, you will have these as a souvenir from me." But after his death I was unable to obtain what the Count had then so categorically promised me.

Can you remember any specific example of the way he taught you?

Yes. In order to make me express my impressions clearly and concisely, the Count sent me to visit the Prado Museum once a week and also to the sittings of the Cortes. I had to write an essay on each, giving my personal views on these subjects. At the *Chambre des Deputés*, sitting very quiet, I could hear all the famous speakers of the *Restauration* period: Canovas del Castillo, Sagasta, Silvela, Remero Robledo, Maura, etc. Also the leaders of the republican opposition: Castelar, Pi y Margall, Salmeron, Azcarate . . .

Did you meet any of these important people?

No, I did not think I had any reason or title to justify any such introduction, although I could have asked the Count to do it for me. However, I did meet Emilio Castelar, the previous President of the

[1] Fortunately for us, Casals has a prodigious memory—and it is as well to realise here that all he told us was never taken from written notes . . . which do not exist!

[2] Casals showed great facility for foreign languages. Besides Catalan and Castilian, he talks French and English fluently—knows German well, and Italian and Portuguese.

first Spanish Republic, when I was at the home of the Marchioness of Alhama.

Which were the painters that attracted you most at the Prado?

Oh, Titian, the Venetians—and, of course, Velazquez and Goya.

What about El Greco? In those days he was hardly known.

I must confess that I was put off by the long shapes of his figures and by the violence of his colouring. But I was very struck by the intensity of expression in his portraits.

What about the theatre?

I got very interested in certain plays given by the Maria Guerrero-Fernando Diaz troupe at the Classical Theatre. The Count used to do the musical accompaniments for some of the plays.

Of course, the Madrid people have always been passionately interested in bull-fighting.

I wasn't. I never went to one in Madrid. Later, before settling in Paris, finding myself in San Sebastian with the *Orquesta Sinfonica de Madrid*, I was begged by my colleagues to go with them to the *Corridas*. So I did, in order not to appear unsociable, but I suffered horribly and could hardly look at it.

The Count was, I believe, a great connoisseur of music?

Yes, he had been a pupil of Fetis and a personal friend of Gevaert, the famous Belgian musicologist. At Court he was known as *el musico* (the musician). He had composed a cantata, a Mass, some piano pieces, three operas and a well-known book on Spanish folk music. He was interested in all young musicians if they were gifted and enthusiastic. He was especially keen to liberate Spanish Opera from Italian influence in order to restore national character to the music. He himself had set an example in *Los Amantes de Teruel*, and he was very happy to see Tomas Breton going the same way.

What did he think of your compositions?

He liked them very much. Every day I had lunch with him at home and after the meal he used to ask me to a drawing-room and make me improvise at the piano. In those days I was attracted by unusual harmonies, but when the Count, who sat next to me, thought I was going too far, he would tap me on the shoulder, saying, "Pablito, do keep to more common language." It was the period of *fin de siècle*, when extravagance was the fashion. Long and untidy hair, melodramatic attitudes. One day the Count took me to Sarasate's place. We were offered brandy but did not accept it, so the great violinist said: "Count, I understand it at your age and with your delicate constitution, but this young man? Do you mean to say he wants to be an artist and does not drink brandy!" Such was the fashion, the way of thinking of that period. Of course, this does not mean Sarasate was not a remarkable artist when you compare him with those of his generation.

I understand that the Royal family was very kind to you?

More than kind. I have already told you how good the Queen always was to me, and until her death she was the same. I was received at the Palace without ceremony and at least once a week I went to play my compositions and the 'cello. I also played duets on the piano with the Queen. Once when I was ill she sent me her own doctor.

Was she a pianist?

She was a sensitive player and, like most Austrians, possessed a real love of music.

And what about the young King Alphonso XIII?

He was seven or eight, cheerful and pleasant. We played games together and I gave him stamps. He was very fond of lead soldiers. While the Queen and I were playing the piano he was so absorbed in playing soldiers that when I asked him after we finished, "Does your Royal Highness like music?" "Yes," he said, "it pleases me. But what I want most is to be given some guns!"

And what about the atmosphere of the Court?

Well, my connection with the Royal family was of a strictly personal character. What I saw of the flattery and hypocrisy of the courtiers revolted me. I did not belong to that world. I used to talk to the Count about my feelings on the subject quite openly. He advised me to judge men from their acts, not from the rank they occupy or their attitude towards the people.

What effect had this contact with the grandees on you?

I have never forgotten the debt of gratitude I owe to the Royal family of Spain. In 1941, when I was already exiled in Prades, I went to play in the cathedral at a memorial service given after the death of Alphonso XIII. I simply thought of him as the son of a lady whose kindness to me had been endless. But, in spite of the personal gratitude and affection I have for these people, the contact I had with them never influenced my thoughts or my behaviour.

How long did you stay in Madrid?

Two and a half years. The Count, who thought of me at nineteen as a future composer of Spanish operas, wanted me to become a composer. But my mother thought differently and it was decided that my 'cello playing should come before everything else. She would say, "If he is really gifted as a composer the 'cello will not stand in his way, but if he neglects or abandons this instrument, it will be very difficult for him to make up for lost time." (And I must say she was right.) Since my studies were practically finished my mother thought I ought to have a change. But the Count did not see eye to eye with her and a very strained situation ensued. "Well," she said, "we shall go back to Barcelona." After months of arguments, the Count agreed to our leaving as long as I promised to go to Brussels and study composition with his friend Gevaert. He gave us a letter of introduction to the Director of the Brussels Conservatoire and arranged for my allowance of 250 pesetas a month to be renewed by the Queen.

So this was your first journey abroad?

Yes, for the first time I crossed the frontier, in the company of my mother and my two younger brothers. My father could not understand and felt desperate: he would say, "What is this woman thinking about?" Neither my mother nor myself could guess what adventures awaited us when we left Spain. As soon as we reached Brussels I took my letter of introduction to Gevaert. He had a long white beard and was certainly pretty old. After looking at my compositions and congratulating me, he said he was too old to give me any lessons and advised me to go to a big city like Paris where one could hear good music. This was my first disappointment, and I was just going to take my leave when he said: "I understand you also play the 'cello, and I should like our professor to hear you. Will you come tomorrow morning?" Next day, feeling full of apprehension, I presented myself at the 'cello class. In those days the Brussels Conservatoire had a name for being the best in the world for string instruments. I sat on a bench at the back and listened to the pupils with long hair down to their shoulders and I did not think their playing was exceptionally good. When the class ended the teacher called me and said, rather sarcastically, "Eh, you, the little Spaniard, will you play something?" "I will try." "What will you play?" "Anything you like." He proceeded to name a great many works, and as I knew them all I said "Yes." Then he said, "Well, this boy knows everything, he must be extraordinary." Everyone was laughing and I was red with indignation. "Now will you play the *Souvenir de Spa*?" (A *bravura* piece which was a kind of "warhorse" of the Belgian School.) "Have you brought your 'cello?" "No." "What instrument are you going to play on?" "Any one which could be lent to me." "What a boy . . . he can play on any instrument." Bursts of laughter from the students punctuated the words of the teacher. I was getting very cross. I seized a 'cello some pupil was handing to me and asked the teacher for silence before I could play.

All this must have upset you just before playing.

Quite the opposite. I was so disgusted with their behaviour that I felt completely sure of myself. After a few bars I could see from their faces that these students were a bit surprised, and when I finished playing there was complete silence. The teacher got up, took me to his office and said, "Although it is against all the rules, I can promise you that you will get the First Prize at the Conservatoire if you consent to be in my class." I answered, "No, you made fun of me in front of all your pupils, and I don't want to stay here another minute."

Next day my mother, my brothers and myself left Brussels.

And you went to Paris?

Yes, I immediately wrote to the Count and told him what had happened, and I stressed the fact that Gevaert could not give me lessons in composition. Our troubles began! The Count accused me of disobedience and forced me to choose between losing my allowance and returning to Brussels. When I told him that although I was very sorry to upset him I would not return to Brussels, he lost his temper and the 250 pesetas were stopped.

You must have been very upset to have to break off your relations with your protector.

Yes, I was extremely sorry to have to do so, but what else could I do after I found Gevaert would not teach me? My stay in Brussels would not have had any meaning! Also, when I was in Monasterio's class I had learned a sense of discipline and musical devotion which did not fit in with what I found at the 'cello class of the Brussels Conservatoire. The Count thought that it was because of my mother's influence that I acted in that way. But he was wrong. I made the decision myself and felt very strongly that I should have wasted my time in Brussels.

You have not very happy memories of your first stay in Paris?

Alas! I went through hard and anxious times. You see the situation into which we had suddenly fallen. A woman, a young man of nineteen and two children, and no means. I had to find some sort of job, however small. Luckily I met a friend from Barcelona called Ainaud (who years later played in my orchestra). He told me there was a competition for a second 'cellist at the *Folies-Marigny*, a music hall where the French can-can was in great vogue. I went, and won the competition. I played the whole of the Saint-Saëns concerto, though the candidates were supposed to play only one movement; but when my turn came, they let me play through the whole work. My salary was only four francs a day! We lived in a hovel near the Porte St. Denis. I had to go to the theatre twice a day on foot, carrying my 'cello, to save the fare of fifteen centimes, a small sum, but one which in those days could buy a pound of bread. My mother and I had decided to live on a strict diet. But the winter was very cold and as I was not used to such a low temperature I fell very ill with a sort of dysentery complicated with enteritis and haemorrhage. We really were in distress.

Luckily you had your mother with you.

She was wonderful—sweet, courageous and firm. Her spirit of self-sacrifice knew no limit: in order to earn a few sous—enough to feed four and buy the medicines—she took on any sewing jobs she could find and worked late at night if necessary. My father also sent us something, although it was very little. One day, from my bed I saw my mother come in with her hair cut short. I looked at her in astonishment.

"What's the matter?" she said. "This is nothing."

For a little money, she had sold her magnificent hair. But she did not make any fuss about it, and thought it had no importance at all.

As days went by and our situation became worse, I said to my mother: "What are we going to do? Shall we stay in Paris?"

She said that that would be difficult, because she knew I couldn't stand the cold winters.

"So, shall we go back to Barcelona?"

"It seems to me the best thing to do."

And in this way it was decided, without more talk or complaint, that we should return home. Of course, my father was in a frightful state, and all the family's savings had melted away.

I did not feel discouraged, however, and went on with my studies. I had a growing conviction that musical performance, at its best, should not be an explosion of feeling only, no matter how sincere, but it should be held together by severe and tenacious discipline.

Had you decided by that time to stick to your own conception of music, rather than make concessions to public taste?

Yes. What I was driving at was based as much on constant simplicity of expression as on the rich variety of forms to be found in nature.

Did you think, all the same, that this sort of interpretation would please the listeners?

Well, I remembered that when I was twelve and I played at the Café Tost, perhaps some dance piece by an unknown composer, the public had reacted perfectly. In any case, don't forget, as I told you before, that you get the best result if you give the best of yourself and try to express the music sincerely.

When you got back to Barcelona some surprises awaited you?

Luck, this time, seemed to be with me. First, I had a kind of legacy, as a result of the departure of my old teacher, Garcia, for the Argentine. I took over his place as a professor at the *École Municipale de Musique*, as principal 'cellist at the *Liceu*,[1] and also private pupils and engagements to play in churches, and so on.

There was then a group of enthusiastic music lovers who founded the Wagner Association . . .

I took part in this craze for Wagner (I had been enthusiastic when at the age of twelve I heard Wagner for the first time). However, I have always preferred to remain eclectic in my taste instead of following one line blindly, however fascinating this line might be. For instance, I had already acquired a great admiration for Brahms' music, although he was considered the *bête noire* of the Wagnerian fanatics.

Can you tell us any anecdotes connected with the Liceu?

If you like stories, I can tell you an amusing one. During one operatic season the conductor was an Italian called Mugnone, who had once taught Toscanini. He was one of those Italians who seem to be born conductors, who don't have much to do with the production. I think we were rehearsing *Lohengrin*. The curtain was down and apparently there was an old man sweeping and whistling at the back of the stage. Mugnone, who had not realised where this strange noise came from, shouted, "*Silenzio, corpo di Bacco!*" But as the noise went on Mugnone ordered the curtain to be raised. When he caught sight of the stage-hand he was on to the stage like lightning, shouting at the top of his voice and all ready to attack him. The other, not realizing who it was, thought a madman had been let loose, and received him with his broom—imagine the scene! They had to be

[1] The Opera of Barcelona.

separated and, of course, Mugnone wanted the sweeper to be sacked, but the whole orchestra protested.

Did you go on tour in Spain during these years?

Yes, with a string quartet led by the Belgian violinist, Crickboom —also with my great friend Granados and some other musicians. We went to Madrid, Bilbao, Valencia and other places which I have forgotten.

Did you go abroad again?

Until 1899 I only went to Portugal, in the first summer after I returned to Catalonia. As there was no engagement to be had in Barcelona at that time, I accepted one for Espinho, which was the fashionable seaside resort in Portugal. The Casino was simply a gambling place. I belonged to a septet and I played solo once a week as I had at the Café Tost. There were quite a number of important Portuguese personalities on holiday there who got interested in the concerts, and these were such a resounding success that I received an invitation to play for the King and Queen, Carlos and Amelia, at the Royal Palace in Lisbon. I left Espinho in such a hurry that I forgot to take my 'cello . . . and there I was, in the presence of Their Majesties, without an instrument: I had to excuse myself as well as I could and postpone the concert to the following day—a very embarrassing situation! As I had to go through Madrid to get to Espinho I immediately wrote to the Count de Morphy to say I terribly wanted to see him. He wrote back very cordially and our reconciliation was most moving. Queen Maria Cristina with her usual kindness asked me to give a concert at the Palace, and after I had played she said, "Pablo, I want you to have a life-long remembrance of me," and showing me a bracelet she was wearing on the left wrist she added, "Which of these stones do you prefer?" "Oh, Majesty, I think they are all wonderful!" "Here, take this one." It was a magnificent emerald, which I had inserted into my bow. The Queen also gave me a lovely Gagliano 'cello, and I was made a *Chevalier de l'Ordre de Carlos III*.

Returning from Portugal, I stopped in Madrid again and for the first time in my life I played a concerto with an orchestra. It was the Lalo concerto and Tomas Breton, my old teacher, conducted.

In those days the Queen Regent must have had a lot of worries with the rising in Cuba and the Philippines, followed by the Spanish-American war of 1898, and the loss of the Spanish Colonies. Do you remember this war?

Yes, as if it were yesterday. The optimistic propaganda in the Press, the news of defeats, the Treaty of Paris. One horrible recollection survives in my memory, the landing of a group of soldiers at the Port of Barcelona. It was like a procession of ghosts: they were so disfigured by hunger and disease.

Did you stay in Barcelona much longer?

Until 1899. I felt it my duty to look after my family, and before leaving Barcelona and the good position I had acquired there I wanted to earn money and economise sufficiently to leave them comfortable and free from anxiety. In 1899 I thought I could go to Paris with my mind at rest. (I had practised French with some French people in Barcelona and, in fact, I was much more fluent in it than when I went to Brussels; it gives one so much more confidence.) I had a letter of introduction to Charles Lamoureux that the Count de Morphy had given me.

Did your mother go with you again?

No, I was then twenty-two and she rightly thought I could travel by myself and that her company was not as necessary as it had been before. It was due to her complete self-denial and her faith in my artistic future that I had been able to go straight on with my career. She was an exceptional woman! Just think what she did when we lived in Madrid: she studied foreign languages and more or less did the same lessons as I did, partly because she thought it would help my work, but mostly so that the deep feeling we had for each other should not be affected by any difference in our education.

What about your introduction to Lamoureux?

I shall never forget it. I was taken into his room where he was looking at some papers on his writing-table. He did not notice (or pretended not to notice) the visitor who had come to disturb him in his work. The fact was that he was giving up all his time and care to the preparation of *Tristan and Isolde*, which was to be produced the following winter. Realizing that time was going by, and as Lamoureux remained silent, I said: "Sir, I don't wish to disturb you. I only came to give you this letter from the Count de Morphy." He took it, read it, and said bluntly, "All right, you come tomorrow with a pianist and your 'cello." When we turned up the next day, I thought we were in for another séance of the same kind: he seemed absorbed in some papers and grumbled in an undertone about visitors who always disturbed him.

So I said, "As I don't wish to disturb you I shall go immediately." Then Lamoureux looked up at me and said: "Young man, I am interested in you. Play me the Lalo concerto." (You remember that

I had played it in Madrid on my way back from Portugal.) He started writing again . . . I tuned up and my friend sat ready to play. Once I began, Lamoureux dropped his pen and slowly turned round. After we had played the last notes he embraced me with visible emotion and said, "My dear child, you are one of the elect." He asked me to play at his first concert on 12th November, 1899. It was my *début* in Paris as a soloist (and also the first occasion I wore evening dress).

Were you nervous before this memorable concert?

Yes, as always.

Was it a success?

More than I could have hoped for.

III

Journeys, Concerts, Friends

After this first concert with Lamoureux, did you decide to live in Paris?

Not immediately. I went back to Barcelona, but soon afterwards I returned to Paris and settled there.

Did you play again under the direction of Lamoureux?

Yes, in December of the same year and, I think, this second concert was even more successful than the first. I asked Lamoureux if he would let me play in his orchestra for the first performance of *Tristan*. I thought he was a great conductor. He only thought of the music he conducted, not the effect he could make with it. He was very exacting about intonation and would not be satisfied with anything short of perfection.

I remember what he said to a bass-clarinet player during a rehearsal of *Tristan*. He had just finished playing a solo when Lamoureux said, "Brenoteau, it is out of tune." And after trying the same passage again a few times, the clarinetist said he thought it was in tune. "Well, if you think you play in tune," said Lamoureux, "I'll tell you a story of what happened to me when I went to see a friend who was ill in rather a miserable little room. Coming in, I exclaimed, 'What a stink! How can you live here?' 'I can't smell anything,' said he. Brenoteau, do you know why my friend could not smell? Because he was used to it."

Lamoureux was not very patient?

No, and when he lost his temper he could say some pretty biting things. Once, during a rehearsal of *Tristan and Isolde*, the tenor did not seem to pay any attention to his remarks. After trying two or three times without better result, Lamoureux laid down his baton and shouted: "Sir, as a tenor you have the privilege of being stupid, but now you are abusing it!"

Unfortunately you were not able to collaborate very long with Lamoureux.

No, alas, he died in December 1899, a few days after my second concert with him. But while I lived in Paris I always played at the benefit concert given every year by his orchestra to promote their

42

social work. I had it very much at heart to honour the memory of my first conductor in Paris. (I used to do the same for the Colonne Orchestra, whose founder had been a good friend of mine.)

In the summer of 1899 I was invited by the famous singer Emma Nevada to stay at her country house in Pierrefonds, and when I got there I heard that the Count de Morphy was gravely ill in Switzerland. I wanted to go and see him, but I had no money and could not think how to borrow any. The news of his death, however, came soon after, and I could only lament that such a highly-placed man had died in poverty. I have his portrait in my house at Sant Salvador, together with those of my relations and dearest friends.

In Paris, you lived at the Villa Molitor.

Not at first. I only went there in 1905, and lived in it until 1914. So many friends came to see me there: I have endless recollections of those years and they still linger in my memory.

When did you begin touring abroad?

Two or three years after my *début* in Paris. I must say I was in great demand and I travelled and travelled!

So composition went overboard?

No. I never ceased writing. When I lived in Madrid a great deal of my time was taken up with theory and composition. More than once I thought that later on I might, perhaps, give myself up freely to composition. But, alas, I guessed that as a musician I would have to become a 'cellist. I have written symphonies, string quartets, pieces for violin solo and 'cello solo, sonatas for piano and violin and for piano and 'cello, songs, motets and a few choral works; a Miserere called *La vision de Frère Martin*; an oratorio entitled *La Crèche*. I finished a sonata for piano and violin only a few days ago. But I have never allowed any to be published: I am quite firm about that. When I am dead and these works are found, someone will see if they are any good. I made an exception for a few religious compositions I wrote for the Montserrat Monastery, to which I am very attached, as you know. The Benedictine monks of Montserrat, who for centuries have done important work on musicology, have published my works.

You went on tour with the pianist Harold Bauer?

Yes. I had met him at the house of an English lady, Mrs. Ram, a good pianist herself, who received painters and literary people. She had fetched me out of a small hotel in Montmarte where I had fallen ill through cold, and took me to stay with her, saying I should be well looked after. There I met Ravel, Lenormand (father of the dramatist), Moreau, Bourcherit and other musicians. Bauer, who came regularly to these artistic parties, suggested we should play together, and I agreed. We first went for a tour in Spain, then to Holland.

For many years we toured through Europe and the two Americas with great success. I remember that in 1917 Bauer and I played the Beethoven *Triple Concerto* with Kreisler, at a concert of the New York Symphony Orchestra, conducted by Damrosch.

I thought of Bauer as a pianist of the first rank and also gifted with a rare intelligence.

I believe it was in 1917 that you landed in New York and Fritz Kreisler said to the Press: "The monarch of the bow has just arrived."

Well, Kreisler and I were always good friends, and in 1917 I was not unknown in America for I had toured the country about a dozen times already.

When did you start the famous trio with Thibaud and Cortot?

I don't know exactly, but I do remember we played together in public for a few years before the 1914 war. Our association, which was really based on music and friendship, lasted many years. We travelled all over Europe together and although it is a long time ago I remember it vividly and associate it with the cult of music and friendship. Poor Jacques Thibaud; we never dreamed that he would die so tragically in a flying accident!

Your recording of the Schubert Trio in B flat which you played to us last week sounds very fresh still after so many years.

Yes, there is no mistake about it; both from the artistic and commercial points of view it has been one of the great successes of recording. We played that most, but, of course, we also had Haydn, Beethoven, Schumann and Ravel in our repertoire.

Of your French friends you talked to me about the Menard Dorians.

Yes, they were great friends of mine, of rare kindness, and they received the *tout Paris* of politics, art and letters. There I met Briand, Clemenceau, Viviani, Colonel Picquart, Albert Thomas (who was Jean Hugo's tutor) and Léon Blum, who was then secretary to Madame Dorian.

What was Léon Blum like in those days?

He looked very aesthetic and was chiefly known as a literary critic. None of us could have guessed he would have such a career as a politician.

What about Clemenceau?

One could not help being impressed by his appearance and manner.
Colonel Picquart played a very important part in the Dreyfus affair?
Yes, he used to tell us some of the secrets which raised such a
storm later.

What was your attitude?
I have always sympathised with victims of any injustice.

*You had quantities of friends in Paris: you mention Fauré, d'Indy and
Saint-Saëns, Zuloaga, Carrière, Ravel, Enesco, Moor, Huré, Casella,
Sandoz. . . .*

And many more! But I am particularly indebted to Fauré, d'Indy
and Saint-Saëns, whose affection had been so precious to me when
I started. Zuloaga lived generally in Paris—I have one of his pictures
in my house at Sant Salvador. Eugène Carrière, for whom I had great
affection and admiration, painted my portrait, and he used to say that
this one of me and the one he did of Verlaine were the two he liked
best.

I heard that you played to him just before he died.
Yes, a very sad and moving occasion. Carrière was dying of
cancer of the larynx and he suffered horribly. I had visited him many
times since he became ill and found that his philosophy enabled him
to rise above any pain he had to endure. When it got too acute he used
to bring his Marcus Aurelius book from under his pillow and read.
A few days before he died, when he could not speak any more, he
indicated that he wanted to hear me play. I got my 'cello and played
some of the quietest movements of the Bach Suites. The glow of the
sunset added to the solemnity of the moment. The few friends sitting
round the bed were silent in anguish and I was crying. When I stopped
he wanted to embrace me and then raised his arms to show how grateful
he was to have received such consolation.[1]

---

[1] In his book *Trois crises de l'art actuel* (Fasquelle, 1906), Camille Mauclair
describes the scene.

"*I shall never forget one of my last visits to Carrière when he was on his death-bed.
A wintry twilight filled the room with the mysterious colours he liked so much. A touch
of light still caught the side of a vase where some faded flowers were drooping. There
were some study drawings on the walls—the last ones. In the half-light one could guess
the faces of a few friends sitting round like shadows. In the middle, the rectangular shape
of the bed where Carrière was lying motionless, like a statue of himself. An admirable
lady, whose portrait was the last Carrière painted, had brought Casals and his 'cello.
He sat near the bed and played some Bach with the emotion, power and charm of that
unique quality of his.*

"*We all sat there in gloom and silence, listening only to the glorious instrument
which seemed to pray for Carrière and also to carry our inner thoughts, which mere*
(Continued at foot of page overleaf.)

I could write endlessly about all the friends I had in Paris before the 1914 war. There was such a marvellous atmosphere there in those days and I felt so rich with so many good friends. Alas, most of them are dead now.

Fortunately, Enesco lived until very recently.

With him I had a friendship which existed for half a century, and I always had a most tender affection for him. I also considered him one of the most important composers of the present generation.

It was through your friend Dr. Sandoz that you met Bergson?

Yes, Dr. Sandoz, a pure and childlike character, used often to come to the *Villa Molitor*, and one day he introduced me to the great philosopher, whom he knew. This was the beginning of one of the friendships I have most appreciated in my life.

Bergson, I knew, was always taken up by the studies and preparations for his lectures and books. But whenever I was in Paris, I used to go and see him because we were both so pleased to see each other. I used to say to him, "How is it you take pleasure in talking to a man like myself who knows nothing?" "My dear boy," Bergson would say, "you have taught me a great deal." "What, in musical matters?" "Not only in those," he said—and I began to understand what he meant, because of my own discovery, namely, "learning while teaching".

Bergson must have been interested in the part played by intuition in the performance of music.

Of course, and we often talked about it. Once he asked me what was my feeling while playing great music like Bach or Beethoven— and I said that what I found was that if, after a good performance, I felt satisfied, I had a special feeling which could only be compared to carrying a weight of gold inside me. He was very interested in this remark and whenever we met he used to talk about it. One day he said, "This weight you talk about, is it equal or similar to the one we should feel when we have done a good action?" I also knew the feeling one has after a good action, but it is of a different nature. In that I feel something outside my own self, whereas the one which comes from

words could not have expressed. And we felt almost guilty in realising that our absorption in so much beauty was rising above our sorrow.

"In fact what we were contemplating was as beautiful as a Rembrandt . . . as beautiful as a Carrière! Shadows, waves of sound, the ghostly knowledge of an agony relieved by the comfort of the music, all contributed to make us realise that these minutes would be remembered as a kind of extraordinary perfection·given us by Carrière. Not until we left the place did we dare to shed bitter tears."

artistic creation seems to belong to the inner self, as if one's participation had been deeper and more definite. There is another difference between the two sensations: a good action with me is followed by a desire to forget it, so as not to lapse into a state of self-admiration, but a successful performance seems to become a part of me, even to evoke a feeling of self-recognition.

Was it not the Prince of Broglie who said that when he discovered the principles of quantum physics he felt that an inner peace and clarity gradually took possession of him?

I feel something of the same kind, but with it I have a more physical sensation, which is why I use the image of the weight of gold.

Did you discuss religion with Bergson?

Yes, and although I knew he did not belong to any religious persuasion, I always felt he was very spiritually inclined. I knew our views on the subject were almost identical—but although I read a few years ago that he was approaching conversion at the time of his death, I must say that he never mentioned it in the course of our discussions.

Since we talk of Bergson, let me tell you of my great admiration for the type of man known as the "French *savant*". Their modesty, their wit and their humanity leave them indifferent to public opinion, but all the same they remain the glory of their country and of all mankind.

I read in a biography of Fritz Kreisler that you and some of your friends used to meet in a "private circle".[1]

It is true. We met in the summer before the 1914 war. Ysaye, Kreisler, Enesco, Thibaud and myself used to gather at Thibaud's place.

Were you by yourselves?

You can imagine, with the life we all led, how we were longing to make music for ourselves. One would arrive from Russia, another from America or somewhere else. When we played string quartets Ysaye always liked to play the viola.

But you also met at Ysaye's country house in Belgium?

Yes.

I hear that you played piano quintets there with Busoni, Cortot or Pugno at the piano, and for the strings Kreisler, Thibaud, Ysaye (viola) and Casals: combinations of this kind would have made the impresarios go off their heads!

But impresarios were not admitted to these meetings!

[1] *Fritz Kreisler*, by Louis P. Lochner. (Macmillan & Co., New York.)

Do you remember when you started your classes at the École Normale de Musique *in Paris?*

It was before 1914. Cortot, Thibaud and myself started the School with Auguste Mangeot[1] as Director.[2]

During the first year of the *École Normale* the public was admitted to the classes on payment. But it was discovered that this audience upset the pupils. (Pierre Fournier was one of the first who came to play at these classes.) I was against this. In fact I did not teach at the School but every year, during the spring, I used to come and hear every 'cellist, one after the other. I decided to have Diran Alexanian as a professor of the 'cello at the School, and when he went to America Maurice Eisenberg took his place.

Did you play for Queen Victoria before or after your début *in Paris?*

Before. I had been in London on different occasions playing at some of the "at homes" society people used to give during the season, and my first public appearance in London was at a concert at the Crystal Palace under the direction of Auguste Manns. This vast place seemed to house a permanent fair where music had a place in the middle of countless other attractions.

The concert where I played in front of Queen Victoria was given at her residence in the Isle of Wight. Her son, the future Edward VII, the Duke of York and other members of the Royal family were also present.

What was your impression of the great queen?

That of a very respectable old lady inclined to plumpness, surrounded by silence and reverence, etiquette being very strict at the Court. I remember the white veil she wore on her head and the Hindu servant who placed a footstool at her feet.

Did she speak to you?

Yes, she got up after the concert and came to congratulate me.

[1] Auguste Mangeot wrote in the *Monde Musical* in 1910: "*What we don't understand is why Casals should be unique, why work and thought should not produce many performers of his value. Is it so very difficult nowadays to be natural and simple? Is it our education, our way of living, that produces so many great talents which seem false or awkward? It is a complex question rather difficult to answer. But what we can wish for is to see that Casals creates a school—and those who like music would find it a noble task to contribute to its fruition. It seems useless to try to reform the present situation, which is made up of the mistakes, flatteries and errors of the past, but we can ask Casals to try and form some better mentalities in the artists of tomorrow.*"

[2] *Translator's note:*

This is not quite accurate: it was my brother Auguste who founded the *École Normale de Musique* and asked Casals, Cortot and Thibaud to be artistic directors.

She said that the Queen of Spain had spoken to her about me and added that she hoped that my artistic career would fulfil the honour and trust that had been placed in me. When I returned to Spain I saw Queen Maria Cristina; she showed me the telegram she had received from Queen Victoria about the concert and specially about my performance of Bach.

Did you keep up your friendship with Maria Cristina?

Every year when I went home, I had to go and visit her in Madrid. She used to say, "Pablo, you sit here and tell me all that happened since we last met." I did not and could not keep any secrets from her.

It was in England that you met Hans Richter?

Yes, and he became one of my great friends. It was during one of my first tours. I was playing in Manchester under his direction, and a performance of the Schumann Concerto with him was one of those that most satisfied me. He was a great conductor. I played with him every year and he always said before the concert, "Remember, we must have a long talk after the concert." He used to take me by the arm and we would walk to a tavern (always the same one), where we talked till the small hours of the morning. The owner of this place used to lock the door at the appointed time and leave us in peace, waiting patiently until we went home. He obviously had a great respect for Richter! And we discussed all sorts of musical subjects.

Did you often agree with each other?

Always! And the fact that we had so many ideas in common used to excite me in a delightful way: I felt intoxicated. In spite of his age he always spoke with the enthusiasm of a young man, which always pleased me so much. It was when he spoke about Wagner that I was most thrilled, for I knew how intimate the two had been. Whenever he quoted any observations Wagner had made to him during rehearsals, I collected them as a treasure. I gazed at him, taking in every word.

You have some of his scores, I believe.

Yes, after his death I bought a large part of them.

Did you meet Joachim in England?

No. When I met Edward Speyer and Donald Tovey, who were Joachim's great friends, he had already retired. But I was present at the ceremony in the Queen's Hall to celebrate his seventy-fifth birthday. Joachim was in his decline, but his performance of the Beethoven Concerto was still full of vigour and, of course, of wonderful artistic value. At the end, Lord Balfour presented him with his

portrait painted by Sargent. And the speech Joachim made showed
how deeply touched he was.

Was Edward Speyer the founder of the Joachim Society in London?

Yes, Speyer founded the *Classical Concert Society* which replaced
the Joachim Society. Their programmes didn't include anything
later than Brahms. Speyer and other members of the Committee
came to ask for my help at a time when the Society was in a difficult
position. I was delighted to help them.[1]

Speyer and I became great friends and one could always count on
music at his lovely house called Ridgehurst. He had been an intimate
friend of Joachim, Brahms and Clara Schumann. He remembered
having heard Mendelssohn at a concert when he was five years old.
His father, who died at ninety-five, had been a personal friend of
Beethoven and of Mozart's eldest son. So you can imagine what
interesting anecdotes and memories he brought out in his conversations
with me.

Was it in 1901 that you went to America for the first time?

Yes, and what a journey it was! We sailed for a tour of eighty
concerts, with Emma Nevada, the great singer.

*To a young European of twenty-five, as you were, some parts of America
must have seemed strange.*

You are telling me! Once, when the French pianist Moreau
and I were having a "look round" in a town in Texas which might

[1] "*My co-operation with the Classical Concert Society brought me in touch with
Pablo Casals. I had not heard him but the foreign papers I had read were full of praise
for him. I wrote to him explaining the origins and aims of the Society and asking for his
collaboration. I got a charming letter from him in which he said he felt honoured to help a
Society that had been brought about by the art of Joachim. It was on October 20, 1909,
that Casals played for the first time at our concerts. The programme included the Brahms
Trio in C minor and the Schubert Trio in B♭ major, which Casals played with Marie
Soldat and Leonard Borwick. In between the two Trios, Casals played the C Major
Suite of Bach for 'cello alone. From the moment he started with the magnificent descending
scale of C major which opens this Suite, the audience followed his performance with a
kind of exalted attention. The enthusiasm rose with each movement until the end, when
it burst into a kind of demonstration rarely heard in a London concert hall. Casals had
captivated an English audience by his playing of Bach. We had been persuaded by the
erudite that Bach had to be played in a dry and lifeless way, whereas Casals, while
observing a great respect for classical form, played it with real spontaneity of feeling and
lively expression. From then onwards Casals was a regular visitor at Ridgehurst, and
when he came he was always the first to suggest making music, which, of course, delighted
us. He is an example of the rare combination of great virtuosity with supreme musicianship. The extent of his knowledge in any branch of music is astounding, and as reliable
as his critical sense. In 1926 we were fortunate to hear him conduct the L.S.O. His
performance was beautiful and he proved that he was also a great conductor.*"—Sir
Edward Speyer, *My Life and Friends.* (Cobden Sanderson, London.)

have come out of any cowboy film, we went into a "saloon", where we began to play dice with the sort of men who wear large hats and carry an ammunition belt with a revolver at the ready! I was "unlucky" enough to win a certain amount, and as the coins mounted up in front of me I noticed how "menacing" the faces of our friends were becoming! I also got into trouble when I persistently refused the drinks I was offered: one man said to me, "Here we bet *and* drink." I kept my eye on the revolver with apprehension, thinking that anything might happen, when, fortunately, luck changed and I began to lose. Then I noticed the cheerful looks that spread over their faces, and when the time came for them to go we all embraced in a most friendly way.

(*Although Casals did not say so, I suspected that he had to cheat in order to lose on this occasion. . . .*)

Every time we went back to America, my colleagues and I were looking forward to some adventures, and there would be no ending if I tried to relate the countless ones we got involved in.

I read somewhere that when you first went to America, some impresarios were rather shocked to see a young performer nearly bald, for it was very much the fashion for musical virtuosos to wear long hair in those days!

Yes, one of these impresarios actually told me that he would raise my fee considerably if I agreed to wear a wig during the concerts.[1]

And what was the accident you had in San Francisco?

It was during the first tour. We had decided to climb the Tamalpais at San Francisco. Fortunately as we were coming down I noticed a piece of rock was on the point of falling. As a matter of fact it did fall on my path, but as I had been warned I had time to get out of the way. But my right hand got smashed and, if I had not been careful, I would have been killed. Do you know what I said when I saw my hand in that state? "Thank God, I shall not play the 'cello any more." You see, if one decides to play an instrument conscientiously with all seriousness, one becomes a slave for life (not to mention the stage-fright I have always suffered from before playing). I thought I would give up my life to composition and conducting.

My colleagues went on with the tour and I had to stay in San Francisco for four months while my hand healed. You can still see the scar now. Before leaving this great Californian town I gave a concert

[1] *Another impresario made an announcement to the audience to the effect that "if you notice the great 'cellist Casals is bald, although he is so young, it is because he left a lock of hair as a souvenir to all the women he has loved".*

where I realized that the use of my wrist and fingers had, luckily, not been impaired.

Were you pleased to be able to play again?

Very pleased indeed.

It all reminds me of Georges Enesco, who called the violin his "intimate enemy". . . .

Did you go on tour again the following year?

No. In 1904 I went again to America, when I gave with the New York Symphony Orchestra the first performance of Richard Strauss' *Don Quixote*, conducted by himself. Quite recently a friend of mine sent me an account of this performance written by Strauss himself: a most illuminating document.

During this tour I played at the White House at a reception given by President Theodore Roosevelt. After the concert the President took me by the arm in a very friendly way and introduced me to all his guests. He was then a man bursting with strength, vitality and sympathy, but when I met him again, many years later, at the house of the millionaire business man, Mackay, I could hardly recognise him. He looked very old, sitting down in a corner of the drawing-room, and when I tried to cheer him up by telling him stories of the past, he just looked at me in a sad way: he was only a shadow of himself.

I have read somewhere that you saved the lives of thousands of people in a theatre where a fire started while you were playing.

Ah yes. I think it was at a place called Wale-Wale. The auditorium began to fill with smoke and the crowd was starting to panic. As it was just at the time of the intermission, I told the Director that his duty was to tell the audience that it was a small fire and that the concert would continue after a short interval, during which time those who wished to go out had plenty of time to do it quietly. So I got the pianist to sit at the piano and the programme went on, in spite of a good deal of coughing caused by the smoke; but anyhow the panic was avoided and the crowd got out without any accident. The next day there was nothing left of the theatre, and when the Town Council came to thank me for the coolness of my action I told them it was, to my mind, the least thing I could have done to save my audience from being crushed to death.

And what about the charity concert you gave for Granados' children?

Yes, I was deeply shocked when I heard of his tragic death (crossing the English Channel during the 1914–18 war in the *Sussex*, which was torpedoed by the Germans). Granados was a great friend, whom I admired tremendously. Being in America, I thought I would do something for his children who were left destitute after both their parents had died. I had no difficulty in getting the kind of help I needed: both Paderewski and Kreisler immediately agreed to play with me at a benefit concert given in the Metropolitan Opera House in New York, which was filled to capacity. This produced a very large sum, which was sent to the orphans.

Was this the first time you played with Paderewski and Kreisler?

Yes: we played the *Archduke Trio* of Beethoven.

Do you remember when you first met Paderewski?

My first contact with him was astonishing: I was staying with Mrs. Ram in Paris and she took me to hear Paderewski at the *Salle Erard*, where he was giving a recital. We were sitting in the front seats and when she took me to the artist's room to introduce me after the concert, she went to talk to him first. Pointing to me with his finger, Paderewski said, "I know this young man and, tonight, I played for him." He fixed me with a penetrating gaze and added, "This young man is one of the elect." How could I explain this?

He had never heard you?

Never.

Had anyone spoken to him about you?

No.

It is amazing, really. And when did he hear you play the 'cello for the first time?

A few years later in Montreux. In the interval I was introduced to a charming boy who must have been nine or ten. He was Yehudi Menuhin. As for Paderewski's homage to me, it was most moving. When I had finished he came forward to greet me, and putting out his hand said only, "*Maestro*". I was a bit confused, for Paderewski was then at the height of his career, but it did not inflate my vanity for I felt he was paying homage to my work and my musical endeavour.

Did you see him again in Warsaw when he became President of the first Polish Republic?

No. After the concert of Granados at the Metropolitan I never saw him again. He was a wonderful man. But fate led him also to a tragic end!

What do you think of musical life in America?

Very intense, and they have the means to organise things in a way that does not exist in Europe. For instance, at Cleveland it was Mrs. Taft who made up the yearly deficit to the tune of thousands of dollars.

In Boston, a rich patron spent fabulous sums in order to give the city one of the best orchestras in the world. The same thing happened in Philadelphia and in many other cities where this American way of patronising opera houses and symphony orchestras has been the origin of their success. Again, in New York, we find that in order to raise the expenses of the popular orchestral concerts he organised at the Metropolitan Museum, Mr. David Mannes (Leopold Mannes' father) simply put an advertisement in the papers. (These concerts, at which I often played, were most interesting. Thousands came and sat on the floor.) To show you the intensity of the musical life in the States— one day when I was playing at the High School at Richmond with an excellent orchestra, the Director asked me to guess how many orchestras of this kind I thought there were in his State. Thinking of our school orchestras in Europe, I suggested twenty to thirty. He said: six hundred!

And what of American mental outlook?

Well, considering I have gone across the States many times and stayed there for considerable periods, I think I have acquired a certain amount of knowledge of American mentality. I think that many European people who judge the Americans of today don't realise enough that the bulk of the people is made up of an extraordinary mixture of different races, religions and nationalities, which is still in a state of fermentation and is not yet moulded into a stable type. There is no doubt that they breathe a dynamism and exhibit a youthful strength which we old Europeans find surprising and upsetting. This display of so much varied energy produces some imposing material creations, as well as a conception of life which is not always in accordance with ours. The problem of harmonising these very opposite conceptions has led me, personally, into some unfortunate situations.

When did you last go to the States?

In 1928. As my work with the orchestra took more of my time, I had to reduce the periods of my tours abroad. After the Second World War, I meant to visit my American friends again and play to them. But, as you know, there were moral reasons which prevented my going.[1]

Tell me about your first journey to Russia.

It was in 1905. Just at the time when the first revolution was shaking the Empire of the Tsars. I was bound for Moscow, but when we reached Vilna the train stopped and everyone had to get out. I

[1] *See especially Chapter XI.*

went to the waiting-room, wondering what I should do, when a man came to me and introduced himself as a general and at the same time a high official of the railways. "You are Mr. Pablo Casals?" he said. As I answered in the affirmative he went on putting questions to me and I realised he knew all about me . . . even more than I knew myself (actually he had just come from Berlin, where he had heard me play). "You won't be able to go to Moscow," he said. "The train is not going any further, but, if you like, I can take you to St. Petersburg in a special train." I accepted his offer since I immediately thought of Siloti, who I knew was directing one of the orchestras there.

Did you know him personally?

No, but we had exchanged letters and that was a sufficient reason for me to share a compartment reserved for the general and his wife. We went on without any knowledge at all of what might happen to us.

But we reached St. Petersburg, where Siloti received me in a most friendly way, and as a soloist he had engaged was unable to reach St. Petersburg because of the railway strike, he asked me to take his place. I shall never forget my introduction to a Russian audience. Such was the success that Siloti and I decided to give a series of concerts, which took place in a curious atmosphere because of the state of affairs: we played in the magnificent Hall of the "Noblesse", which was all lit by candlelight because of the general strike. As I had lost my suitcase I had to play in my ordinary suit. The posters were written by hand as the printers were also on strike. One evening after the concert I asked Siloti if I could not witness some scene of a revolutionary character. So we crossed one of the bridges over the Neva and got near the riot. I saw a good deal of shooting in the distance, when suddenly a man rushed by screaming in Russian (as Siloti translated it to me), "Long live the Republic of the Tsars!" They could not even imagine that a Republic was possible without their Tsars!

Do you think that the more enlightened Russians thought the revolutionary spirit was incompatible with the beliefs of the Slavophiles?

That is something one noticed when speaking with a Russian: even if he was a supporter of autocracy, you realised he had a conviction of a redeeming mission assigned to Russia in which the whole universe was involved.

How often did you go to Russia?

I went every year until 1914.

Did you meet any Russian composers?

I met Cesar Cui, Rimsky-Korsakov and Glazunov when I stayed with Siloti, and in Moscow, Scriabin and Rachmaninov, who was Siloti's cousin and under whose direction I played many times.

I remember one evening at St. Petersburg when I was listening to a first performance of a work by Rimsky-Korsakov, where Chaliapine was singing the title part, Glazunov came to me to say that the composer was feeling very nervous on account of my being in the audience. In the interval a friend of Rimsky-Korsakov came to ask me what I thought of the work. I thought that was a most friendly and modest gesture on his part.

What about the group formed by the younger generation, like Stravinsky, Prokoviev and Diaghilev?

I think I met them later on, although I met Diaghilev in Russia. When I came across Prokoviev he was only seventeen or eighteen, and I was very impressed by his gifts as a pianist and composer.

Did you see any productions of the Russian Ballet before it became known outside Russia?

Yes, and you must realise that over there the ballet is a necessity to compensate for the light and warmth they miss for such long periods: the shining lights of the theatre make up for them and the excitements of the show produce a wild elation, serving in the place of the sun.

You told me once that upon entering Russia you felt a sense of suffocation.

Yes, it is true: when you go through the Customs you find these enormous officials who look at you with suspicion and you feel immediately as if you were entering a prison.

The Marquis of Custine, who was French Ambassador in St. Petersburg when the Bourbons were back in France, wrote that the air he breathed there seemed filled with fear and suspicion.

And, one century later, it was just the same!

Was there much apparent distress?

You met it at every step, all the time—and you felt that the poor were completely under the yoke of the aristocrats who flaunted their luxury in the most provocative, scandalous way. The Russian students I met seemed to belong to a Dostoievsky novel: they wished to work for their people and to open up new horizons for them, but, at the same time, you found so many of these students who, realising their impotence, took refuge in an art like music, which was a mental comfort to them.

When the cataclysm burst in 1917 I was not surprised. But I must say that the way some great people I knew were treated made me loathe the new *régime*.

What of Italy?

I began to go there two or three years after my *début* in Paris.

What did you think of the country, the buildings and the museums?

Who could forget them? I had a special weakness for Venice and I did not hesitate to travel twenty-four hours each way in order to spend a day there!

Was Italy still the land of bel canto?

Symphonic music only started about fifty years ago and the *bel canto* you speak of, the Opera with all the appealing melodies, was part of a very lively tradition.

But how did the Italians look at their famous ancestors, like Frescobaldi, Scarlatti, Corelli, Tartini?

They were very proud of them, which does not mean that they knew them or played them, except in a very small circle, of course.

What was rather curious in those days was the fact that their famous poets like Dante, Boccacio, were widely known, for you would hear the most unexpected people reciting their poems by heart. But nothing was played of the music of the glorious composers you named. Today, all that has changed.

What about your tours in Holland?

I went back there almost every year. Julius Röntgen was a great friend of mine and I admired him as a pianist and a composer.

Didn't you have trouble with the Dutch Police?

Yes, once as I was entering Holland, the police authorities kept me and questioned me (it was the year of Queen Wilhelmina's coronation). Apparently I bore a striking likeness to a very dangerous terrorist they were looking for because of his participation in some anarchist plots. In spite of my explanations the police would not be convinced of my identity. Finally I was allowed to proceed to The Hague, where I said I was going, but an inspector accompanied me right to the hotel at which I was staying.

Twelve to fourteen years later, I was dining with my friend Röntgen at the house of Delange, the Director of the Amsterdam Conservatoire. During dinner, a manservant came to say something very discreetly to Mr. Delange, who immediately went out looking rather worried. When he came back he was bursting with laughter: the police had come to enquire about me. Not having received any countermanding order from their chiefs all this time they had, naturally, followed me up all over Holland. But Delange assured them I was not dangerous and the affair was closed. This sort of thing happened to me in Russia also. Coming back from Finland (before 1914), the Tsarist Police began to search me very thoroughly and to question me in what was, obviously, very rude language. But as I talked German to them and they talked Russian, we hardly understood each other. They wished me to sign a paper printed in Russian, which I refused to do without knowing what it meant. They treated me so roughly and I was so furious when I arrived in St. Petersburg that I immediately went to Siloti to tell him. He knew Polit, and when this chief heard the story he took it to the Duma where it was discussed: a few days later I received an official explanation. But this sort of terrorism goes on just the same in our country. I was sitting in a carriage at Barcelona ready to go abroad when a Spanish police officer came to me and said I was arrested! I told him who I was but he looked at me with very suspicious eyes and began to question me. I smiled at him and the people travelling with me began to laugh: one said to the policeman, "Don't you know this is the Maestro, Pablo Casals?" The inspector was very apologetic, but he nevertheless made me sign a paper to the effect that I admitted having been threatened with arrest but that I told him I was Pablo Casals!

Did you meet Ysaye in Belgium?

No, I met him in Paris at the beginning of my career and our friendship grew from day to day. The more I knew him, the more I liked him, and what a great artist he was! When he appeared on the platform, one felt the presence of a king. He had a fine presence and was of great stature, looking like a young lion with piercing eyes. His gestures also; the way he moved about; he was a show in himself.

As for his performances, I did not agree with many colleagues who would say that he took too much liberty with the text and could not control the flow of his fantasy. But if one thought of the surroundings where he developed, and the period of his formation, one could not fail to be carried away by the strength of his personality.

His début had not been very striking?

It was Joachim who discovered him in a café in Berlin, where Ysaye played every evening—and you must remember that it was a fashion for music-lovers to go to places of this kind to hear good music: Jacques Thibaud, for instance, played for a long time at the Café Rouge in Paris.[1]

I think I have read somewhere that it was Anton Rubinstein who had organised his first tour in Scandinavia?

I don't know, but Ysaye told me that Joachim had heard him play in this café in Berlin and was so enthusiastic that he told him he should see to it that he left this job and become an international artist! And, of course, he did!

Did you play under Ysaye when he conducted the Cincinnati Orchestra?

Yes, and also in Brussels with his own orchestra. I even played there for his farewell concert when Queen Elizabeth came. It was a solemn occasion which I shall never forget, the last concert he conducted. I had a strong impression he would not live very long, but he was so keen to show me his esteem, that as I came in to play the Lalo Concerto, he got up and signalled to all the orchestra to stand and made the brass play a fanfare in my honour! And I knew how painful it was for Ysaye to stand up!

Was it in Brussels that you deliberately provoked an incident which had certain repercussions in the world of music?

Yes: you might even say that it was an "organised" incident. I had known for some time that at these concerts it was the custom to play the programme through at the dress rehearsal as well as at the concert. As the public paid for their seats at the rehearsal, and the artist only received one fee, I thought it was most unfair and a bad precedent for young artists to be treated in this way. So when I began to rehearse my Concerto in front of an enormous audience, I simply behaved as one does at a rehearsal, stopping and discussing points of interpretation with the conductor as I thought necessary. I could feel the audience getting restive, and when the concert manager came to me after the concerto asking me to play the Bach Suite I had put down for the second half of the programme, I refused to play it, saying there was no need for me to rehearse this alone. He insisted, but I did not give way and the public became more restive and started shouting. I waited until the Director came to me, saying, "Please, Mr. Casals, will you play the Suite to this audience, who expect to hear it, and you will be paid for two concerts." I had won on this question of principle and the following evening, when the Director and the Treasurer came to pay me for the two concerts, I asked them to be good enough to

[1] *And so did I!* (Translator's note.)

allocate my second fee to the benevolent fund for the players of the orchestra, and, in order to avoid any misunderstanding, I repeated very clearly all the reasons for my protest—and, I am glad to say, the result of this incident was that they decided to do away with this deplorable habit.

I suppose it would be too much to question you about your tours in Hungary, Switzerland, South America, Germany and Austria?

It would be an endless story, but in Hungary I had the pleasure of meeting Molnar, Béla Bartók and Kodály . . . I think Bartók deserves the great name he is making for himself, but I have the greatest admiration and liking for Kodály, who is one of the simplest and most charming artists I have come across. I think his works will last.

I understand that you were interested in the tziganes?

Yes, enormously. All Hungarian musicians got interested in the wealth of their folklore. They have created a Magyar school of music, which must not be mixed up with the songs and the music of the *tziganes.* This is the kind of music based on Hungarian popular tunes, which the *tziganes* flavour in a very characteristic way. These players all possess a most wonderful sense of music, and I never missed a chance of hearing them when I was in Hungary. Many of them knew me and seemed to like me! I think no musician can help being interested in their playing. But looking at it from a purely instrumental angle, the *tzigane* art is almost miraculous. One of the leaders (*Primas*) I had heard was a 'cellist called Toliansky and, to my great surprise, I saw him using all the fingering by extension, which I had elaborated in the course of my studies! He had come to it by pure intuition. I have never met a 'cellist who, technically speaking, could be compared to him. His tone was also marvellous, both in quality and intensity. It sounded like four 'cellos playing together. This fingering he used was the same as on the violin, even in the first or half positions, such was the size of his hand.

(I once went to hear the *tziganes* play with David Popper and I was astounded to hear the old maestro telling me that their way of playing did not interest him.)

As for Switzerland, it is a country I have always been very fond of because of its beautiful scenery, its liberal traditions, its political institutions and the respect of its inhabitants for eccentricities, such as the love of music!

Zürich is like another Vienna: everyone seems to have been born with the love of music.

I also have a deep admiration for the Scandinavian nations, which remain a model of civilisation in the middle of our tormented world.

What about your tours in Central and South America?

I went many times to Mexico, Cuba, South America, Argentina, Uruguay and Brazil.

My first stay in Mexico coincided with the restless period which began after the fall of the dictator Porfirio Diaz.

One day I asked some friends to take me in a car towards the Sierra de los Leones, where the rebels were encamped. They were not very keen to go but agreed to my request. When we got near the forest I could see a party of *Zapatistas* sitting round their tents. As we left we came across a dashing-looking horseman of the Zapata Army, who looked at us with a very suspicious eye. I shall never forget the looks on the faces of my friends, who were gripping their revolvers with anxiety . . . but nothing happened.

In spite of this situation, the Mexicans accorded me a most warm welcome: music-lovers used to come to the hotel and push my carriage to the concert hall, repeating this performance after the concert was over.

The last concert took place at the *Plaza de Toros*, where music and plays had replaced the "*corridas*" which were not allowed by the new government. How lovely it all looked, the audience sitting in their colourful costumes up on the grandstands and shouting enthusiastically.

You also took part unexpectedly in a ceremony dedicated to Anna Pavlova?

Yes, I did. I had read in the papers that a benefit performance for Pavlova was to be given by the Russian Ballet in the Federal City. Of course the *Mort du Cygne* was on the programme, and it gave me the idea of paying my own homage to her in a rather special way. When I arrived in Mexico I went to see Smolens, the conductor of the orchestra, and said, "Pavlova does not even know that I am here and I want to give her a surprise." It was arranged that as Pavlova came on to dance the *Mort du Cygne* the first 'cellist of the orchestra should stop and I should play the solo off the stage, where they had a piano. It so happened that while all this actually took place Pavlova noticed there was something unusual and began to look at the side of the stage . . . as soon as it was over she ran into the wings and embraced me many times! Diaghilev also threw himself into my arms. And

Pavlova took me by the hand and forced me to come on to the stage, although my face was covered with the marks of her make-up.

I feel that if one day circumstances altered for me, the first country I should like to visit would be Mexico, as I should like to pay a tribute to the loyalty she showed towards democratic Spain.

What do you think of German audiences?

In Germany one finds immediately that music is an essential part of the people's life. I have played at hundreds of concerts in the land of Bach and Beethoven and I have always been struck by the atmosphere of devotion to be found in the public. An artist tries to create such an atmosphere in order to get in more direct and intimate communication with this audience. I must say that he finds it ready to hand in Germany.

How did the German public react to your Bach interpretations?

It understood immediately, as well as any other audience did, in fact. I must add also that not only most of the critics and audiences accepted my ideas on the interpretation of Bach, but they also seemed to welcome them with a sense of deliverance. Of course I did not escape reproaches from the minority of so-called "traditionalists", who will stick to this nonsense they call "purism". But this minority is disappearing fast and must disappear completely. So-called "objective" performances of Bach's works, stripped of any life, are just inconceivable. It was in Germany that I received a tribute which touched me deeply. I had just played the Schumann Concerto with the Berlin Philharmonic Orchestra conducted by Arthur Nikisch. After the concert two men advanced towards me, and I could see that one of them was blind. The other, who was holding the blind man by the arm, said to me: "Don't you know him? He is Professor Wirth." (The viola player in the Joachim quartet.)

I imagine that Joachim's death had left his colleagues inconsolable. Professor Wirth began to feel my arms, hands and chest, he then embraced me and murmured in my ear, "Joachim is not dead."

I understand the emotion you must have felt.

I would prefer it if you did not mention this in your book.

But why not? I feel that homage of this kind should be recorded.

I suppose that Vienna was the last of the European capitals you visited?

Yes, and only God knows how I wanted to go there, but it was only seven or eight years after my *début* in Paris that I decided to go.

The first work I played in Vienna was Emmanuel Moor's *Concerto in C♯ minor*, with the Philharmonic Orchestra conducted by Schalk. I felt so terribly nervous that at the moment I started playing I felt my bow slipping through my fingers. Instinctively I tried to turn it in my hand but I had done it too violently and the bow fell in the ninth row. Someone picked it up and, in complete silence, it was passed from one row to the other until it reached me. During these precious minutes I had regained the control of my nerves and could begin properly. After this the musical élite of Vienna honoured me by organising a chamber music concert in which I played with Bruno Walter (who had not yet begun to conduct) in the "Bosendorfen Hall".

From then onwards I went to Vienna every year and always loved it: one felt as if one was in a town made for music.

Yes, it has produced Mozart and Schönberg.

I have known Schönberg well and I'll talk to you about him another day. Vienna, more than any other city, has lived through the history of music from the Classical School to the most modern one. One could imagine that the young generation, having gone so far in their search for new music, would look back to their musical ancestors with a certain amount of disdain. But that attitude does not exist in Vienna. The Viennese and the Austrians, generally speaking, have reached such a high level in what may be called "musical civilisation" that their interest in new music has not altered their love for the great masters of the past.

You cannot imagine how very much alive one finds Haydn, Mozart, Beethoven and Brahms in Vienna. As for Schubert, one might meet him coming out of a brasserie!

In Austria, you feel that music is not the privilege of a group or class of people. Everybody has a natural need of music, just as much as the need for conversation. One day, when I was coming out of the Bristol Hotel in Vienna, I noticed that the porter was humming a tune while he put letters in their boxes. I said to him, "Do you know what you are singing?" "Of course," he replied quite naturally. "The third Brahms Symphony." And as I questioned him he told me he belonged to a music society whose concerts he attended twice a week. And he added, "So do most of the clerks and cab drivers and carpenters."

In 1932 in Vienna I took part in the festivities given on the occasion of the two hundredth anniversary of Haydn's birth. One of the items in the programme was a visit to Rohrau, the village where he was born. President Miklas and the highest authorities of the Republic were there, as well as a number of Austrian musicians, including Furtwängler. As I was crossing the square of the village I found two natives of Rohrau arguing passionately about some disagreement between Haydn and a copyist: one supported Haydn, the other the copyist. Think of it! I met Miklas, Dollfuss and Schuschnigg, and they were all great music-lovers.

I know that in 1912, you and Ysaye gave a memorable performance of the Brahms Double Concerto which, you said, remained one of the most moving recollections of your career.

Yes, this performance was like a revelation and Vienna published a postcard to commemorate it! On one occasion I was invited by the *Gesellschaft der Musikfreude* of Vienna to visit the exhibition dedicated to Beethoven and his contemporaries. There I saw the portrait of Beethoven by Mahler and also the violin method written by Mozart's father, Leopold. I was greatly impressed by these exhibits and the next day, after the concert I was giving, the Director of the Society presented me with a copy of this precious violin method I had so much admired. He also said that he was ordering a copy of Beethoven's portrait from the most highly-qualified artist that could be found, and would send it to me when done!

In fact this copy is unique and it hangs over my father's harmonium in my house in Sant Salvador, next to Beethoven's birth certificate which had belonged to Joachim.

Some friends of mine in Vienna, who were always charming to me, also gave me a piece of stone from the room where Beethoven died, which I greatly cherish.

The celebration of Beethoven's centenary in 1927 in Vienna was specially brilliant, wasn't it?

Yes, and very moving. This commemoration, in which I took part as a 'cellist and also as conductor of the Philharmonic Orchestra, has left me an imperishable recollection. I can still see Edouard Herriot standing next to me, singing with his lovely voice in front of Beethoven's tomb during one of the ceremonies.

But, believe me, the Barcelona commemorative celebrations were also memorable. This was the occasion when Ysaye played, for the last time in public, as a soloist, the Beethoven Concerto with my orchestra, which I conducted. He then took my place to conduct the *Eroica* Symphony and the *Triple Concerto* with Cortot, Thibaud and myself.

You have witnessed the end of many great periods: the Paris of the belle époque; *the Texas of the Westerns; the Russia of the Grand Dukes; the Vienna of the Blue Danube ...*

... And Victorian and Edwardian England, when the aristocrats spent fortunes and engaged the most famous artists to give the best parties to their guests. . . . Well, at my age it is very comforting to have such wonderful memories.

Have you ever been to the Far East?

I could never make up my mind to accept the many offers I had to go to these remote countries, mostly because of the nerve troubles I felt in my head after 1920, which forced me to be careful. I regret not having been to Japan, since all the musicians who went told me of the public's high esteem for them.

Would you believe that it is in Japan that my recordings have had their highest sales?

You told me once that you had never postponed a concert.

It is true, although there was a time when I had an average of 150 to 200 concerts a year. But the fact that I always fulfilled my engagements does not mean I have always felt at my best when coming on to the platform. One evening in Berlin I felt so run down that I fainted while playing.

Was the concert adjourned?

Not at all. After an interruption of half an hour, I resumed the concert: an artist has got to face these situations and be ready to put his will above his physical troubles.

Who were the pianists who accompanied you most often?

In America, Edouard Gendron, Nicholas Mednikoff and Jean Verd. In Europe, Conrad Bos and mostly Otto Schulhoff.

Gendron was a friend of Charlie Chaplin and one day at Hollywood he introduced me to the celebrated actor. He was at the time making a film, and was dressed in his well-known get-up, with the bowler hat and old boots.

What is your opinion of Charlie Chaplin?

My admiration for him is boundless and in these days it is comforting to be reminded of a virtue which should never be forgotten: love for the humble people and pity for the poor. Whether Chaplin does it from an angle of fun and pantomime or not, his intentions are all the more laudable, and it is rather pathetic at the moment to see the administration wrangling about his political views, etc. Fortunately the public knows better, and we all know how great an actor Charlie

Chaplin is. But talking again of the pianists who accompanied me, I must say that Otto Schulhoff, who played with me in Europe and America, had a very remarkable feeling for music and a special gift for accompanying a 'cello. We were always in perfect agreement.

Was Horszowski ever your accompanist?

No, but we gave numerous chamber music concerts together. He first came out as a dazzling *enfant prodigue*, after which he came to live in Paris to study at the University. I encouraged him to resume his career of pianist. He had played a good many times with my orchestra in Barcelona, where the public loved him. For the last five years you have heard him at the Prades Festivals and you have had the chance to see what a simple, modest and retiring man he is. But what a great and real artist!

Of the great conductors you have played with I remember your naming Bréton, Lamoureux, Colonne, Richter, Mottl, Steinbach, Nikish, Siloti, Rachmaninov, Richard Strauss, Damrosch, Mengelberg, Weingartner, Furtwängler, Bruno Walter, Stokowski, Ansermet, Koussevitski, Ysaye, Tovey, Pierre Szel, Sir Adrian Boult, Sir John Barbirolli.

There are many more!

Toscanini?

No, I have never played with Toscanini, although I have known him a long time. We have had many very interesting and cordial talks. I remember once discussing with him certain points in the interpretation of Beethoven. After the Second World War, when he came back to Italy, he invited me to play with him, but there were so many invitations at that time that I could not be everywhere at once. Besides, after 1946 I took on the attitude I have kept ever since.

Have you always agreed with the conductors?

Always. Far from being upset by other people's remarks, I have always tried to compare them with my own views. I must add that on the whole I have met with the greatest understanding from the different conductors I have played with. There has been one exception, however, and the only incident in my life when I had to go to law to settle it.

As you know, I played once a year for the benefit concert of the Lamoureux and Colonne Orchestras. The chief conductor of the Colonne Orchestra came to see me to fix up our programme some time beforehand, and it was decided I should play the Dvořák Concerto. I arrived in Paris one morning for the dress rehearsal, having spent the night in the train. I was waiting in the artists' room for my turn to go on, when the conductor came in. We were looking at the score together, to decide the tempo and some details of performance, when he suddenly threw the score on the table saying, "What horrible music!"

I thought he was joking and asked him what he meant, and he repeated the same words slowly. "Are you mad?" I said. "How can you insult such a magnificent work. Do you know that Brahms considered it a masterpiece?" "Ah," he said, "Brahms is another one, and if you are a musician yourself you must know how bad this music is." I did not know how to contain my feelings: my hands and legs were shaking and I said: "When I think I have travelled all night in order to introduce this magnificent work to your public, only to find you not only scorn the work but detest it! In the circumstances it is obvious that you don't understand it, and I don't see how I can interpret it with you. I see it is impossible and I shall not play."

My refusal to play was a bombshell. While we went on arguing the public, who had paid for admittance, were filling up the hall. The audience broke on to the stage arguing and shouting, and then I noticed Debussy, who was standing near us. I said to the conductor, "Ask him if he thinks an artist can possibly play when feeling as I do." "Come on," Debussy said, "if you wanted to play, you could play." Such was the answer of the artist who wrote *Pelléas and Mélisande*, and it pained me greatly. I said to him, "Monsieur Debussy, I assure you, it is impossible for me to play and I will not play."

I was just getting ready to go when the conductor, wanting to interfere, said I could not go until he had got a bailiff to serve me with a summons.

But it was a charity concert?

Yes. The bailiff put down the facts of the incident and the case was heard a few months later in a Paris court. The barrister who was prosecuting, curiously enough, said in front of the magistrate that I was right. But I was made to pay a fine of 3000 francs and costs.

Thirty years later I still think I could not have played in such circumstances: when a conductor himself despises and insults the work he˙has to interpret with you, in what physical and mental condition can you be to play the work, and who would be responsible for the musical slaughter which would follow? Later on this conductor repented having been the cause of this incident, and said to some friends of mine, "What would Casals say if I went to apologise?" They said, "Of course you should go." But he never came.

Would you have told him again he had been wrong?

Without the slightest hesitation.

And now, living as you do in this quiet little town of Prades, you can rest after so much travelling and the agitated life of great cities to which you have been accustomed. I know that you have imposed this retirement on yourself in order to keep faith with your moral convictions.

Yes, but this retirement has lasted a long time, alas.

But what of all the great musicians and music-lovers who come to Prades every year, as a sort of pilgrimage during the Festivals?

Yes, I am immensely grateful to them all and their company is a great comfort to me.

IV

Casals as a Conductor—The Pau Casals Orchestra

How early did you feel the desire to conduct?

When I was a child and played the organ. I was already longing to conduct the choir in the church: I felt like saying to the tenors "Do this" and to the sopranos "Do that".

When did you actually begin to conduct?

I must have been fifteen or sixteen when Granados asked me to conduct the rehearsals, in Barcelona, of his first opera, *Maria del Carmen*, because, he said, he felt so nervous.

You conducted many orchestras besides your own in Barcelona?

Quite often I conducted the Lamoureux Orchestra in Paris, the London Symphony Orchestra, the New York Symphony Orchestra, the Vienna Philharmonic Orchestra, the B.B.C. Orchestra. I have also conducted many concerts in Rome, Milan, Madrid, Mexico and Havana.

The more I went on conducting, the more I was asked. One invitation I accepted every year was from the London Symphony Orchestra.

It was this orchestra which offered you an imposing collection of pipes?

Yes (*Casals gave a rather wicked smile*). I had been to see a doctor as I was not feeling well, and he told me I ought to stop smoking.

I was very affected by this gloomy prospect when, on the same evening, the Committee of the L.S.O. sent me a magnificent collection of English pipes as a present! What could I do but use them?

What were your intentions when you created your own orchestra in Barcelona?

My first intention was not to create an orchestra but to help one of the existing ones which were in a state of decay. I wanted to raise one orchestra to a level worthy of the capital of Catalonia.

Emil Ludwig says in his book that when you started to do things for your country in 1920 "You were not going to gain anything by it."

Of course not. I was convinced I was going to lose a lot, but I was also convinced that it was my patriotic duty to take an active part in the musical life of my country. I had always had this idea, although

69

my profession took me abroad nearly all the year round. But, at that time, I decided to fulfil the task I had planned because I could now afford it.

I heard that you had a very difficult task?

At first there were too many difficulties in the way and it looked quite hopeless. The two orchestras of Barcelona had not got any solid financial basis and in spite of good material in the players and conductors their organisations and ways of working were entirely ineffectual. I talked to the conductors, telling them I would finance them and play with them in order to form a really first-class ensemble, but they kept on saying that it could not be done and that I had been away too long from Catalonia to know the real conditions there, and they thought that my views were only idealistic ones! I went to see all sorts of personalities and I must say that the result was disappointing to say the least: I remember an aristocrat saying to me that music interested him as little as bull-fights did. Faced with such a gloomy prospect I called a meeting of important people in Barcelona and said, "I am taking charge of this project myself and hope to make a success of it." They all thought Casals had gone mad and said, "It is all very well to go about the world playing the violoncello, but why does he want to create a great orchestra in Barcelona?" Luckily I had a few faithful friends. First, Felip Vidal, who was enthusiastic about my idea and put himself entirely at my disposal. He became the treasurer and dealt without respite with all the financial problems. His wife, Madame Francesca de Capdevilla-Vidal, did all the correspondence and the markings in the orchestral scores. They both went through the most tiring and thankless period with me.

The secretary of our committee was an admirable man called Joaquim Pena, who joined us more through idealism than conviction. He had a good deal of experience in the field of art but was carried away by his optimism. He had already spent all his capital in support of musical events in Catalonia. He had a vast culture, talked many languages and was a great Wagner enthusiast, going to Bayreuth every year. He had been president of the Wagnerian Association of Barcelona and had translated all Wagner's operas into Catalan, as well as librettos of French and Italian operas. He translated the text of Schiller for the *Ninth Symphony*, *The Creation* of Haydn and all the songs of Schubert, Schumann and Brahms. When I think that such a man as Pena fell a victim of the military rising which swept Catalonia in July 1936, I can hardly contain myself.

The President of the main committee was Mr. Vidal-Quadres, who had great social prestige which helped considerably in consolidating the position of the orchestra.

It was at his home that I had played my first string quartet when very young. He had music regularly at his house. He said to me, "I am with you and I'll give what I can." He gave so much and he gave it in such a wonderful way, that, in fact, it was as if he had given everything.

When was the orchestra constituted?

In 1920. With my own money I engaged eighty-eight musicians, the best I could find. They had previously been badly paid and came to rehearsals as they pleased. I promised them a good salary but told them they would have to rehearse every morning and afternoon punctually.

On the first day I talked to them seriously, but in a friendly way, about the importance of the work we were about to begin. Unfortunately I then became seriously ill. I realised that all these preparations would not lead to anything if I were unable to carry on. I suffered from inflammation of the iris, and the well-known oculist who treated me made a mistake in the number of injections he gave me. I had three, and a doctor friend told me that one would have been enough to kill a horse! (It resulted in a contraction of the blood-vessels of the head which causes the headaches I still suffer from periodically.) I had to stay in bed for weeks and weeks, which coincided with private worries as well. But I realised that unless I went forward with my scheme the dream I had of forming this great orchestra for Barcelona would not materialise.

The scepticism I had met when I took the first steps turned into organised hostility in certain quarters when it was discovered that I was going ahead with my plan. Surreptitious attacks were made while my enemies prepared to boycott it. In order to avoid a collapse of the whole scheme I sent a message to my musicians asking them to meet twice a day, according to their contract.

And what were they doing without a conductor?

They only met. Sometimes my brother Enrique, who was my leader, would make them rehearse some pieces, but most of the time they remained idle. After a few weeks I was visited by a delegation from the orchestra who saw me in bed and said they could not go on being paid without working. "You must be spending enormous sums," one said, "and we don't know what to do." "Don't worry," I said, "you have signed a contract with me and you must keep it. Your fees will be paid regularly and, in the meantime, will you please meet and make suggestions about the orchestra, in fact form a feeling of community."

Summer came, the spring season was over and everything was in the air. I felt a bit better and against my doctor's orders I wanted to pay a visit to my musicians. After congratulating them on having kept faith, I wished them a good holiday and told them we should give our first concert in the autumn. In fact our first concert took place on the fourth of October of that year.

We all remember how the orchestra took root in Barcelona's life and how it became an object of pride to all Catalans.

Nevertheless the first few years were a great struggle. At first the audiences were small, mostly because some influential people had circulated what was virtually a command to ignore the concerts. As a rule we gave twenty concerts a year: ten in the spring and ten in the autumn. As we found that ordinary subscriptions would not produce enough money, my friends formed a group of "protector" members who paid double. There were over a thousand of them. Once a year I gave a 'cello recital for them, my only appearance in Barcelona.

At no time did I take any salary for my work with the orchestra. After seven or eight years it paid its own way but until then I made up the deficits.[1] This orchestra had cost me a terrific amount of work, but I felt very proud of it and working with it was my greatest pleasure.

What motives did you have besides the patriotic ones that urged you to create an orchestra?

Some people may be surprised to hear it, but I have never been quite satisfied with only playing the 'cello. The responsibilities involved mean a most exhausting amount of work and concerts are a terrific tax on the nervous system. I feel as much at home playing the 'cello, sitting at the piano or holding the conductor's baton. Making music is what interests me, and it is as necessary to my mind as bread is to the daily diet. And what better instrument is there than an orchestra, since it includes them all?[2] It is the supreme medium for anyone who feels music deeply and wants to translate the form and shape of his most intimate thoughts.

[1] *Although Casals does not want such details to be published I know that he spent over 2,000,000 pesetas (about 320,000 dollars at the rate before 1929).*

[2] *In the days of his early tours Casals had once written to his great friend Julius Röntgen: "If I have been so happy scratching a violoncello, how shall I feel when I can possess the greatest of all instruments—the orchestra?"*

In Bucharest, 1937

Casals, aged twenty-one

The cloister, Chester Cathedral, 1945

Beethoven's sonata for piano and cello: Casals and
Rudolf Serkin at Prades Festival, 1954

I feel enormously attracted by team-work and the human element near me. I delight in it. I always feel the need to possess the limitless treasury of orchestral music and the desire to perform it according to my ideas and my conception, for the benefit of the audiences of my country.

What were your guiding principles at first in your work with the orchestra?

My first preoccupation, knowing the bad habits of orchestral musicians, was to create an atmosphere of artistic endeavour, to awake or to reinforce their sense of responsibility and to obtain maximum efficiency, so that each player could feel like a soloist.

In the first place I wanted to get perfect intonation and would explain patiently how to get it without shouting at them or losing my temper. Then I would deal with accent and expression suitable for the work we were rehearsing. I was never satisfied until I could obtain the most exact reproduction of the tempo and rhythm required, in fact, until the "music" spoke. I did not mind repeating an explanation as often as necessary, and I do believe more in the efficacy of *convincing* a man than of *imposing* my will upon him like a dictator. It seems to me that if the conductor himself is convinced, he ought to find the means of convincing his orchestra.

The first work we rehearsed was the *Ride of the Valkyries, note by note.* First the players seemed surprised—but they soon realised the importance I gave to the performance of *each* note. I advised the string players to use my own technique and to all the others I suggested what I thought was the best way. The fact that I had played many instruments myself proved invaluable through this period of preparation. But all the time, I took great care not to use any language that might seem ungracious or humiliating. And after a short time I was happy in the certainty that all these players understood that I did not wish them to be at my service but at the service of the music they were playing.

I can remember that your orchestra gave a concert every year for the Associacio de Musica da Camera *in Barcelona.*

Yes. A few years before the period we are discussing, the supporters of this Association, who were friends of mine, told me of the difficulties they were encountering. So I offered to give a 'cello recital to the Society in the hope that it would bring in more subscribers to the Association, especially as I had not played in Barcelona for a number of years.

Later on, this Society engaged us in return to give two concerts a year to their subscribers. It even became so prosperous that it could engage in the year 1929 more well-known artists than any other society in the world. However, their audience was not entirely made up of music-lovers. To belong to the *Associacio* had become a fashion and I know that during the concerts some people liked to talk rather than listen to the music: there were even some who went as far as playing a game of cards during the concert.[1]

You gave some concerts with the Orfeo Gracienc?[2]

They were most interesting. This choir was mostly composed of young men and girls, workers and clerks, who sang with the greatest enthusiasm and who were very persevering under the direction of a friend of mine called Joan Balcells. With them and my orchestra we performed the *Ninth Symphony* of Beethoven, *The Creation* of Haydn, the *Mass in B♭* of Schubert, the *Faust Symphony* of Liszt, *Christ on the Mount* of Beethoven—and some other works. I used to give them a few last tips just before the concert, and spent some delightful moments talking to these simple folk who loved music for its own sake.

What about the Orfeo Catalan?

I would have been delighted to give concerts with them but, as in any collaboration, the goodwill of one side is not enough.

I know that your orchestra performed in all the principal towns of Catalonia until July 1936, especially since most places wanted to pay homage to you. Do you remember the occasion at Vendrell in 1927?

Of course I do! Of all the distinctions I have received the one which made me a *fill predilecte* of Vendrell was the one that touched me most. In order to show my gratitude to my fellow citizens I conducted my orchestra at a concert given in the village square and, in the afternoon, I gave a 'cello recital. At the close of the ceremonial unveiling of the commemoration tablet, I walked to the Town Hall through rows of people and, as I stood on the balcony, I saw the *Castells*[3] arrive, reaching my own level. When a child I had so often

---

[1] *I personally remember playing with my string quartet at one of these concerts in Barcelona, and being warned by the manager that the audience would probably consist mostly of young ladies who used the concert as a meeting-place with their boy friends. This manager included in the programme a loose sheet of green paper on which was written a short story of young people talking during a concert. The effect of it was stupendous: we played through an exacting programme in complete silence to our great surprise and to the delight of the manager!* (Translator's note.)

[2] *A choir from a suburb called de Gracia where at the Café Tost Casals had made his début in public.*

[3] *See p. 19.*

admired these *Castells*. I had even practised how to do it, but I had never thought that one day I would contemplate them from the balcony of our Town Hall.

So you were once a potential Casteller?

When I was six or seven my godfather used to stand me on his shoulders and we went for a walk! I had to keep my balance very carefully.

Were you frightened?

No, every boy in the village did it.

I also remember a charming episode at Vendrell in 1929 on the occasion of the restoration of the old organ in the church. It had been silent for a great many years, but I had not forgotten how I used to be carried away in a world of dreams when I heard its deep and sweet tone. With all the pipes eaten away by rust and the fabric dilapidated it was ónly a shadow of what it had been. The new organist used a harmonium. One day when I was visiting the church with a friend he asked me to play on it and as soon as I heard its tone again it went straight to my heart. So I decided to get it restored. When it was done they had a ceremony to inaugurate the new instrument. It was very moving and they presented me with the old music-stand which I keep in my house. At the same time they also restored a lovely statue of an angel which stood on the top of the tower. It was an 18th-century work and the Angel had lost an arm, and one leg was broken. Curiously enough a small wild olive tree had grown on the top of the bell tower (a bird must have dropped a seed from which the tree had grown). We used to call it *El Rabell* and it became a sort of habit for the village people to greet each other by saying, "How is the Rabell today?" When they restored the statue the workmen had to take this olive tree away and they wanted to make a conductor's baton of it for me. But I preferred to have the tree carried to my house at Sant Salvador, where it is still growing from a wall and waiting for me. I only wish the chance of seeing it again were not so uncertain!

In the book by Lillian Littlehales[1] where she describes your attachment to Vendrell she writes that "Having seen Pau Casals talking to Jaume Nin, the village carpenter, with his hand on his shoulder and having observed the way these two men looked at each other, I think one can realise better the traits and character of our great artist."

I don't see why. My friend Nin and myself sat on the same bench

[1] *Pablo Casals—A Life*, by Lillian Littlehales. (W. W. Norton & Co., New York.)

of our local school. I went round the world and he stayed in the village as a carpenter. When we meet again with some other old friends, it is just as it was in the days we went romping together among the vines and the fields outside the village.

When you spent the summer at Sant Salvador you must have done a lot of swimming, which I know you like.

Yes, I have always been very fond of swimming. And tennis also: I had a court at home where I played with friends. Some of them were great players like Panchita Subirana, the greatest woman player I have known. She had reached the finals in an international contest in Paris and if she did not win, it was only because she was paralysed with "stage-fright". I have known three generations of tennis champions and I prefer those of thirty years ago, but the connoisseurs do not share my opinion. A few years ago in Paris when I was watching a match, I asked my two friends Russell Kingman (President of the International Tennis Association) and Jean Borotra if the aces of Decugis' and Cochet's time were not superior to the ones of today; they smiled at me and said "No"!

I have also been very fond of riding. When in Sant Salvador I rode on my horse Florian every morning. He is still one of my most faithful friends. Poor old thing: he has waited for me fifteen years. He is not able to go about now, but my brother keeps him and looks after him for the sake of the affection I had for him.

Did your mother live in your house in Sant Salvador?

Yes, and my brother Lluis also. He has the task of running the estate, which he does with love and great knowledge.

My mother was known all round for her kindness: when someone asked her anything she never refused. She was the daughter of a Catalan family which had emigrated to Puerto Rico, where she lived till she was eighteen. She always had a nostalgia for her native place and in the last years of her life she longed to return. "How I should love to see Puerto Rico again," she said to me. "Well, let's go," I said. "No, son," she answered, smiling and resigned. "You owe your time to your career."

Did you ever go to Puerto Rico?

No, but I should love to go. You must have seen that touching letter I received last year from the Rector of the Puerto Rican University inviting me officially to stay there. This journey would be the realisation of one of my life dreams. But before I go I must realise that other things have got to come first.

Were you able to have your parents with you for a long time?

At the time we speak of, my father had been dead some years. A curious thing happened while I was taking part in a performance of the *St. John Passion* of Bach in the cathedral of Basle; I had a terrible foreboding that he was dead. I stopped my tour and came home immediately, and realised that my presentiment had been only too true: he had died exactly at the time I had thought of it.

My mother died on the 13th March, 1931, and I heard of it after a concert of the Trio with Cortot and Thibaud at Zürich. She was seventy-seven. The older I grow, the more I realise what I owed her!

Could you tell me about the famous concert at the Liceu with your orchestra, when Primo de Rivera was dictator and Alphonso XIII and Victoria Eugenia visited Barcelona?

This concert had some interesting consequences. But before I tell you about it I must remind you that Alphonso XIII (who had probably been ill-advised by some courtiers) had made a very unfortunate speech in which he declared himself to be the successor of Philip V. This was resented by all classes of Catalans.[1]

I could foresee the consequences of these grave utterances all the more because the dictatorship was pursuing an anti-Catalan policy. All the time I was wondering what I could do to prevent the worst happening, and I ended by deciding to go and talk to the Queen Mother about the speech her son had made.

As I was touring the North of Spain I received in Bilbao a letter from the Secretary of Doña Maria Cristina, who said she wished to see me. So I immediately went to Madrid. When I entered the Palace the Majordomo made a mistake and directed me to the King's apartments. I told him of his mistake but he said he knew that the King wished to see me. The latter appeared immediately and greeted me very cordially. I told him I had come to see his mother, to which he replied that he knew about it and she was waiting to see me. It looked as if I had good prospects of success, and I decided to talk frankly to her. I found her in one of the Palace galleries. "What has happened to you, Pablo? I have been waiting for the last twenty minutes." I explained to her what had happened, and we started talking. My

[1] *In 1714 Philip V, who was the first Spanish king from the house of Bourbon, had taken Barcelona after a siege and imposed a rule of iron on the Catalans, doing away with all their institutions with a stroke of the pen.*

intention was to use any pause in our conversation to stress the consequences that the Barcelona speech could have, since it had outraged the Catalans in their most intimate feelings. (I felt all the more inclined to broach this burning subject since the Queen had always told me she was especially fond of Catalonia.) So when the first silence came I started, but the Queen pretended she had not heard me. We went on talking of one thing and another and I had not lost heart, but when the next silence came, the same thing happened. So, this time, I gave up.

It is a queer thing: there I was, talking to a woman who had always shown the greatest affection for me and with whom I had conversed on every subject under the sun. And as I approached this Catalan question, which was a very legitimate case of injustice and grievance to be settled, she would not even listen! And so, the great ones of the earth often prepare their own downfall! They are so often surrounded by flatterers and courtiers who never tell them the truth, that they fail to grasp realities and cannot face the facts as they are. And as I knew that Maria Cristina was the only one with any real ascendancy over her son I had hoped that through my warning she would convince him of the great dangers which were so obvious.

I read somewhere that the Liceu concert took place before your interview with the Queen Mother.

No. Someone must have made a mistake. Shortly after this interview, Alphonso came again to Barcelona with all the Royal family, and he sent me a message to say he would like to hear a concert of my orchestra with me as a soloist. Of course I answered that I would do it with pleasure. The concert took place at the *Liceu* where there was a packed audience. The moment when the Royal guests came in coincided with my starting the Concerto (probably the Schumann) I was playing.

Had there been an incident about the Marcha Real—the official Spanish Hymn?

No. It had been understood that my brother Enric would conduct the orchestra, which he always did when I played solo. What happened was that the public accorded the Royal family an icy welcome; obviously the Catalans had not forgotten the speech, and wished to show their feelings. The March was received with equal indifference; but when I appeared on the stage a wave of applause burst out, and after it had gone on for some time the royalties decided to get up like all the audience had done when I came in! Shouts went up, and one soon realised that the concert had turned into a political affair and an occasion for a protest against the speech. The police made some arrests amongst the public. When I had finished playing the demonstration started again, even more heated. I felt rather upset that a family that had been so good to me should be so badly treated, although I had resented the speech as much as all my compatriots.

I wondered what was going to happen and what reaction there would be among the royalties. As I was not asked to visit them in their box during the interval, which I always did, I thought, "Here is the end of my relations with the Royal family." I felt it deeply, especially because of the Queen Mother, but considering the fact that my feelings in the matter were exactly those of all Catalans, I did not think it was necessary for me to apologise.

Did Alphonso ever talk to you about this?

Yes, but in a very curious way. Some two years after the concert incident I was in Paris, when I received a letter from the Spanish Ambassador asking me, on behalf of the King, to give a concert at the Royal Palace in Madrid on the occasion of an official reception for the Italian King and Queen.

This concert took place in the *Salle d'Armes* of the *Palacio de Oriente*, an absolutely gorgeous place. Apart from the two Royal families there were present all the highest dignitaries as well as the *Corps Diplomatique*, all wearing uniforms and decorations. At the end of the concert Alphonso came to me while all the audience stood up. He began by thanking me for my participation in this ceremony and the beauty of my playing. I guessed at once that he wanted to provoke a mild scandal against all the etiquette practised at this sort of reception. He then started talking of our young days at the Palace when we played games together; he enquired after all my family and all sorts of details. All the audience was still standing, including the Italian royalties, and for at least twenty minutes this went on. I looked at the Queen Mother with a question in my eyes: "How will all this finish?" The King looked at me with an understanding eye, to which I replied with a smile, and then came the words I was expecting: "Well, Pablo, I want to tell you how happy I was to see how the Catalans love you." I answered with a few polite words—we looked at each other and laughed, and I think we both had the same thought: "We understand each other." This breaking of all the rules of etiquette made a sensation when it got to be known; Alphonso had preferred to ignore the incidents of Barcelona, and counter them by being nice to me. It was a lovely gesture from him and also a proof of the consummate politician he was.

Did you see him after the Spanish Republic had been proclaimed and he had left Spain?

No. In 1938 at the end of the civil war, and during the period of concentration camps in the South of France, I wrote to him from Prades to tell him of the tragic situation of so many of our compatriots, and I thought I ought to tell him that so many of these refugees had put their trust in him. He sent me a very affectionate reply but said he was really too ill to be able to do anything. In fact, he died a few months later.

Were you in Spain when the Republic was proclaimed?

Yes. The day after the installation of the new *régime*, the 15th of April, 1931, I conducted the *Ninth Symphony* of Beethoven with my orchestra and the *Orfeo Graciene* at Montjuic. The Catalonian president, Francesc Macia, who was present, declared that the Republic had come into Catalonia to the sound of the *Hymn of Brotherhood* from the Beethoven Symphony.

Did your relations with the Spanish Royal family create any difficulty with the new régime?

None at all. As I have told you, my relations with the Royal family were exclusively personal and did not affect my feelings or convictions. The Queen Mother died in 1929, and Alphonso himself had bowed to the popular verdict. But I have always kept my gratitude to the Royal family. In 1935, when I was made an honorary member of the *Academia de Bellas Artes* and "honorable citizen" of the City of Madrid, they organised entertainments to celebrate the occasion. One evening Arbos, who was Director of the *Orquesta Sinfonica*, asked me to conduct his orchestra. At the end I had to speak to an audience mostly composed of personalities of the new *régime*. I briefly retraced the important stages of my career and I remember saying, "I, who owe so much to the late Queen Maria Cristina, who was a second mother to me . . ." the audience did not allow me to continue. Everyone got up and applauded frantically. This ovation went to my heart as it proved that they all appreciated my sincerity and, next morning, I realised that the Press had agreed with my declaration.

You have been President of the Junta de Musica (*Music Council*) *of Catalonia, haven't you?*

Yes. I have never belonged to a party or occupied any political position. But I was happy to preside over this venture in art which had been created to revive the cultural manifestations of our country. When it began the Spanish Republic made a worthy attempt at renovation. National feeling showed unequivocally that the people wanted a real democracy in which institutions like the Army and the Church would be given their proper place, and where the social economy of the country would find its own level again after it had been for so long in the hands of the rich families whose selfishness made them grab all the profits of the State orders.

The new governing bodies tackled energetically all the problems of public instruction which had been so long neglected. It is true to say that the majority of Spanish intellectuals were Republicans and that their views had contributed to the fall of the monarchy. As a Catalan I felt particularly grateful towards the new *régime*, which had given us our autonomy, which all our people desired and which was not incompatible with a Spanish fraternity.

Like so many well-known artists, you could have ignored the problems of your country and only looked upon it as a nice place where you could take a rest between two concert tours!

That would have been extremely easy, but I am afraid my conscience would have told me that to act like this would be unworthy and that I should not do it!

In the years preceding the civil war, all your countrymen had realised more and more your devotion to the cause and bestowed all their admiration on you. You must remember the memorable homage Barcelona paid to you in 1934?[1]

How could I ever forget it, especially since I have been exiled?

---

[1] *This ceremony, in which more than 200 Catalan Societies and Institutions took part, grew into an imposing demonstration. The name of Avenue Pau Casals was given to a big thoroughfare of Barcelona. He was proclaimed "honorable citizen" of Barcelona. The municipality struck a medal which was presented to him and an exhibition of some of his possessions was opened at the Arts Museum of Catalonia. At the same time America staged some celebrations connected with the Hispanic Museum in New York. The founder of this Museum, Mr. Archer Huntington, had commissioned a sculptor, Brenda Putnam, to do a bust of Casals and he opened a subscription (which was covered by 700 'cellists of the United States) to reproduce this bust and present it to the town of Barcelona in admiration for Casals. At that time the XIVth International Festival of Contemporary Music was taking place in Barcelona, and it was a good occasion to present the bust at a ceremony where Dr. Carlton Sprague Smith, Head of the Music Library of New York, delivered a speech in Spanish. At the Palace of Montjuic a great concert was given by the three orchestras of Spain: the Pau Casals Orchestra, the Symphony Orchestra of Madrid, conducted by Arbos, and the Philharmonic Orchestra of Madrid conducted by Perez Salas.*

What I do remember most are not all those tributes (although I have always been deeply touched by these marks of affection) but the realisation of the task I had set myself to accomplish and which was so savagely interrupted.

In your opinion, which are the principal qualities a conductor should possess?

Before anything else, a great conductor must be a great performer. The most convincing proof of his value can be found in his ability to get in touch with his musicians in order to communicate and convince them of his personal ideas. An absolute necessity is that each word of the conductor must be understood and accepted by the orchestra. If this condition is fulfilled he can rely on the goodwill and enthusiasm of his musicians; in this way there is no necessity to be over-forceful, a practice which I utterly condemn.

What about the lack of rehearsals?

On that subject I have always been uncompromising. If I am asked to conduct a concert I ask for three long rehearsals. Even when you deal with a good orchestra, it is not enough to "conduct" it. All the details must be gone into and absorbed into a harmonious whole. This requires time. I want to do with an orchestra what I do with my violoncello.

And what of the routine, which is so characteristic of orchestral players?

That is one of the principal dangers. The conductor must know how to fight against the bad habits which can always creep into an orchestra, the feeling of automatism which always ends in routine. To counteract this, the conductor must know how to preserve the artistic feeling of his players so that they all end by putting technique at the service of music. The highest aim is to *make the music speak.*

All this requires a great deal of patience. Yours is proverbial!

The thing which counts for the conductor is that he must be very severe towards himself and ask himself if he has succeeded in making his ideas comprehensible. One cannot expect everything from others.

(*Casals has a habit of singing aloud during the rehearsals and waving his arms and body in a way which leaves no doubt of his intentions.*)

Toscanini says that orchestras are prone to think that a work is easy because it is very well known; that, of course, means they will not bring the necessary attention to its performance.

That is true, and I shall give you an example. When I was conducting the Vienna Philharmonic Orchestra in 1927, on the occasion of Beethoven's centenary, we were rehearsing the *Eighth Symphony*, for which I could only get an hour on the day of the concert. So I decided to stop as little as possible, until we got to the Minuet where the horn plays the melody. I thought he did not play it in the right way and I told him how I thought of it. He was so offended that he packed up his instrument and went. Think of it: the first horn player in the Vienna Philharmonic Orchestra, a grand personage, and when he was playing a work as well known as a Beethoven symphony, which he and all his colleagues could have played by heart!

I went back to my hotel after the rehearsal, when I was asked to receive a delegation from the orchestra, led by the leader of the violins, which had come to apologise. "Please don't be surprised at what has happened. We did appreciate all your remarks and tonight our horn player will do as you asked him." In the evening the performance was magnificent, but if I had had more time at my disposal I should have corrected many details that I had not approved of. It was exactly this question of routine, which can play havoc even with the best orchestra in the world.

Many people have noticed how you address your players with a certain amount of congratulations and encouragement, followed by a "but".

No one could be hurt if after recognising their goodwill you make some further remarks connected with the expression of the music itself. The players are generally happy when they feel that the remarks of the conductor are fair and based only on an artistic consideration of the work played.

The rehearsal work must often be irksome.

Not for me. Rehearsing is the sort of work I like and enjoy. It is the moment when I can communicate my views and my feelings. I have never been disappointed in the reactions of my players. They realise very soon that I look on them as collaborators instead of slaves. And in that way the work of a rehearsal becomes a pleasure to all.

But when you conduct an orchestra which is not yours?

When you are on tour and you have to deal with an unknown orchestra, I think you realise right away if your authority is going to tell or not. One look sometimes is enough to judge the new "boss".

Rudolf von Tobel says in his book:[1] *that you belong to the category of the*

[1] *Pablo Casals.* (Rosapfel—Verlag, Zürich.)

"orchestral educator" and that anybody who has not seen you doing this sort of work, which you prefer above any other, cannot get a clear picture of your personality.

It is not for me to judge the opinions of other people, but I do know that the 'cello is not my only domain.

Do you ever conduct from memory?

No, for I do not see the use of useless accomplishments. Richter was of the same mind.

I see that your scores are covered with notes.

I never start rehearsing a work until I have studied every note of it, and marked all the points I think necessary.

A good many conductors seem to think that they should keep their musicians at a certain distance and not get intimate with them.

I don't agree with this. Every player of *my* orchestra in Barcelona was my friend. They used to consult me over problems or preoccupations they had. And you have been able to see for yourself the atmosphere which exists in the Prades Festival orchestra, although the players belonged to totally different parts of the world.

Ludwig asked you this: "When you conduct an orchestra one day and the next day play the 'cello under some other conductor, how do you manage to pass from being the 'general' to being the 'private'?" And you answered: "I remain the general."

It is quite possible that I said that. What I meant was that I saw that my ideas were shared by the great conductors. This intimate communication which is essential is immediately established. Therefore I feel that from the strictly musical angle there is no difference for me between being the director or the soloist.

When you play as a soloist you don't feel disturbed by the conductor that exists in yourself?

The fact is that it does not disturb me actually, but I cannot get rid of it. However concentrated I may be on my 'cello playing, I hear everything else; a second violin entrance coming a bit too soon or too late, some unsteady rhythm, a bad intonation. I get surprised, but I cannot do anything about it.

In Barcelona, you had other conductors to take your orchestra.

Yes. I had Ysaye, Tovey, Cortot (when Thibaud and I recorded the Brahms Double Concerto), Kleiber, Fritz Busch, etc., and also some Spanish and Catalan composers when their own works were being played.

Tell me about the concert where Ysaye played in public for the last time.

That was a very moving occasion. It was in 1927. We were at the time preparing the Beethoven centenary. I saw Ysaye and told him he must come and play the Violin Concerto. He refused (he had ceased to play in public for a considerable period). I insisted. "But do you think I could?" he said. "Yes," I replied, "it is quite possible." Ysaye took my hands and said, "As long as the miracle happens." The concert was to take place in five months. But soon after I received a letter from Ysaye's son. It said: "If you could only see my dear father, working every day, playing scales slowly by the hour. It is a tragedy and we cannot help crying over it."

The appointed day was at hand. We had prepared the concert most carefully (and the audience also a little). There were some unforgettable moments in Ysaye's performance and the audience was delirious. When he found me afterwards in the artists' room, he kneeled down, took my hands and said: "Resurrection. Resurrection!" It was an incredible moment of emotion. Dear Ysaye, I went to say good-bye to him next day at the station. Leaning out of the carriage window he was still holding my hands as if he did not want to part with them.[1]

Was that the occasion when he gave you this photograph?

(We were looking at a photograph fixed on the wall, showing Ysaye playing the violin near the sea on a sandbank. "La Panne 1916. The modest seaside resort which became a Royal residence." The photograph is signed by Queen Elizabeth of Belgium.)

No, this portrait has a long story attached to it. In 1939, soon after the war was declared, a queer person dashed into the modest "Grand Hotel" of Prades. He looked athletic, with peculiar manners, and the

---

[1] *This is what Ysaye wrote about the concerts of the Beethoven Festival in Barcelona.* "In order to realise the enthusiasm and the warmth of a Catalan audience one must have heard these model performances. They seem to have such an instinct for beauty. I heard Casals conduct the *C Minor Symphony* twice. It is due to his energy and the genius of his interpretations that Barcelona has become a centre for music *par excellence*. Casals conducts the orchestra he founded with such vigour, such a refined aesthetic sense, and such a spacious comprehension of Beethoven's spirit that one cannot help being moved to the quick. I had the honour of conducting the *Eroica* and of playing the Violin Concerto. I also conducted the *Triple Concerto* performed by the "Holy Trinity"—Cortot, Thibaud, Casals. It became a quadruple collaboration full of cordiality and I shall never forget the frenzy the audience got into. They were all delirious and one had a sensation of something which only happens once in a lifetime and also the highest artistic lesson. I could write reams about this but I shall only add this aphorism which will tell all my thoughts: 'All is possible when the man is there'." *(Action Musicale: Brussels. July 15, 1927.)*

gendarmes watched him carefully. As they questioned him, he produced a revolver and said that as an Englishman, and therefore belonging to an Allied nation, he had a right to carry a firearm. Then he said: "You and I are swine. But in Prades there is a . . ." and there he applied a very flattering adjective to me! Just imagine what French gendarmes look like when they are called swine! After long and complicated explanations at the police station this Mr. Philip Newman ended by coming to see me. His very aspect made me jump with the memories he roused in me. We became great friends, and for days we played music together. He was a great artist with a strength and an irrepressible originality. The day he came to say good-bye he said, "I know you are in a precarious financial position," and out of his pocketbook he produced an enormous bundle of banknotes and insisted on putting them in my pocket. We had a sort of fight and when he realised I would not accept them he said, "I shall give you a thing I hold as my most precious possession," and he gave me this photograph which had been given to him by the Queen herself. I shall never forget his generosity.

What should one do to become a good conductor? I have read that Toscanini began to conduct by accident, so to speak, at Rio de Janeiro during a performance of Aida. *You cannot become a good conductor if you cannot use a good orchestra, and a good orchestra will not be lent to you if you are not a good conductor. The problem seems impossible to solve.*

If a musician feels he has a vocation for conducting he can begin with a group of amateurs, or a modest orchestra in the provinces. It is a necessary training and it becomes an excellent way of practising. Supposing the orchestra is a bad one and the new conductor succeeds in making it improve a little, it gives an indication that he is capable.

Herman Scherchen declares that the conductor has at his disposal three principal means: "representative gesture", "expressive mime" and "explanation by word of mouth". What do you think of "expressive mime" to help the musicians in finding the kind of expression suitable to the music they play?

I agree with this as long as the mime is a natural one and not studied.

One day a young musician asked Furtwängler, "What is, in fact, the rôle of your left hand when you conduct?" Trying to answer this question,

*the great German conductor said: "After over twenty years of conducting,
I must say that I had never thought of it."*[1]

Neither have I. It seems to me a trifling question. The conductor's
left hand, as well as his right one, contributes towards the expression
of the work he wishes to convey to the orchestra.

*I have read that your old friend Bruno Walter sometimes stops a rehearsal
and instead of making observations to his players, he just says—please let us
play this again, it sounded so lovely.*

I do understand that—and it reflects the sweet nature and the
cordiality of Bruno Walter. It is a pity he has abandoned his piano
playing, because I think that besides being a very great conductor he is
also a very great pianist.

Toscanini and Furtwängler are the two conductors you admire most?

I admire a great many conductors, even if I don't always agree
with their rendering, but I certainly place Toscanini, Furtwängler
and Stokowski at the top of the living conductors.

*Howard Taubman, who wrote Toscanini's biography, says that Tosca-
nini "holds his tempi". Sometimes when a performance of a classical symphony
was timed with a stop-watch, it was discovered that there was only a difference of one or two seconds in performances of the same work given many
years later.*[2]

I don't understand what conclusion should be drawn from this
assertion. Toscanini, like all great artists, does not lack in creative
fantasy. And since a musical work does not always appear to the artist
in exactly the same way, without the slightest difference, it follows
that a great interpreter can be carried away by some inspiration of the
moment, where the idea of the stop-watch has no place at all.

*Furtwängler writes: "A small orchestra that has no pretensions but has
become a real ensemble will be without doubt more efficient than the most
'virtuoso' orchestra in the world."*

In a small orchestra, as well as in a great one, the result always
depends on the power of communication the conductor can establish
with his musicians. It goes without saying that Furtwängler can
impart his magic to a big or a small orchestra just the same.

Have you always agreed with him when you played under his direction?

Yes, always. Our respective musical conceptions always seemed to
coincide in a perfect way.

[1] Wilhelm Furtwängler: *Entretiens sur la Musique.* (Translated by T. G.
Prod'homme. *Editions Albin Michel,* Paris.)
[2] Howard Taubman: *Toscanini:* (*The Maestro.*)

And which conductors did you appreciate most some fifty years ago, when you began to play all over Europe and America?

Richter, Lamoureux, Steinbach, Nikisch.

Which works did you like to conduct best?

Besides the well-known ones, any work that has a musical interest.

Could you tell me about the Associacio Obrera de Concerts (Workmen's Concert Association) in Barcelona, one of your most daring foundations which had some unexpected results?

This Association was founded in 1926 or '27. I had thought of it for a long time but I did not think I could start it before my own orchestra was established on a sound footing.

And what about the popular concerts?

That did not interest me: I had heard and played at such concerts in different countries and I had noticed the people who profited from them were not those for whom the concerts were given. What I wanted was an association entirely run by the workers themselves. They had been kept outside the musical movement of my country and I wished to alter that. I wanted the men and women who spent most of their days in the factories, the shops or the offices, to be able to participate in our musical life and in such a way that their outlook on life and general culture of the mind should benefit by it.

On a more modest scale we had had an attempt of this kind started by J. A. Clavé.[1]

That is what I meant: I wished to continue his work. His idea was to take the workmen away from the "pubs" and give them the joy of choral singing instead. Clavé was a great man and composed some fine popular songs.

Did you get in touch with the workmen themselves?

Yes, I got the leaders of the *Atetenu Politecnic* of Barcelona (a Workmen's Cultural Society) to come and see me. They turned up one evening after work and as I told them of my plans I said that the first thing was to organise the Association on a basis of a small yearly subscription paid by the members. I said: "Nobody besides yourselves will interfere with the direction and administration of your Society. You will have my orchestra, with well-known soloists, and I'll play for you." They listened to me and looked at me with a certain amount

[1] *Josep Anselm Clavé 1824-1874. An autodidact musician, author of many songs and especially instigator and propagandist of choral singing in Catalonia.*

A performance
at home

of suspicion. They probably thought I was hiding something from them. It was not surprising, for it was all new to them. They were simple people and could not imagine they would get something without being asked to give something in return. At the end of our talk they said they would think it over, and would send me an answer. A few days after I received rather a stern letter asking me for more precise information on some points. We had four or five meetings and gradually they understood what I meant. I told them that, for the moment, they could use a room of the *Atetenu Politecnic*, "but later on, you will have your own place. Your Society will spread and have branches all over Catalonia. You will not lack furniture and office equipment. An important music library will be at your disposal. You will have a music school, a choir and an orchestra all of your own." "And all this will cost us six pesetas a year?" "Yes." (They were looking at me with an expression on their faces which seemed to mean, "This man is half mad.") "Moreover you will publish a music review written by yourselves." "And what shall we write in it?" "Just describe what you felt and thought while listening to your concerts."

On what basis did you think of creating this Society?

The first basic idea of mine was that the workman should feel at home. If he goes to a concert or a theatre, occupying the cheaper seats upstairs from where he looks down on the luxury of the audience in the stalls and boxes, he will be absorbed by thoughts and reflections that have nothing to do with the music he is listening to. I wanted the workman to develop his aesthetic sense without the interference of class consciousness. Another basic thought of mine in connection with this Society was that simple-minded people don't like to feel that they are being given things out of charity. I said to them, "When you spend six pesetas a year, you will really be spending more than the rich people who pay twenty pesetas for one concert at the *Liceu*."

What was the result?

Miraculous. The chairman of my orchestra committee agreed to help organise the beginning when I asked him. They had all the furniture, typewriters, music scores and instruments they required. The enthusiasm amongst the workmen was extraordinary. They had decided that only those who did not get a salary higher than 500 pesetas a month could belong to the Society.[1]

---

[1] *In those days in Barcelona, an expert workman earned about ten pesetas a day and the basic salary of a professor at the University was precisely 500 pesetas a month.*

The yearly subscription was fixed at six pesetas a year as we had suggested. Soon after the Society was founded, we gave the first concert with my orchestra. It took place on a Sunday morning (as they all did afterwards) at the Olympia Theatre at Barcelona, with an audience of 2500 people (it must be remembered that only members of the Society could come to these concerts). The Association consolidated itself gradually and there was a wonderful driving spirit about it. All the things I had predicted were realised: the library, the music school, the choir were formed. The monthly review called *Fruicions*, written in Catalan, had very interesting articles with opinions which revealed the enquiring minds of the writers. All the concert programmes had extensive introductory notes about the composers, the works and the performers. And do you know which was the composer the public preferred?

Bach! This is a fact which will make certain people think again about the apparent difficulty for an audience in understanding certain works of Bach.

My orchestra gave six concerts a year for the Association. The members also had an amateur orchestra which got to a very decent level. I remember that one of the double-bass players, who was a carpenter, had made his own instrument and used to walk to the rehearsals all the way from the suburbs where he lived, carrying it on his back. This is the sort of thing which makes life worth living: the love and enthusiasm we put into a thing we have created ourselves.

Did they have any upsets?

Yes: there came a dangerous period which I had anticipated. The members of the committee came to see me one day and their President retraced the history of their Association, which they thought had been miraculous: "All happened as you said, Maestro," and he went on to say that they were feeling strong now and wanted to extend their activities beyond music. They thought they had a mission to fulfil in the cultural line, and therefore ought to participate in the municipal councils and the Parliament of Catalonia. They asked me to represent them—in fact they wanted me to become a member of parliament. Even before they started this conversation, I had guessed what they wanted. I said: "You have fallen into a trap: if you start in this direction, all we have done will collapse. From the day you begin to interfere with the elections you will have enemies everywhere, and all your understanding and the collaboration you have built up will automatically fall to the ground." They were not very pleased, but they accepted what I said because of my ascendancy over them.

As I had predicted, their Association had formed branches in Sabadell, Terrassa, and the big industrial towns of Catalonia, and when the civil war started they had thousands and thousands of members everywhere.

All the great artists who visited Barcelona always wanted to play for them. Their success and their influence were so well known that different countries such as the United States, England and Germany got interested in their activities and asked me for information on the organisation and on its work.

And now?

Now, it has all gone: my orchestra, the Workmen's Association, the Music Council. But if things altered and I felt strong enough, I would start again with the same enthusiasm I had when I began.

V

Three Unknown Masters

Amongst your friends who were great musicians, and whom you admired, you have often named Emmanuel Moor, Sir Donald Tovey and Julius Röntgen.

Yes. These three great musicians are almost forgotten. When do we see their names in concert programmes? Although I can assure you that the names of the many composers you see on programmes nowadays, mixed up with Bach, Mozart or Beethoven, would be nowhere in comparison with those of Moor, Tovey and Röntgen, if only their music was played—and in saying this I weigh my words carefully.

When did you meet Moor?

It must have been in 1907 or 1908 at Lausanne. I had given a concert there and went to a café afterwards. There I recognised a Mr. Brandoucoff, the Director of the Moscow Conservatoire, whom I had met in Russia. He introduced Moor to me as an "amateur composer". I looked at him and found in his eyes signs of a personality, as if he had something to say. As we went on talking together, I tried to address him personally. "I should like to know some of your compositions," I said. He agreed immediately and we arranged a meeting at my house in Paris. When he turned up he had reams of paper under his arm. He sat at the piano and played me his 'cello concerto. The way he dealt with the piano, the way he looked, and the music he played during the first moments convinced me that I was in the presence of a remarkable man. And while he played I thought more and more: "What? An amateur composer!" He went on, playing marvellously well, and his music had such quality that I began to suspect the tragedy of this man. When he stopped playing he turned towards me. I looked him straight in the face and said in all sincerity, "You are a genius." At which he fell upon me, sobbing, holding me tight in his arms. And with deep emotion he told me the tragedy of his life, a tragedy indeed. He said that nobody understood his music except his wife. His creative power had dried up since no one

92

would understand. He had been told so often that what he wrote was devoid of interest, that he ended by being convinced of it and had not written for ten years. As his wife had means he had become a landed proprietor in the country in England. Our interview created such a commotion in him that he decided to compose again. Every month he came to Paris from Switzerland, where he often stayed, to show me his new compositions. Every month he brought either a symphony, or two string quartets, or a Mass, and so on. His output was endless, almost monstrous: his capacity made one think of a Haydn or a Boccherini.

And so you decided to make his compositions known, since you admired him so much?

Yes, I really admired him and became more and more convinced every day of his great gifts. I began to busy myself about getting his works played and I succeeded, after a great deal of trouble, in making such conductors as Nikisch, Steinbach and Mengelbert insert a work of Moor in their programmes. I conducted some concerts in Paris with the object of making some of his works known. I organised chamber music concerts of which I undertook the expenses. Out of consideration for me such performers as Ysaye, Kreisler, Cortot, Thibaud, Pugno and Dumesnil would play his works, although they did it without pleasure or conviction. They did it out of respect for my convictions. But there was a general antipathy towards Moor himself and for his compositions.

And what did people think of his music, apart from the man himself?

I'll give you a factual example which will enlighten you on this subject. There was an international competition in Paris for a Trio (the first prize went to Leo Vainar, a remarkable Hungarian composer who ought to be more well known than he is outside his country). Amongst the judges of this competition were people like Fauré, d'Indy, Bruneau, Colonne, Chevillard and our Trio—Cortot, Thibaud and myself.

(There was a general feeling of antagonism towards me in the musical world at that period because of my insistence in praising Moor's works.)

There were ten competitors left after we had sifted all the entries, and we decided to take a rest. I went to a room where there was a piano and began to play. All the members of the jury came in one after the other (the first one was Colonne). When I had finished I found they were all standing round the piano and I heard one say, "It must be a composition of Casals: it is a beauty." I took my hands off the keyboard and they applauded saying, "What is it?" "It is a composition by Emmanuel Moor," I said. There was general consternation.

Did Moor have a difficult temper?

Yes, he was a strange character. He got on the wrong side of anyone he met, with the result that people always wished to get rid of him. He talked to anyone, either a celebrity or an unknown person, in a brusque direct way. However, one found that what he said and did (although not pleasant) was often true. Others did not understand him because they didn't know him as well as I did, and because the admiration and sympathy I had for him (which I alone felt) allowed me to penetrate the intimacy of his mind. I'll give you an example: Moor ate like a lion, and to tell the truth, it was not very pleasant to see him at table, when, with his teeth protruding like an animal, he gobbled the food as if he were starving. However, I knew what reason there was behind the mind of this man, who devoured what was put in front of him. Moor did not sleep: music disturbed and absorbed him with so much intensity that it took his sleep away. And because of this an excess of food was necessary to him.

I believe you succeeded in getting one of his works played at the Classical Concert Society in London?

Yes. This is what happened, and you will judge how Moor's character always came into conflict with everybody. The programmes of the Classical Concert Society never went further than Brahms, and so it was quite a success to have arranged that a work of my friend should be included in one of their programmes. This Society only engaged artists of the highest rank. They had Jelly d'Aranyi (a relation of Joachim), Donald Tovey, Leonard Borwick (the best English pianist of that period), Fanny Davies, etc. (Borwick and Fanny Davies had both been pupils of Clara Schumann.) Moor and I went specially to London for this concert. I am not telling you of all the incidents of the journey: it would be too long a story. When we got to London I went to see Borwick to fix up the programme: a Beethoven Sonata, a Bach Sonata, a Bach Suite for 'cello alone, and a Sonata by Moor. Moor and I went together to Borwick's house for the rehearsal. It was a lovely house, full of the refinement characteristic of a distinguished Englishman. We began the rehearsal. Borwick, sitting at the piano, had his back to Moor, who was on his right. As I was to the right of Borwick I could see them both, and I realised pretty soon that Moor was not pleased. It was Beethoven we were rehearsing, and

Moor's attitude was getting troublesome and I signalled to him to stop. He took no notice. We went on to do the Bach Sonata; just after the first page I saw Moor get up and, with a frightful look on his face, push Borwick off with savage energy, saying, "I am going to show you how to play Bach": and he sat at the piano. You can imagine what the situation was. At the end of the movement Borwick just said, "Thank you, sir, I shall do my best."

What a dignified way to behave.

Yes, like the real gentleman he was. But no one could get on with Moor, or even understand him, when he behaved in that way.

Was he a good pianist?

Well, he was a thrilling pianist. Of course his appearance and manners were rough and ready, but all the same he had genius. He always said what he thought, bluntly, which created most embarrassing situations. I'll tell you of what he did during one of his monthly visits to me. Although he had played all day different compositions he had brought with him, when it was time for supper he still had an opera in one act! At that moment there was a knock at the door: it was Szanto, a Hungarian pianist, very well known for his Bach transcriptions for the piano. Moor immediately seemed upset by the arrival of Szanto, as he thought it was going to stop his playing. We started talking, and in the course of the conversation Szanto asked Moor (who was also a Hungarian) if he knew his Bach transcriptions. (As I knew how impatient Moor was, I felt there was trouble coming!) Moor answered in the negative in a rude way!

Szanto, however, sat at the piano and began to play. He played through one work and Moor did not say a word. He played a second one: same silence. So Szanto said to Moor, "What do you think of these, Mr. Moor?" On which Moor got up and shouted at him, "I think you are an ass!"

I took Szanto on one side and apologised for Moor's behaviour, saying he was a man who got easily upset and would he come another day. I saw him off and when I returned to the room I told Moor what I thought of his behaviour. He put his head down like a child who has been scolded and murmured: "Don't you think as I do? Well then?"

Is it true that Moor had invented a piano with two keyboards?

Yes, it was an instrument that brought some interesting technical solutions and had been built by Pleyel. He had also conceived a string instrument which included all the registers from bass to that of the violin. And he invented different mechanical tools. He was gifted in every way. Look at this reproduction of his self-portrait. Doesn't it look like a Van Gogh?

You have played his Concerto for Two 'Celli with Guilhermina Suggia, haven't you?

Yes, very often.

And the Triple Concerto?

That is a work which deserves attention. Moor had written it for our trio, Cortot-Thibaud-Casals, and we worked at it through a whole summer (before the 1914 war). We were supposed to play it in many Swiss towns with the Romand Orchestra (which was perhaps already conducted by Ansermet). The programme of this tour was supposed to include a Schumann Trio, one by César Franck, and the Triple Concerto of Moor. Cortot had rented a country house in Switzerland for the summer, and there we worked. As soon as I thought the rehearsals were sufficiently advanced I suggested we should get Moor to hear it and say what he thought. During the rehearsals neither Cortot or Thibaud made any comments, probably on account of my friendship with Moor. However, Cortot suddenly said bluntly that he would not play this work unless he could rewrite the piano part himself. So I just said that if any change was made Moor must be consulted. Cortot wrote to Moor about it and Moor accepted his indications, which did not please me very much, but I abstained from any comment. (A few years later the work was published in its original form—which, of course, did not meet with Cortot's approval.) Cortot invited Moor to come and when he heard the work with all the modifications, he agreed to everything. While we played a terrible storm got up. It was getting dark, so I asked Cortot, in case the storm went on, if Moor could be put up for the night. He refused. It was a long way to the station, so I thought l would walk with Moor, but they would not let me go and even held me by the arm in order to stop me. However, when the first Swiss concert took place, this Triple Concerto, as well as the rest of the programme, had a great success. After the second concert I noticed that Cortot and Thibaud did not seem so hostile to the work as they had been, and as the concerts went on the success of the Moor work was confirmed. I had gone to bed at my hotel after the last concert when I heard a knock at the door, and when I opened it I was surprised to see Cortot and Thibaud, who, after apologising for the late hour, said they wanted to have a word with me! They explained that during our rehearsals of the

Moor work they had not shown any enthusiasm, but they said that after these four performances their interest in the Schumann and the Franck Trios had decreased, whereas the value of the Triple Concerto had increased until they could now share all my admiration for this composition.

It was a belated gesture, but a very definite one.

This was not the only one (you remember what had happened about the Trio Competition). Here is another opinion from a great artist on Moor's music.

Coming back from England one day I met Ysaye on the ship. He said he had something important to tell me, so we went to the smoking lounge and he said, "Do you remember when we met in Berlin once, and you asked me to play a composition by Moor which left me cold!" "Yes, I remember." "And when you asked me again at some other time, I was still very unwilling." "I had noticed it, but did not want to bother you further with my suggestion." "Well, I must tell you now that as time goes on, I admire Moor's music more and more. I have just been on tour in England, during which I played his Violin Concerto nine times, and my liking for it has increased so much that when I played it last night at Plymouth I began to think it was as fine as the Beethoven Concerto."

Such was Emmanuel Moor!

I have noticed that your admiration for Sir Donald Francis Tovey increases with time.

Yes. He is another great musician who was not generally understood during his lifetime nor, until now, any more recognised after his death.

When did you first know him?

When I began to take part in the concerts of the Classical Concert Society, in which Tovey was very interested. I soon realised that I had met an exceptional personality. Joachim, who knew Tovey, had once said that he could discuss music with Brahms and the two Schumanns but not with a young Englishman called D. F. Tovey. "He knows too much."

I understand that Tovey had known Joachim since he was a child?

Yes; just think that, at the age of thirteen, at a private party, he had already played a sonata of his with the great violinist. It was in 1909 that I played for the first time with Tovey, a composition of his called *Elegiac* which he wrote in memory of Hausmann, who had been 'cellist in Joachim's quartet.

I have read that Tovey went to Bayreuth in 1897 and, although he did not think much of the performers, he found himself impressed by Wagner's music, which he did not find at all difficult to understand.

I am not surprised to hear it, since I think that Wagner's means of expression are very clear.

Until that date we don't find Tovey talking about Wagner. Would it be because of his having been brought up in the Joachim circle?

That is possible. Joachim was a great friend of Brahms and it is well known that the great writer and the apologist of lyric drama moved in different spheres.

In 1901 Tovey gave a concert in Berlin with Joachim, at which he played the Goldberg *Variations. His biographer[1] says that this interpretation of the Bach work made a sensation in the German capital, where the audience seemed to be hearing it for the first time, however incredible this may appear.*

It is not so surprising. Something of the same kind happened to me with the Bach Suites. It was necessary to show the Germans how mistaken they were in their conception of how to play Bach. The *Goldberg Variations* played by Tovey sounded like a new work. Those who doubted his personality as a great pianist did not, or could not, understand him. He tackled the most imposing and difficult works for the piano with a science and a mastery that were almost baffling.

Eugène Istomin was telling me the other day of his admiration for Schnabel and Rachmaninov as pianists. I have known and admired them also. The Brahms Concerto played by Schnabel was remarkable but Tovey's rendering was superior to his.

Richter was surprised by the choice of Tovey's programme for his first recital in London: the Goldberg *and the* Diabelli *Variations.*

Everything depends on one's conception of the works played. When I made my *début* in Vienna—as I told you before—although I felt how important the occasion was for me, I chose to play a work of Moor quite unknown to the Viennese audience.

What do you think of Tovey's critical notes in concert programmes?

These were so profound and concise that they all become works of art in themselves. Also his work for the *Encyclopaedia Britannica*, as well as his articles on musical subjects in reviews and newspapers,

---

[1] We have consulted the book by Mary Grierson, so accurate and well documented, *Donald Francis Tovey*. (*A Biography Based on Letters*.) (Oxford University Press.)

were remarkable in every way. He showed such widespread knowledge and such penetrating vision that one could say he was without
parallel as a critic. It is all devoid of pedantry or obscure formulae,
probably on account of the kind of wit which was one of his characteristics. And his memory! Tovey was capable of quoting and
playing by heart any work of Bach, Haydn, Mozart, Beethoven,
Schubert, Brahms and others. Listening to him one almost got
frightened!

*I see that at the time you knew him Tovey was already a target for some
London groups, who accused him of creating a sort of "monastic order, an
order of reactionary purists who had elected him as their Pope". Was there in
his character anything approaching scornfulness?*

I never heard him say a word of this kind. His difficulty, as far as
his artistic career was concerned, was his enormous superiority, which
cast a shadow and frightened most of the English musicians of his
period.

Did you play with him outside England?

Yes, I remember that in 1912 Tovey, Enesco and myself played the
Beethoven *Triple Concerto* in Budapest.

Did Tovey live a long time in Edinburgh?

I think it was in 1912 that he accepted the Chair of Music at the
University, where he stayed till he died, but he went abroad regularly
during the vacations, and he also played occasionally in other towns
in England.

All his lectures and his writings are crammed with brilliant ideas,
and one looks in vain to find another man in our time who has written
on musical matters with such competence.

*Did you hear the Reid Symphony Orchestra which Tovey created in
Edinburgh?*

Yes. I even conducted it once. This was how it happened: Tovey
admired the works of Juli Garreta, a Catalan who had taught himself
music and had composed some lovely *Sardanas* and some remarkable
symphonic works. He had included one of Garreta's compositions in a
programme, and during the rehearsal he came to me and said he did
not feel he was getting the real character of this work, so would I
conduct it! So I did, and the *Pastoral* of Garreta had a great success.

This orchestra of Tovey's had something in common with those
I had in Prades, in that the "spirit" of it was different from that of the
usual organisation of this kind. There were some great instrumentalists
in it as well as ordinary professional players, but it was the almost

ferocious work he put into it, as well as his great knowledge, that gave to this orchestra a unique quality.

What do you think of Tovey's editions of Bach and Beethoven?

They are wonderful. So accurate and showing all his knowledge. I use his edition of *The Well-Tempered Clavier* (this is dedicated to our dear friend Dr. Schweitzer). I also use the Röntgen edition. Both these seem to be as perfect as any edition of this kind can be.

And the Beethoven piano and 'cello Sonatas?

I also use Tovey's edition.

Elgar wrote about Tovey's edition of The Well-Tempered Clavier, *saying how proud he felt that an Englishman had done a work that no German had been able to do!*

Elgar had every reason to feel proud of it.

I see that your friend Tovey went to give concerts in America in 1925.

I was in America at the time. Tovey gave four recitals at which he played the greatest piano works in existence. The great music critic, Aldrich, wrote that these concerts stood as the most important manifestation of piano playing that the United States ever had.

I also read in Mary Grierson's book that Tovey had given three concerts in London after having been away for a considerable period, and that some critics had said that Tovey took liberties with the tempi. And Mary Grierson goes on to say: "Even by the metronome, Tovey remained round the tempo all the time. What really happened was that people were not used to hearing his version and thought he was taking liberties with the time."

I am not surprised to hear that.

According to Mary Grierson, Tovey thought that in Beethoven "a real fundamental tempo suggested two different aspects, one fluent and the other large, but both of which were connected with the time of a metronome". Neither the rubatos of his Chopin nor the "big gestures" of his Brahms ever disturbed the fundamental rhythm.

We felt alike on this subject, but that is something that some musicians will not understand.

Of Handel, Tovey said: "Beethoven was right when he called him the greatest of the Masters and without parallel for producing great effects with the minimum of expenditure."

Bach and Handel were born in the same year: Tovey liked to find analogies and differences between Bach and Handel. Now and then, when he was feeling slightly frivolous, he made up little musical games. One of them was laughing at Handel. He would sit at the piano and sing and play in the style of Handel in the most amusing fashion.

But he would not do that with Bach: and that showed the distinction he made between these two great composers in his estimation of values.

I heard that in his late years Tovey became very sensitive to what he called "the sublime simplicity of Haydn".

How right he was.

As for modern composers, he included Debussy in his programmes?

Yes, Debussy and Ravel.

You had friends in common?

I told you of my friendship with Edward Speyer and the principal artists of the Classical Concert Society, also with Julius Röntgen and Dr. Schweitzer. But I must add Mr. Trevelyan, the famous English historian who wrote the libretto for Tovey's opera called *The Bride of Dionysius*; the Busch brothers, Adolf and Fritz, and many others!

After the first performance of his opera, *The Times* wrote again saying that Tovey was more of a theoretician than a *practical musician*! He was very pained by these assertions, which showed how misunderstood he was.

Was it Tovey who proposed you for the title of Doctor honoris causa at Edinburgh University?

Yes. It was in 1934, and the title was conferred on Albert Schweitzer at the same time. It was also on this occasion that I met this wonderful man. He had already published his book on Bach called *The Poet Musician*, and I realised how our two poetical visions were alike on this rare subject. Of course, I had already formed a great admiration for Dr. Schweitzer, the man who had taught us all what virtue there was in self-sacrifice. During these festivities a number of private and public concerts took place in Edinburgh and Schweitzer showed great enthusiasm for my playing of Bach. On the last day he begged me to stay, but I had some engagements to fulfil and I had to go. After the last concert, I was leaving the concert hall by myself when I heard someone running behind—I turned round—it was Schweitzer. He stood in front of me and said, "Listen, since *thou* must go, thou must at least say *thou* to me before we part." Of course I said a few things to him, after which we embraced each other, rather overcome by emotion. My friendship and my admiration for him increases from day to day. Not so very long ago, in 1951, he was kind enough to come and see me in Zürich, where I was conducting a concert given on the occasion of my seventy-fifth birthday.

Albert Einstein thought that Schweitzer was the greatest man of our day.

So do I, and in spite of all the lamentable happenings we see going on in the world today, it is enough to think of a man like Schweitzer to keep some hope and faith in humanity.

Will you tell me what you think of Tovey's 'Cello Concerto?

This work, dedicated to me (for which I feel very honoured), is in my opinion the most important of his compositions and should stand high in 'cello literature.[1]

The first performance of the Concerto took place in Edinburgh in the autumn of 1934, where it was enthusiastically received. A number of important people heard it, and many critics who had come from London.[2] (I remember that, on this occasion, I had to try hard to pull myself together for I had been suffering for some time from pains in the left thumb which none of the great specialists I consulted in different European capitals had been able to diagnose. It was the pleasant Dr. Ernest Vila of Figueras—a small Catalan town of 10,000 inhabitants—who later on discovered what it was almost immediately; he looked at my hand and, getting a pair of pincers, pulled out a bristle from a nailbrush which, having got into my thumb, had kept it inflamed.)

After the concert I got into a carriage with Tovey, who was most deeply moved and said, "Today I had what was never granted to me before—to be thought of as a composer." I was supposed to record

[1] *Casals had written to Tovey thus:* "Dear Donald, The day I received your concerto will remain one of the most important of my life. It caused me a great joy and I do appreciate the words you wrote in your dedication, which I hope I shall be able to do justice to." *The date of the first performance was fixed for 22nd November, 1934.* "This date," *Casals says,* "will be the most important in my career as a musician. Joachim must have felt the same . . ."

[2] *The Times said:* "Señor Pau Casals wished to give London the chance of hearing the fine violoncello concerto by Professor D. F. Tovey, which he produced in Edinburgh on Thursday evening with the Reid Symphony Orchestra, the composer conducting" (. . .) "Professor Tovey is honoured as a musician of profound learning, but not as a composer to whom Queen's Hall need listen. The loss in the case of this violoncello concerto is to the Queen's Hall audiences. In the B.B.C. Symphony Orchestra we have one of the most richly endowed orchestral institutions in the world. In the Royal Philharmonic we have a society which for over a hundred years has claimed to represent, among other things, the best products of native composition. If both decide to ignore a work which is clearly one of considerable power and intimate beauty and which, moreover, is sponsored by the greatest exponent of violoncello playing in the world, they will be very foolish. . . . The whole concerto grows out of the genius of the violoncello, and it takes all Casals' genius to display its qualities. That in itself is worth going to Edinburgh to hear."

the Concerto in the autumn of 1936 with the B.B.C. Orchestra conducted by Sir Adrian Boult, but, owing to some regrettable complications, it was not done.

Tovey often went to Barcelona, didn't he?

Yes, he came to Barcelona many times and during the Festivities for the centenary of Beethoven he played a Concerto and conducted my orchestra. Later we made him an honorary member of the orchestra. When I asked him to lecture he said to me, "Casals, do make me play." Those who always thought of Tovey as a "theoretician" never knew how much he loved his "clavier"! When I played his Concerto at Barcelona he also conducted my orchestra.

What was he like as a conductor? I read that when you played his Concerto in London with Tovey conducting, the critic of the Observer *wrote that, as a conductor, "he became an enemy of his own composition".*

Tovey was very nervous on that day, but all the same he was a great conductor, a very great conductor. I remember that he once conducted one of the *Leonora* overtures in a way that was finer than any interpretation that I have ever heard. In an interview I had with the *Daily Telegraph* I declared that it was an honour for all of us to be sitting on the same platform as he was. The curious thing about Tovey is that he never managed to be understood as a composer, a conductor or a pianist. It is true to say he did not possess the sort of brilliant and superficial facility which belongs to "born" conductors. But his interpretations possessed another kind of quality which reflected the depth of his thoughts and the burning sensitiveness of a great man.

What, do you imagine, are the reasons why his compositions are not understood?

First, one must be aware that in England most artists acquire a label which it is extremely difficult to get rid of. And, further, the English are inclined to think that an Englishman cannot be a good composer. And yet the musical renaissance in England, marked by the works of Elgar, Tovey and Vaughan Williams, has been very important, not to say the most important, in connection with the general development of music in the last epoch. Here we find a strongly original product in which there is great diversity of style and character, always stemming from the deep roots of its national inspiration. English music of that period has definitely turned its back on the so-called modern tendencies, about which we'll have further occasion to speak. It has remained faithful to natural and human principles.

In 1945, when I went to England for the last time, I visited Tovey's

Museum in Edinburgh. It is beautifully kept by his friends and admirers. I was very deeply moved. I sat down at his old piano and, unable to hold back some tears, I played the opening of his 'Cello Concerto. When I got up, I said to those who were around the words I always repeat, "Tovey was one of the greatest musicians of all time."

When did you meet Julius Röntgen?

Early in this century. He was one of my dearest friends and one of the great musicians I most admired.

I have read[1] that he belonged to a family with an old musical tradition.

Yes, his ancestors, both on his father's and his mother's side, were distinguished musicians. The well-known 'cellist, Julius Klengel, was a cousin of his. His father had been leader of the Gewandhaus Orchestra in Leipzig, and also professor at the Conservatoire there.

When Röntgen was fourteen, his father and Joachim played his duo for viola and piano at Düsseldorf during the Rhine Festival of Music. Young Julius was sitting next to them on the platform listening intently to the performance of his composition and completely oblivious of the audience. And Joachim said, "He will be a great master."

The prophecy was realised, for he certainly was a great master.

Do you mean as a pianist and a composer?

Yes, and also as a musician of the highest rank. The term "Master" is often used as a figure of speech, but in the case of Röntgen it becomes a statement of fact. He was a great master by the depth of his mind and by the breadth of his knowledge, by the commanding position he occupied in every branch of the art of music, by his admirable gifts of interpretation and his remarkable creation as a composer, by the value of his teaching and by the mark he made on all those who were lucky enough to come into contact with him.

Tovey absolutely agrees with you: when he wrote an article on Röntgen, in The Times *after he died in September 1932, he said of him, as a composer: "Only the greatness and the richness of Bach's art would not suffer by comparison with the extraordinary facility and enormous activity of Röntgen as a composer."*

I do not remember this article in *The Times*, but think what it means coming from a man like Tovey.

When Röntgen was fifteen he went with his mother to see Liszt at Weimar (this was in March 1870), and he gives a very amusing account

[1] Madame A. Röntgen: *Brieven van Julius Röntgen*. (H. J. Paris, Amsterdam.)

of this visit in one of his letters: "On the way," *writes young Röntgen,* "we had a look at Weimar. I have never seen such a place for bad taste: Goethe's and Schiller's statues look like two commercial travellers. After walking for about half an hour we reached the Allee in Belveder, a pretty place where Liszt and Preller live. Waiting until Liszt sent for us, we had coffee with Preller. But we waited in vain, and the next day Preller told me he would not accompany me to see the 'Devil', as he called Liszt, so I decided to go alone. I did not feel embarrassed and when I got there I found that his butler, although born in Bonn, did not understand a word of German. However, I managed to explain to him what I wanted and he took me to his master. Liszt was occupied with a visitor and he treated him with such haughtiness that I quite lost heart. But I asked Liszt to tell me when he could possibly hear me play a little piece of mine, and he told me immediately to sit at the piano. I rushed downstairs to tell my mother to come up, and sat at the Bechstein and started playing my Prelude in D♭: I had not played three bars of it before he stopped me and began saying how original and masterly he thought it! I started playing again, and he stopped me and talked in the same vein. So I thought I had better play something else, and started my Prelude and Fugue in B Minor. He liked it so much that he invited us immediately to come to one of the matinées he held every Sunday morning at half-past eleven. In any case he wanted me to play something else, and he said I was to come and visit him in Leipzig. You cannot imagine how charming he was to us, especially to me. I don't think anybody has ever enjoyed this fugue of mine in B Minor as much as he did. At every bar I played he made some flattering remark, which was always so true and musicianly that I developed an enormous respect for him.*

"At the matinée all the compositions were his. The brothers Fern began with Festklänge, which was not too bad on two pianos, Liszt conducting with his finger. Directly after, Scario sang a few songs, then an ugly woman singer sang an even more ugly song of Liszt's with him at the piano. Then Brassin played the Concerto in E♭ major, and a Polish Countess, the Mephisto Waltz. Well, allow me to tell you, these people can play the piano! It is incredible. And yet the idolatry they have for Liszt is enough to make you sick: they kissed his hand after each bar, they shouted bravo furiously. When the music séance was over we bade farewell to Liszt, who had introduced me to all these people as 'pianist and composer' and who kissed me in such a ridiculous way."

Yes, I remember how Röntgen used to talk to me about the *Liszterriens* in rather a sarcastic way. even jeeringly. What he did not like was the fuss, the atmosphere and incense and exaggerated flattery which surrounded Liszt. But, of course, one must not forget (as Siloti used to) that Liszt was an elemental force, whose passage raised a storm of frenzy and veneration quite unintended by him.

Röntgen himself, and his parents, were also great friends of Clara Schumann, Brahms and Joachim.

It is fascinating to study the evolution of Röntgen in connection with Brahms. In 1873—when Röntgen was eighteen—he could not understand the blind worshipping of Brahms' followers. ("I don't think this is music for all time. It requires too much effort without reaching the summit. But time will ultimately decide.") But, through Röntgen's letters we can perceive a change of mind—especially after he had heard the Second Symphony—and he became a fervent admirer of Brahms' works. (In 1885 he wrote about the *Trio in B major*: "I see now that, if I did not like this work at first, it was entirely my fault, as was the case with many other works of Brahms.")

This evolution is all the more interesting when we realise that Röntgen also became a friend of Brahms and that his compositions, although they have a strong personality, are nevertheless closely related to those of Brahms. This friendship and admiration are reflected also in the names he gave to his sons: Johannes (in memory of Brahms), Joachim (in memory of the great violinist), Edward (in memory of Grieg).

I believe it was at Röntgen's house in Amsterdam that you met Grieg?

Yes. We spent an unforgettable afternoon together.

What impression have you kept of Grieg?

He was a man who looked old, with a large head which reminded me of Einstein, but better looking, and two blue shining eyes with a surprisingly soft expression. He was very small and looked even smaller because of a slightly bent back. He had a winning sympathy of the most delicate kind and he seemed to live in that noble dream of a patriotic ideal which you find reflected in his music. Röntgen had honoured me by dedicating his Piano and 'Cello Sonata to me. We played it to Grieg on that day, and I also played the *C minor Suite* of Bach for 'cello alone. Grieg wrote the same evening to his friend and publisher to give him his impression of my performance ("a drama," he said).[1] Afterwards Grieg sat at the piano and his wife Nina sang a cycle of songs Grieg had written for her when they were engaged. It was delicious.

[1] Grieg wrote about this performance by Casals: "*This man does not perform, he resuscitates.*"

Can one describe Grieg's music as "folklore"?

No. Grieg's music primarily suggests the character and the pictorial side of his nation, Norway. Of course there is also a side of rhythmical folk dance in his music.

Can one bracket Grieg and Sibelius together?

Well, we can detect a certain kind of national character in Sibelius, but his art is altogether on a much higher plane and I think his musical contribution is one of the most important of our generation.

It is a great pity that the book of Röntgen's letters does not contain those he wrote to you.

Do you know why? In 1914, just before the war started, I gave up my *Villa Molitor* in Paris and left a few packing-cases full of books, letters and various kinds of documents in a repository. When I returned to Paris at the end of the war I realised that the police had been searching all these cases and all the papers were spread on the floor in the most awful mess, and I could not find Röntgen's letters any more than those of Strauss, Fauré, Saint-Saëns, Moor and many other friends.

Have you given any concerts with Röntgen?

Yes, a great many.

Tovey wrote: "An audience capable of appreciating the purely musical value of the Sonata of Röntgen for piano and 'cello at a good performance of the work, would share Mendelssohn's opinion when he said that music is much more precise in its meaning than words are."

This Sonata stands comparison with the best ones written for the 'cello. I remember so well when Röntgen arrived in Paris with his wife and gave it to me. They spent a few marvellous days at the *Villa Molitor*! On the day of their departure we were all sitting in the garden, when Röntgen went back into the house to play the Beethoven Sonata (*Les Adieux*). It was a magnificent performance, a thing one could not forget, and what a master he was at the piano!

It is Tovey who says: "No one who has seen him dealing with young people could avoid thinking of the Hans Sachs of Wagner."

That is true: welcoming, generous, unselfish, always ready to help young musicians: such was my friend. Jealousy and intrigue simply passed him by. However, Röntgen's judgment was always very carefully weighed and had nothing facile or complacent in it. His sincerity and independence were well known.

I saw him shortly before his death. He had been taken for a few weeks to a clinic at Billthoven before he came back home. But his health was worse and his wife wrote to me asking me to come as soon as possible. When he saw me his strength seemed to return and he looked a different man; we spent the whole day in his room playing music. The next day, after I had gone, he became unconscious and he died a few days later. I had felt when I was there before that it was the last time I would see him.

The list of his compositions is impressive.

What he has written is big in quantity and quality . . . a very hard worker. Röntgen left behind a series of works most curiously neglected, but which give him a place next to the most remarkable musicians of our time.

Moor, Tovey and Röntgen. Here are three very great minds still unrecognised. But I feel sure that their time will come. Only the mediocre are impatient. The great know how to wait.

VI

Johann Sebastian Bach

This Chapter and the two following are planned to demonstrate the opinions of Casals by opposing them to the statements of other musicians and critics as expressed in their published works.

At the time of the 1950 Bach Festival at Prades you wrote: "The miracle of Bach has not appeared in any other art. To strip human nature until its divine attributes are made clear, to inform ordinary activities with spiritual fervour, to give wings of eternity to that which is most ephemeral; to make divine things human and human things divine; such is Bach, the greatest and purest moment in music of all time."

Yes, Bach is the supreme genius of music. I have reached this conclusion, so easy to state, and of such enormous significance. This man, who knows everything and feels everything, cannot write one note, however unimportant it may appear, which is anything but transcendent. He has reached the heart of every noble thought, and has done it in the most perfect way.

I have been told that for many years you have been in the habit of starting the day at the piano, playing Bach Preludes and Fugues.

That is so. At my house in Sant Salvador my maid Thérèse used to hum most of the themes of *The Well-Tempered Clavier* from having heard me play them so often.

This music is the perfect elixir of youth. It refreshes the spirit and induces a calm and cheerful frame of mind for the day's activities.

One critic has called the composer of The Well-Tempered Clavier *the least psychological musical genius that ever existed.*

A complete fallacy, since every psychological nuance is to be found in this work. Quite simply, the Preludes and Fugues are great music, and it is inconceivable to think of them as "objective" pieces in which the performer's personality should not play any part.

What gives them vitality, in spite of their form, is the freedom of their construction. Cherubini did not accept them as Bach had conceived them. According to him, they were not real fugues because

109

they were free. It shows that Bach thought of the fugue as a means of expression, and not as a dry and formal thing. He held that when a part had nothing to say it should remain silent—splendid, not to overdo anything. The Master only brings the part in again when the sense of the music demands it. That is the right way to create.

"*Never did any teacher make his pupils a more precious gift* (The Well-Tempered Clavier), *never has there been an educational work of such artistic value. In this kind of composition, which because of its complicated form seems to put technical skill before poetry and inspiration, Bach is able to express his personality with great eloquence. Each of the ninety-six pieces has its clearly-defined individuality, each one a physiognomy of its own, as characteristic as the profile on a medal.*"[1]

Bach's intention in this work is to convey various impressions of tonality—sometimes with such extraordinary significance as in the *Prelude in B♭ Minor*, which overflows with feeling; a most poignant movement, which could have come from the *St. Matthew Passion*. Bach also gives us all qualities inherent to the major keys—grandeur, joy, simplicity, even high spirits. To hell with the notion that these pieces should be played as if they were just exercises, or little models of "technical cleverness"! In every note I can detect the throbbing sensitiveness of their author.

A critic has said that this collection reflects Bach's soul in all its greatness.

Yes. Bach being the universal genius, there is no emotion that has not been expressed by him, except stinginess, meanness and all that is incompatible with a noble mind. In his works you find some feelings which words cannot describe or classify. I have got used to saying that Bach is a volcano.

What of The Art of Fugue?

It constitutes a peerless monument to his musical science. We can hardly imagine such greatness. It is rather as if Bach had said, "Now I'll show you who I am and what I can do."

Your friend Tovey, as one among many, had completed The Art of Fugue, *hadn't he?*

Yes.

Dr. Schweitzer does not think that The Art of Fugue *was unfinished. He thinks the error arises out of the way in which the work was edited after Bach's death.*

[1] This quotation, and the others in this chapter from William Cart, are extracts from his book, *J. S. Bach (1685–1753)*. (Rouge et Cie., Lausanne.)

From what I have read and from what Tovey told me, I am sure my friend followed in his work the plan left by Bach himself.

"*No-one has known how to make the organ speak as Bach has. He was its most astonishing virtuoso, its most learned and poetical composer, its most prolific improvisor.*" (William Cart.)

I entirely agree with this statement. But it should be added that Bach created new resources for the instrument.

"*Theatrical effects were finding their way into church music. Contemporary taste, which was becoming frivolous and worldly, demanded secular tunes, even during services. The true style of religious music was declining. Bach's music seemed outdated. But it is well known that the way of artistic survival is often to appear out of fashion. Bach fought a rearguard action, defending alone the post which his fall would deliver into the hands of the enemy. This sense of isolation makes him disdain the approval of the crowd. He no longer seeks to please others, he wants above all things, his own self-respect and satisfaction as an artist.*" (William Cart.)

When he wants to, Bach knows how to get near the people without using flattery or trying to win its approval by presenting something facile. He knows, better than anyone, how to make use of that deeply rooted tradition of German Protestantism, the chorale. One of the facts that most reflects the character of Bach is that the theatre never tempted him. There was no room for concessions to showmanship in any of his works.

Dr. Schweitzer wonders if Bach's aversion to the theatre would have persisted if he had remained in Hamburg.

I think it would. If the stage had tempted him he would have realised his wish wherever he found himself, whether in a village or on a farm. Once when Bach went to a town with one of his sons (I cannot recall which one), he said to him about some theatrical show going on there, "Let's go and hear this little music." This remark, if not actually scornful, is at any rate detached and ironical and tells us a lot about his attitude to the theatre.

What do you think of this opinion: "*The form of the Cantata Arias lends itself to varied effects and attractive repetitions. But it undoubtedly ends by becoming monotonous. It can be said straight away that of all Bach's output, it is the Arias, cast in the Italian mould, which bear the hallmark of their period and have dated most.*" (William Cart.)

Why think that? You have the contrast between the Arias and the choruses, each bringing out the value of the other. As for the Arias, I don't see how they have dated, either in form or in quality.

You say their form becomes monotonous? It is true that the recitatives of the Cantatas are in the Italian style, but we must not forget the great riches which music owes to Italian recitative.

Dr. Schweitzer also complains of this Italian influence. "The Arioso, pure and simple, as found in the actus tragicus, *is very superior to the ritornello* aria. *It is a free form which represents the ideal synthesis of recitative and melody. This recitative* arioso *is a creation of the German genius, being no more nor less than the original form of what will be brought to fruition on such a grandiose scale in Wagner's music. This is the form, so simple and at the same time so rich, that Bach has abandoned for the recitative aria in the Italian Operatic style. He does not seem to realise that these foreign influences don't suit his genius, and he does not notice that the structure of the* ritornello *will become an obstacle to the natural development of his ideas."* [1]

Bach has made his choice. It is not for me to object. He must have done so because this form attracted him, and if, in this way, he has created marvellous music why should we regret that it was not written in some other way?

"Bach, in following the Italian school, arrested the growth of German music along the lines which Wagner used later. The forms and texts which he accepted in order to conform to contemporary fashion, are not those the very things in his output that have become superannuated?" (Albert Schweitzer.)

I do remember I noticed these criticisms when I read Dr. Schweitzer's book in the German edition, a fairly long time ago. When I see Bach adopting a style or a form it means a great deal more to me than a simple question of influence. But supposing we accept the idea that the Italian recitative acted as an influence on Bach. The very fact of its adoption by such a genius is surely a proof of the excellence of this musical form. And why shouldn't Bach, this man who has created a universal musical language, adopt as his own a method which appeals to him? Furthermore, hasn't he given us proof of his amazing capacity in every kind of composition? It seems to me that there is logic in my argument. What can we do about it if the character of his music does not pretend to be exclusively Germanic and if, prompted by his universal genius, the great master felt a need to absorb all that surrounded him and look to new horizons?

"Things that have become superannuated in his output." I cannot

[1] All the Schweitzer quotations are from his book, *J. S. Bach, Musician and Poet.*

accept this. If a work of art is of a high order its form and the style in which it is presented are, to me, of quite secondary importance. The adoption of one style or another does not matter to me. There is no such thing as an outworn or obsolete form, provided that the music contained in it is of true value. And what should we say about the aria and recitative of Mozart? And of Beethoven? The opening of the finale of the *Ninth Symphony*? Is there a greater monument to the Italian recitative?

Curiously enough Bach never went out of Germany, in contrast to other musicians of his period, who were very cosmopolitan.

No, but he copied with his own hand works by Italian and French composers, looked at everything that came his way, and became a patient and attentive pupil of all the great masters. His genius, which was too powerful to be confined to any particular form or tradition, was always drawn to great art, of any kind or any origin. I don't deny that Bach is a German master, but it is a mistake to try and restrict him with a national label, and an even greater one to connect him with the prickly character of modern nationalism. He is among those geniuses who shine over all nations and all time. And also, as I have said before, the blame for Bach being misunderstood for so long rests with the Germans themselves. They used to, and still do, perform the music of their compatriot without any imagination. I recently heard the *Third Brandenburg Concerto* played by a Berlin orchestra and relayed on the radio of that city. The performance was remarkable in many respects, but Bach, the poet, was not there.

I remember an amusing discussion apropos of the "exclusive Germanism" of Bach. It was during a tour in Germany: in Berlin, the well-known pianist Ansorge and myself were invited to lunch by a distinguished music-lover, Dr. Meyer. Our host had arranged things so that the two guests, Ansorge and myself, would first meet in a drawing-room and get to know each other. We began to talk about Bach—Ansorge would only admit Bach as being exclusively and essentially German. I talked to him about the French and Italian influences in his output. He would not recognise them. Also Hungarian, I said, in a slightly louder voice. This unhinged him completely. I calmly walked to a piano there was in the room and began to play some Bach piece of the same character as the first movement of the *Partita in G minor*. I was trying to give the accompaniment the timbre of a cimbalom. Do you know what Ansorge did? He flew off in a wild temper and went to tell Dr. Meyer and his wife that as long as "this man" was there, he would not come near the house. As a matter of fact my hosts and I had a good laugh about it.

Now about Bach's religious mysticism. Schweitzer says: "If Bach adorned all his scores with his S.D.G., it is because of an essentially religious idea of music. It was his godliness that kept and sustained his laborious existence—and mysticism was the life-spring of his godliness. He felt a deep need for eternal rest and tranquillity. Never has the nostalgie de la mort *been translated into music in a more striking way."*

In my opinion there has been much too much leaning on the exclusively religious side of Bach's music. The intensity of his faith is evident in a great many of his compositions. Bach was a sincere believer and a man whose occupation led him to serve the Church. However, I cannot rally myself to this idea of exclusively religious feeling in his music. I find that very exaggerated. Religious inspiration is not everything. In Bach we find infinite gradations of musical allusion: the simple joy of the people, the popular dances, the elegance, the perfume, the loving contemplation of nature and the rest.

We know that Bach had the most sincere religious feeling: in all the Passions and the Chorales he has given expression to his faith in the most complete and the greatest way, but I insist this inspiration is far from being the only one in his work. I think that Bach was a poet who felt the necessity of translating all noble thoughts into music.

I remember one day, when we were listening to your recording of Komm Süsser Todt, *you said, "I cannot hear this without being moved in the deepest regions of my soul."*

I believe that: one cannot describe the serene expectation of death in a more perfect way, nor can anyone go deeper than Bach in any of the ideas he has translated into music.

About the place the Chorales occupy in the Cantatas, William Cart says: "The instruments mostly reinforce the melody known by the congregation, and if they sometimes seem to take flight into more luminous heights, it is in order to surround it with divine glory. This symbol is clear enough for anyone to understand what Bach means. In spite of all things human art can invent, it is the simple Chorale that becomes the most sincere expression of the Church, and all the Cantata is only a preparation for it."

Yes, the foundation of the work is the Chorale, which comes from folk-song, and through which Bach could achieve the most intimate communion with the faithful. The Chorale, with its religious as well as popular origins, is one of the great musical forms.

"If one begins to study the Cantatas, one gets so accustomed to wonders that one ends by finding the most astonishing things quite natural. The abundance of Bach's thematic resources and the ways in which he combined and developed them remains something of a miracle." (William Cart.)

Truly, they belong to the miraculous, and adjectives are superfluous in trying to describe them. One of my dreams has been to conduct all the Cantatas which are known.

"Bach's nature, with all its strength, was so sensitive and mobile that the slightest shock made it vibrate. Since all the strings of his artistic nature were musical they started singing at the least touch. Bach and Mozart are alike in this respect. Their truest and only mode of expression was through music: whether they wanted it or not they could not help it."

In this respect I think the comparison between Mozart and Bach is right. "Since all the strings of his artistic nature were musical, they started singing at the least touch" is a remark of great subtlety. Whose is it?

It is in William Cart's book, published in 1887.

Then if it was written in 1887 it is even more interesting since the real significance of Bach was little known at that time.

Dr. Schweitzer says: "Yet Bach was a poet because what he looked for in a text before anything else was its poetic content."

Yes, Bach did look for poetry in a text and he knew how to breathe it into a fugue of the most scholarly appearance. Dr. Schweitzer has greatly served the cause of Bach in putting forward the poetical aspect of his writing, for until the appearance of his book there were many people who could only see in Bach a master full of knowledge, but cold and academic.

Another comparison between Bach and Mozart: "Mozart begins by charming our ears in a most delicious way and then gives our body and soul an indescribable feeling of well-being. Bach lifts the soul away from the body. Without trying to maintain a paradox, we can say that in spite of his austerity and the greater age of his forms, Bach is more modern than Mozart." (William Cart.)

Which of the two is more modern? This question is meaningless, all the more so because in their own time, neither one nor the other was understood as they are now.

One of Bach's commentators makes the remark that the Christmas Oratorio *is not in the same style as those of Handel, with dramatic action and real people who each have an individuality of their own.*

In Bach's Cantatas, as in his Passions and this Oratorio, one never thinks of the theatre, whereas in Handel one does: he is much more of a showman.

The unavoidable comparison between these two contemporaries: Handel has a more harmonious beauty. Bach moves you more deeply. Handel imposes himself. Bach makes you dream.

As I told you before, Handel is more of a showman. Bach never is, although he can reach a much higher plane of emotion. In the science of obtaining effects Handel was a great master, maybe the greatest. Bach never thought of an effect: his music came out of the most intimate part of his mind and never aimed at anything but the purest.

In the Christmas Oratorio *about which I spoke, the canticle which greets the child Jesus is the one that will be addressed to Christ when persecuted and beaten in front of Pontius Pilate. So we find Jesus' death glorified in His birth. Isn't there an idea of the same kind in your* Oratorio del Pessebre?

The libretto of this Oratorio is by our friend Joan Alavedra, and, in fact, he was inspired by the same idea. Naturally the music adapts itself to this poetical theme. When they are dancing a *Sardana* in front of the porch at Bethlehem, paying homage to the newly born child, the "Santons" (Moslem religious ascetics) standing by already know that the child will be crucified. Thus the *Sardana* already announces the sacrifice of the redemption.

The Christmas Oratorio *contains some pieces which had appeared in other works, some of them in secular compositions. Some people have wondered how a composer such as Bach could apply the same music to such different words; to which a music critic (*J. Weber, Les Illusions Musicales) *answers that religious music is not essentially different from any other. "It is only separated through nuances, to a greater or lesser extent, not through any principles."*

That is true. One could think first about the Gregorian chant, which has its roots in folk-song. How many tunes coming from the people, which have been passed from one generation to another, have gone into the Chorales!

In the St. John Passion *do you find anything "sombre and agitated"?*

Yes, certainly. And I can hardly avoid telling you that it always brings back to my mind the day when I took part in a performance of it at Basle, and had the presentiment of my father's death, as I told you before.

Furtwängler says about the St. Matthew Passion: *"This masterpiece is the most sublime of all music."*

A thousand times I agree with this. When I heard this *Passion* for the first time in Paris, the impact it made on me was so violent that I felt ill for about two months. I felt stifled and as if I could not cry enough. The bigness of it all had shattered me.

About the Chorale sung by a third choir in this Passion (Agnus Dei....) *William Cart says:* "*Christian art has not produced anything which can be compared to the emotion caused by this voice standing above the harmonic flood of the two choirs and the two orchestras.*"

It is true: the impression made by this third choir is immense. There are the two choirs in the introduction, and suddenly a third one comes in singing in unison an amplified chorale. The impression of this third choir is great, but, to get the real effect, the third choir should be placed higher up.

"*His dramatic instinct,*" *writes Dr. Schweitzer,* "*is not less developed. The plan of the* St. Matthew Passion, *so admirably conceived for a dramatic work, is of his own invention. In each text he looks for contrasts, oppositions and gradations.*"

Bach was lyric as well as dramatic when it was required. His inspiration is sure, without hesitations. I make a Bach-Shakespeare parallel, in the sense that both these great geniuses have explored endlessly the psychological nuances of any emotion.

Some critic has written, apropos of the performance of the St. Matthew Passion: "*It is necessary to avoid sentimentality as much as coldness; one must combine taste with technical perfection, the solemn style of the church with the pathos of the situations, without ever striving for an effect.*"

Especially without striving for effect, otherwise the spirit of Bach would be spoilt. For a long time one of my dearest wishes has been to conduct the *St. Matthew Passion* as I conceive it. I should like that to be my "musical testament". You know that I was invited to do it in Zürich in 1954? To my great sorrow I had to refuse, because of my present attitude. I only hope that circumstances will alter so that I may realise eventually one of my last and most intense wishes.

Dr. Schweitzer writes on the subject of the Mass in B Minor: "*If the* Mass in B Minor *is the most vigorous and grandiose work of Bach, it nevertheless lacks that unity which makes the beauty of the* St. Matthew Passion. *Religious subjectivity, which is like the soul of Bach's music, cannot have a free rein in the Mass. We can say that there are in this work some sections of a very German subjectivity, for instance, the* Et incarnatus est *and the* Crucifixus, *but on the whole the work has a rather objective*

*character. The 'Protestant' sections do not compare for greatness with the
ones representing the Catholic dogma."*

I agree, the Mass is so divided. However, I didn't find there is
anything missing in it. The Master had no wish to write it in any other
way, and felt the desire to compose it as it is. And what has been the
result? That is what we must ask ourselves when confronted by this
great outpouring of feeling and knowledge. We might prefer Bach
to have given it confessional unity, so that the work would have been
ascribed immediately to the spirituality of one or the other creed. Bach
has written it on a dual basis and I think we must accept it as such. And
I repeat: what does interest us musically and what we want to know is
—what has Bach given us in his Mass?

William Cart thinks that the Mass in B Minor *reminds one of a Gothic
cathedral in which the faithful of both confessions can hold out their hands
to each other.*

It is obvious that the Mass suggests a Gothic cathedral. But Bach's
music cannot be Gothic; however, when performing or listening to
certain works of his one can think of a cathedral of the Middle Ages.
In Beethoven's *Ninth Symphony* one would never think of it.

"If we compare the Bach Mass with the Missa Solemnis *of Beethoven
we can realise the abyss there is between the two works. Bach rests entirely
on a biblical foundation. His style was born in the church, his faith is one of
traditional Christianity. Beethoven is a 'modern' in whose heart the theism
of the XVIIIth century and the humanism of the XIXth have replaced the
old faith. But the modern master has his moment in the* Benedictus: *there
he can breathe out all his loving soul. Never has the religion of fraternal love,
of universal charity been sung with more fervour; all the tenderness he showed
to men, and which men reflected, he poured out in this unforgettable violin
solo. A very characteristic detail of this great master of instrumental music;
it is to the violin and not to the voice in this vocal mass, he entrusts his most
intimate feelings."* (William Cart.)

There are some interesting ideas in this comparison, but some of
the remarks such as "Bach the 'old master', Beethoven the 'modern
master'", might lead to confusion. The violin solo of the *Benedictus* is
certainly a sublime and an extraordinary moment and one of the
summits in Beethoven's work. What a responsibility for the violinist
who plays it!

*On the subject of the evolution from Bach to Beethoven, Furtwängler
remarks that the "epic" character in Bach becomes completely "dramatic"
in Beethoven. He recalls the example of Ancient Greece, when Homer*

came before the "Tragics", and he sums up in one paragraph the course of this evolution through Haydn and Mozart: "But it is in Haydn that we first find how the great advantage of the Bach period (which continued through Mozart's happy music) began to disappear. Up till then the wholeness and coherency of a work was, so to speak, in its nature. From then on this unity will have to be achieved: modern music begins. With Haydn, and even more with Beethoven afterwards, we pass from the 'being' of Bach through the 'unfolding' of Mozart to the 'becoming'. A final Chord in Bach only means the end of a piece of music. With Haydn and Beethoven this chord marks the end of a composition, the conclusion of a composer's endeavour. It is the beginning of a new era, which imposes on the composer the necessity to connect musical logic with ordinary logic, and in this way to bring about a synthesis which could hardly have occurred naturally—the movement of the music and the emotion of the soul."[1]

To assert that before Haydn the "wholeness and coherence of the work" would happen of itself—I cannot see that. The composers had to achieve the formal unity of their works through a procedure which might be different from that of a later generation, but always keeping in sight the logic of unification. As for Bach's music, it is neither square nor static. Can one imagine a "becoming" (*Werden*) more intense or more dynamic than his work, since the whole music of the future was influenced through it? It is true that Beethoven puts the accent on the dramatic, and this side of his character is often evident in his compositions. But to say that Beethoven is "nearer" to us than Bach because of this "dramatic" touch, I cannot accept. (I know that a great musician like Furtwängler does not pretend to make this assertion, but his comments could easily be interpreted in such a way.) Bach and Beethoven exist all around us, and they will exist as long as human beings are capable of feeling anything. Every creation of the mind bears, in a way, the mark of the period in which it was conceived. But what characterises great creations is that they project themselves towards the future like a shining star. Bach is one of the great ones who for a long time was put away in a drawer as being too "old-fashioned". That is why I instinctively reject these classifications which, without meaning to, present Bach as an "ancient". When I was young, I found lots of people talking of Bach with great respect, but without any understanding. Even in our day there are lots of performers who believe that Bach is a long way away and make the mistake of looking for "objectivity" and "impersonality" in his compositions. Bach's

[1] *Op. Cit.*

work is fully immediate and real, just as any of Shakespeare, Cervantes and Michaelangelo. We musicians should not lose sight of its immediate vitality and radiance.

Dr. Schweitzer says about Bach's transcriptions of his own works: "From the technical point of view it is curious to find Bach transcribing violin works for the keyboard. It may be that Bach considered the violin style as universal." Schweitzer adds: "When Bach writes for the violin, or rather, for an ideal instrument which would have the power of the organ and the completeness of phrasing of the violin."

Well, if you like, but a violin lacks a low register. In Bach's themes I sometimes hear other instruments than the violin. I do understand this opinion as far as phrasing is concerned, because of the flexibility one can get in so many themes with this instrument, but I would not give it too exclusive a character.

And what do you think about the technical aspect of the Six Suites for 'Cello Solo? Those Suites which had waited for you to reveal all their treasures!

The Six Suites for 'Cello give an idea of Bach's vision of the possibilities of this instrument, possibilities which had not been exploited before. Here, as in so many other branches, Bach was in advance of his time.

The Fifth Suite is entitled Suite discordable, *because it requires the A string to be tuned down to G?*

Yes. This Suite shows the desire and the possibility of new departures and obviously constitutes a discovery, considering the period when it was written.

The last Suite is written for the Viola Pomposa—*an instrument Bach had invented.*

My impression is that, after the Five Suites, Bach foresaw new ways of using the upper register of the violoncello which, so far, were unknown. That is why he invented the *Viola Pomposa*, which possesses an extra string tuned up one fifth above the A string.

Have you heard this Suite played on the instrument conceived by Bach?

No, but with a 'cello built so that it could be played as a *Viola Pomposa*. As far as its sonority was concerned, it did not satisfy me. Now this Suite can be played without the addition of a string. We constantly notice Bach's preoccupation to go beyond the technical limitations of the instruments of his period, in the perfecting of the organ, the research into the intonation of the keyboard, the use of the thumb and the organisation of modern fingering, the technical advance found in the violin and the 'cello Suites and so on.

The richness of Bach's writing does not come from an abundance of different themes, but in the different inflections taken by the same theme according to the occasion?

That is very often what he does (except in a fugal form): work the same theme to its end. How wonderful it is to be able to give with this method so much diversity and yet perfection of form! In Bach we find ourselves confronted with a theme which goes from one end to the other of the composition, and what is admirable is that the listener *needs* this exploitation of the same theme! Bach, if he had wanted to, could have introduced some secondary themes; but what he looks for, and finds, is a feeling of unity, and he proceeds as if the theme was a subject of conversation. He looks for lots of nuances and inflections in his theme but does not get away from it.

Critics and musicians agree in saying that Bach has not changed, and that there is an increasing accentuation of his personality, but that his younger works predict his future development. "Whereas it is sufficient to study a page from Beethoven to give it a place in the chronology of his works," says a critic, "one needs to be very advanced in the knowledge of Bach to distinguish the different periods of his works."

It is very true. It happens to me also. If I did not know it before, I should find it difficult to say which period a particular work belongs to.

Bach is the composer who has made more transcriptions of his own works than any other composer has done.

Yes, and how much art and tact he has brought to these arrangements! I have been one of the few people to defend transcriptions. To spurn them is a mistake. In all work there is the element of music, besides the "colour" of the instruments for which the works were written. The strictly musical value is above the instrumental value, and it should predominate. Why, then, shouldn't it be transferred to other instruments? Bach did it consistently; why shouldn't we do it?

I was talking the other day with a pianist friend of mine about the transcription of the *Kinderscenen* of Schumann for 'cello and piano. He thought that, as these pieces had been written for the piano, it was not possible to hear them otherwise! I know that Schumann thought of them for the piano and I know also how wonderful they can sound just on a keyboard. But since the piano does not possess the inflections of a string instrument, why not play some pieces on the instrument which possesses these qualities, and especially these *Scenes*, which are so delicate and expressive? Of course the effect is different, but why should this difference stop us?

Nowadays nobody minds—although, at first, people objected—to the fact that Ravel has arranged the *Pictures from an Exhibition* by Moussorgsky, which was not a work for orchestra. Supposing anyone felt like arranging a piano sonata of Beethoven for orchestra? Why not!

Edwin Fischer writes:[1] *"In order to understand a great composer and to perform his works as they should be performed, it is important to know also the surroundings this composer lived in. In order to know these things (in regard to Bach) it becomes necessary to obliterate from our minds all the developments which took place after Bach, all the things which in his day had not been discovered, written or achieved. To understand Bach in his day, we shall have, therefore, to forget all the music of Haydn, Mozart, Beethoven, all romanticism and also the philosophy and free thinking, the political and geographical conceptions of the generations subsequent to Bach. We shall have to imagine all the things which, as far as we are concerned, have disappeared in the past, but were active and visible in his day: the religious habits of his century, his symbolism, his connection with the Church. Only thus, shall we understand the Master, not just through ourselves but objectively."*

How can one say that, if you think of the musical side of the question? How can one do away with one's own feeling of the music performed? I don't say that it is not useful to be informed on the general history of the period in which the composer lived and worked: any cultural acquisition, in enriching the artist's sensibility, will make him more able to grasp all the esthetic nuances of the composition he is playing; but the *real* artist must, before anything else, rely on his own musical sense in order to know exactly what the work is and how he is himself affected by it. If the performer begins to think he has to abide by the old methods, and decide what form it was presented in, his mind will become prey to doubts which are bound to spoil this spontaneous expression, which, in a good performance, should come before anything else. As for the performer who plays Bach nowadays, he specially ought not to be concerned with the idea of historical reconstitution. Above all in Bach, because his music belongs to all time and therefore when performing it one does not want to follow

[1] Edwin Fischer: *Johann Sebastian Bach.* (Berne, 1948.)

the prescriptions of one period, even less to be hampered by the obstacles and limitations which existed two centuries ago in the field of technique.

That young man of thirteen who, one day, discovered the Six Suites for the 'Cello in a music shop in Barcelona, could not have bothered his head with historical preoccupations!

This young man was just struck by so much greatness in music, and he applied himself to the study of the Suites for years with all his enthusiasm and his devotion.

Dr. Schweitzer writes on the question of tempi *in performing Bach:* "*The mechanism of harpsichords in those days did not allow the performer to play a modern* allegro. *When playing Bach's works on ancient instruments, we realise that his rapid* allegro *(the maximum of speed one could expect on those instruments) does not go much beyond our* allegro moderato. *This does not prevent us from making use of the better mechanism of a modern piano to play Bach's works quicker than he played them himself. Some compositions would seem to drag if we wanted to stick to the 'authentic' tempo. For example, we find it so in any gigue movements of the great Partitas. But on the whole, one should not go beyond an energetic* allegro. *Similarly, the slow movements of Bach have not got the slowness of our modern performance. His adagio, grave, lento are equal to our extreme* moderato. *The short sound of his harpsichord did not allow him to play his slow movements as slowly as we can do it on a modern piano where sound is prolonged. Quite naturally we shall play certain pieces in a tempo a bit slower than the authentic tempo, although we should not go as slowly as our modern* adagio.*"*

These indications: not to go beyond an energetic *allegro moderato* in a quick movement, not to get as far as a modern *adagio* in the slow movements, are, to my mind, vague remarks. The question of *tempi* is always decided by the intuition of the artist. He may make some difference according to the quality of the harpsichord or the piano he plays on, or else because of the acoustics of the hall or room he plays in.

The "authentic" *tempo* is impossible. The *tempo* should vary with the performer according to the circumstances. What does matter is that he should know how to produce the *tempo* required by his personal feeling and suitable to the spirit of the music.

Forkel relates that Bach played his most austere fugues with enormous freedom.

That does not surprise me.

"*For a long time people thought Bach's works should be played without expression. Bach, it is true, rarely writes any sign of dynamics, but it is because he relies on the feeling and the intelligence of his performers. This ought to be said: 'Bach knows all the modern effects.'*" (William Cart.)

I am entirely in agreement with this.

Dr. Schweitzer talks about a "refined rubato". "If the Bach tempi do not vary from a normal tempo as much as those in modern music, this normal tempo should be graduated in a most subtle way. A sort of rigid and uniform tempo does not suit Bach's music.

Very good.

"*Actually one does not find in Bach the opposition of themes of a different kind, as one does for instance in the Beethoven Sonatas. Bach generally adopts a rhythm in the first bars which will continue throughout the piece.*"

Exactly.

"*But this homogenity of tempo should be simple and expressive. Bach does not ask us to abolish the beat but he intends a subtle rubato.*"

This could constitute a rule for all music. Bach does not require any special rules; it is the general rules of music one should observe when performing his works. Even so, the word "rule" is slightly out of place because it implies too much precision. It is the musical sense, the instinct of the performer, that should decide everything.

"*The impression a piece of Bach should make depends on its clarity to the listener. Whence this very simple general rule, too often neglected by performers: one should hold back the tempo when the design becomes more intricate, and be ready to resume elasticity as this design simplifies.*"

This also could be applied to all music.

Dr. Schweitzer, having told us why Bach so seldom marks the tempo, tells us that sometimes the actual material of the music calls for a special treatment of some part of the piece.

That seems obvious to me. As far as I am concerned, I think that one should notice the particularities of different parts of the same piece. For instance, in the first section of the *Gamba Sonata in G Minor*, there is a moment when I feel the need of a slower *tempo* than the initial one.

Dr. Schweitzer declares: "Let us set down three axioms which represent as many modern principles that one should abandon when dealing with Bach's music.

"*(1) Bach's works begin and end with their greatest sonority. All effects of pianissimo at the start and at the end of the work are alien to Bach's style.*"

Anyone who possesses some musical intuition does that anyhow. However, let us imagine that I begin to play a fugue of Bach; if, at the start, it seems to me that a *piano* is the right thing, I do it without any hesitation; if, at the end, I feel a *forte*, I do it. On the whole the sonority at the beginning and at the end is the one indicated above, but there can be exceptions and in these exceptions I shall follow my intuition without abiding by general rules.

"(2) *The cadence in Bach does not represent a* diminuendo, *but always remains within the sonority of the phrase it terminates*, piano *if this phrase is* piano, forte *if the phrase is* forte. *One must specially avoid spoiling the effect of a* piano *which follows a* forte *by connecting them by a* diminuendo. *The sudden opposition of a* piano *to a* forte *is one of the elementary principles in Bach's music. On this subject, one should study the expression marks in the Brandenburg Concerti.*"

On the whole I agree: there are these sudden oppositions from *forte* to *piano*.

"(3) *It is a mistake in the fugues to play the theme* piano *and gradually to reach the* forte *through the successive entries of the theme. It is not necessary to amplify in this way the natural gradation which comes from the succession of entries.*

"*The logic of a classical fugue does not bear any alteration of sonorities in the first entries of the theme any more than logic in architecture allows the main nave of a Gothic cathedral to rest on pillars of different dimensions. From the first bar the Bach themes come forward with some grandeur, even some pride; it is as if they carried the feelings they represent on a higher sphere, absolutely pure.*"

I agree in principle with what he says about the first entries in a fugue. As for the grandeur with which the subjects come forward, I think it depends on the subject. This "grandeur" depends on the *character* of the subject.

It is only in Bach's ensemble works that we notice how different the sound of our piano is different from that of the harpsichord of Bach. When he wrote the sonatas for violin and cembalo, the sounds of both instruments were completely homogeneous. Nowadays, played with a piano, the sounds do not blend but sound apart from one another. The listener who has a sensitive ear and has imagined the Bach works played with a well-matched sonority is bound to suffer by this antagonism. The difference of tone between a harpsichord and a piano is evident. However, I believe that the ear can adapt itself to the sound of the piano. In any case, as the piano has a power of expression the harpsichord has not, I would always choose it for the performance of these sonatas, since, in my opinion, the possibilities of expression are more important than the question of the *timbre*.

In the works of Bach where the keyboard instrument only has a role of accompanying, filling up the harmonies of a figured bass, I prefer the harpsichord, because its *timbre* mixes better with the orchestra. In any case, a good pianist can get such an effect if he plays discreetly.

Dr. Schweitzer maintains that the editions of Bach covered with expression marks (to save the performer from thinking for himself) do not help the cause of the Master—just the opposite. It is much better to publish them as we got them.

I am entirely in agreement on this point.

The indications added by editors can easily lead the performers along the wrong path. That is why I have always refused to edit Bach's works myself: and I have declined all offers. I think they should be published as we had them. As for the *tempo*, it is for the interpreter to look for it and to create it.

"What satisfaction it is to be able to play the fugues of Bach on an organ that is still intact in spite of its ancient mechanism. Only then can one discover how the modern organ is unable to show the value of the master's works." (Dr. Schweitzer.)

This is an idea one should respect. It is always an interesting experience and a cause for satisfaction to be able to play compositions as they were played two hundred years ago, and to find instruments by which one can revive the past. But that ought not to make us forget that Bach was always looking for improvements in the instruments he had to make do with because there were no others. If an organist can play on a good modern organ, what he should do is not to let himself be seduced by the reconstitution of archaism, but make good use of the new possibilities of his instrument. An organ is of itself a very mechanical instrument. The expressive value of string instruments can only be produced through a kind of phrasing that is done by the advancing or retarding of the notes, by the pauses and by the length of the sound. In rapid and loud passages an organ can be impressive, but its tone cannot vibrate with the rhythm of the organist's hand—and yet, we can recognise immediately if the player is a real musician.

I have read that F. A. Gevaert—your "missing" teacher—was the first to order the reconstitution of the instruments of Bach's time, in order to produce the works of the Master with their real colour. Dr. Schweitzer also wishes to return to the instruments of the period. "In order to bring out all the value of Bach's works, one is obliged to return to the old instruments. Attempts of this kind have been made in many places. The result has been above all expectations."

If one wants to undertake an interesting, though always incomplete, reconstruction of the musical atmosphere of a period, I accept the use of instruments of that period. But in any ordinary performance we ought to make use of the best instruments available nowadays, for, in my opinion, respect for the music we perform must be above all other considerations. We don't want to conjure up the past on an historical basis (which is always only relatively exact) but to produce the best version from the musical viewpoint.

Bach was always anxious to improve the instruments, and his extraordinary vision of what these instruments would be capable of justifies my doubts of his satisfaction with the instruments of his time. What performances he would have given with the numerous and well-drilled orchestras and the good instruments we possess nowadays! In his day all wind instruments were out of tune, now we have them in tune. And can you imagine what the effect of wind instruments playing out of tune would have on the string players, whose ears must have become falsified through hearing the wrong intonation every day? In any case the instruments were played in a different way. For instance, the violinists of that period held their bows in the middle!

Therefore, in order to get an "authentic" reconstitution, we should have to make the flutes and the oboes play out of tune and ask all string players to play in a mediocre way! No, to submit oneself to archaic practice in playing Bach would only do harm to his music, which rises above past, present ... and future.

Talking about instruments, you decided during the Prades Festival to replace the trumpet by a soprano saxophone in the performance of the 2nd Brandenburg Concerto.

What happened on this occasion is very interesting to relate. We got a famous trumpet player for this performance of the second concerto. At the first rehearsal we realised that he could not follow the *tempo* I was giving, which was, in my opinion, the right one to keep the music alive. He had to hold the *tempo* back, he played wrong notes, until he owned in front of everybody that he could not continue in this way. What was I to do? I did not want to change my *tempo*, so this player had to give up the performance. It was suggested that we could try the soprano saxophone which, well played, gave an excellent result. There were some purists who, when they learned of the change, were scandalised. Some years before I had already witnessed what happened to my first trumpet player, who, in practising the part of the same concerto, lost for ever the proper lip contact with the mouthpiece of his instrument. I am not inclined to use our trumpet in these works because it has to be played too much in the higher register. The soprano saxophone, if it is well played, can take its place with advantage.

Dr. Schweitzer, a few pages further on, voices an opinion which I find almost similar to the one you have just expressed. ". . . anything which will enhance the natural beauty of the work, or the plastic value of the performance, anything which will add vigour or delicacy to it, is not only allowed but actually demanded by the score. If Bach had had our resources at his disposal he would have used them in this way . . . We can only 'modernise' Bach. If we perform his works as they were in his day they would not make the same impression on the modern listener, since he is much more exacting than the faithful of St. Thomas Church."

That is exactly my opinion.

"It is not enough to play Bach's works, they must be interpreted."

Very good.

". . . interpret them in such a way that, while keeping the style of ancient music, one brings out the ideas and effects contained in the scores. To reconcile old style and modern effects, such is the problem of performance."

The old style for Bach, I just cannot accept it, it just is great music. If Bach had not lived then, and were to appear now, in the middle of the confusion of our time, he would be proclaimed as the Messiah.

Bach, with his fugues, cantatas, and polyphony?

Bach as he was in his day. His works would be like a sort of *fiat lux* . . . and so, how can we talk about "old style"?

We have not yet reached the full knowledge of his output. The search continues. We have, of course, gone some way towards this complete knowledge since the days when Mendelssohn and Schumann undertook to repair the neglect into which Bach had fallen. However, Mendelssohn and Schumann, in spite of their generous attempt for which they deserve all our gratitude, did show in many respects that they had not understood the greatness of the master. One example: the idea of Schumann's to write accompaniments to the Sonatas and Partitas for violin alone! We, ourselves, can see from day to day the growing of Bach's greatness. As for this question of performing it, of performing it deeply, we are only just emerging from the period of groping. The best advice is to discard deliberately the old prejudices and to get as near as possible in our performance to what the music makes us feel and what inspiration we derive from it. I repeat: there is no special rule for the interpretation of Bach's music.

VII

Music of Yesterday and Today (i)

May I be allowed to put to you further questions on Bach's great contemporary, Handel? How can one explain the fact that Messiah *was written in three weeks,* Israel in Egypt *in fifteen days and most of his* concerti grossi *in òne day?*

Facility is a more complex problem than it appears. I remember what Emmanuel Moor told me on that subject, since he was much criticised for excessive facility. "They don't know that the works I may write today, I may have worked at for some twenty years." How long does the conception of a work go on? The great musician does not compose only when he puts pen to paper; a constant gestation operates in his mind.

When you hear works like the Messiah *of Handel,* The Creation *of Haydn, the* Passion *of Bach, do you feel a religious emotion?*

Certainly. In so far as humility and adoration belong to this emotion.

Romain Rolland thinks that Buxtehude influenced the organ style of Bach and the Oratorio style of Handel.[1]

With Buxtehude we should mention Schutz and many others. Bach and Handel were not obsessed by a desire to be original. Genius is not a closed door; it receives and assimilates influences knowing that they will not weaken its personality. In the case of Bach we can admire his humility, that humility which led him to copy other works and use the ideas of authors he admired.

Richard Strauss opposed the great stream of polyphony and symphony descended from Bach to the homophonic and dramatic one stemming from Handel.

I don't see that very clearly. The dramatic sense appears with Handel in his ability to find one theatrical effect, which later will be the same with Rossini or Verdi. As for the deep dramatic sense, it is a basic element to many musicians.

[1] All the quotations from Romain Rolland are from his book, *Handel*. (Editions Albin Michel, Paris.)

Romain Rolland in his study of Handel makes a reference to Purcell and says that: "because he lacked in invention he did not make enough of his wonderful ideas". Purcell is a very elegant musician, a little Mozart.

Purcell has nothing to do with Mozart. Elegant, yes, and deep and great! Some of his works have been attributed to Bach! When I was young one could have called Purcell "the unknown". It is very different today! For the artist of genius, the hour of recognition always arrives.

About Handel, Saint-Saëns used to say that he was especially keen on the "picturesque", "the colour" and "imitative effect". "He was a painter." And Romain Rolland says of Handel that he was not "shut up" in himself. He, more than any other German, was a "visual" composer.

I quite agree.

It has been said that if Handel in his Oratorios used the stories of the biblical heroes, it was because they were known by everybody.

Yes, I am not very sure of the intensity of his religious feeling.

"Songs of the forest, of the birds, picturesque interludes, almost romantic, Handel was a pre-Romantic, rousing tempests from choir and orchestra like a Wagner or a Berlioz." 'You refuse to let rules constrict your personality' could have been said to him by a contemporary. "He is like a Beethoven in bondage" concludes Romain Rolland.

Maybe. It would be very difficult to explain how one "classical" composer is a pre-Romantic and another is not. . . .

"Language, without any concession to the crowd, can communicate in a popular way feelings that are common to us all. Nowadays this type of art and person has disappeared. We find the pure artist now stays at home, and those who speak to the people are most often entertainers." (Romain Rolland.)

Indeed, Handel had this quality: he would create a work of great artistic value which would be understood by every listener. That is why he was Handel! Now it is different, and the reason is that, unfortunately, we have not any genius to equal him.

In the XVIIth century singers embellished melodies with ornaments and sometimes considerable cadenzas, *a custom which has practically vanished.*

In Handel's day, singers used to improvise in passages where they could show off their voices. It is an Italian tradition. I don't think that, in modern editions of Handel, these improvisations should be rewritten, as Chrysander has done.

"Handel's orchestration reveals a sure instinct for balance and economy. If we want to reproduce his music adequately we ought not to change the

balance of the orchestra in order to make it richer and more modern." (Romain Rolland.)

I have already told you what I think about this subject when we talked about Bach. Handel, like other masters of his time, had to be content with existing conditions. However, we have never seen any indications from him or his contemporaries to the effect that we should play their compositions in this or that way and no other. One can understand that the Sonatas or Trios should be played as they are. But with an orchestral work why not employ the means at our disposal? At the Crystal Palace in London they gave the *Messiah* with a choir of ten thousand voices. In Kansas they also have performances of this oratorio with thousands and thousands of Americans of Scandinavian origin. I really don't see why such performances should be disapproved of.

"*People think that nuances are a privilege of modern art . . . With Handel the nuances are very varied from* pianissimo *to* fortissimo. *If one does not see* crescendi *or* diminuendi *marked, it is only because these nuances were not written in those days, but, of course, they were intended.*" (Romain Rolland.)

Quite right. Dynamics are intended even in polyphonic work, in Palestrina, and in all composers of all periods.

Reviewing the musical situation at the end of the XVIIIth century, a critic says: "*An abyss separated the master of fugue and the devotees of the Sonata. One learnt fugue as a means of improving one's study of music, but the emotion looked for was the sweetness of the Italians. Beethoven accepts Haydn's influence in the Sonatas and the Symphonies but turns his back on its convention and rhetoric.*"

Convention and rhetoric? So many people don't understand Haydn. His music is solidly constructed and full of seductive invention. His enormous output is full of novelties and surprises. I would even say that he is more surprising than Beethoven. With the latter one can sometimes guess what is coming. But not with Haydn. He eludes us, he has something new to say and he offers us another surprise.

Adolphe Boschot thinks that Mozart's music speaks most directly to the "angelic" aspirations of man.[1]

It is possible. I have read M. Boschot's study of Mozart with pleasure and admire it very much.

[1] Adolphe Boschot: *Mozart.* (Librairie Plon, Paris.)

Boschot adds: "For instance, we find Haydn very near him. He might be his brother, but a less poetical brother. Alas, with Haydn charm is only apparent from time to time, and fleetingly. As soon as it shows itself, it is superseded by the galant style and by developments which are too formal and too precise, that is to say unexpressive. Very often Haydn gives us the framework of which Mozart will reveal the content."

It is possible that M. Boschot has understood Mozart better than Haydn. But what about *The Creation* of Haydn? Can one find anything more "angelic" than Haydn's presentation of the marvellous apparition of the world to a child? Haydn has an inexhaustible imagination, and the solidity of his musical architecture—solidity which we also find in Mozart—does not prevent him from being poetical and expressive. I have said all along: the proper understanding of Haydn's music is only beginning now. With him (the "father" of the symphony) the same thing will happen as has happened with Mozart in the last fifty years or so. One of the revelations which will emerge from the present chaos will be the rediscovery of Haydn, and the well-deserved consecration of his greatness, which has been so little recognised for so long.

"Haydn has never attempted to renew the syntax and the vocabulary of his day."

Always this mania to discover if there has been innovation for the sake of innovation! How many works of art has Haydn given us by using the vocabulary and the syntax of his time? That is what matters. Bach, Handel and Mozart copied out, and even sometimes imitated, the works of the masters of their period or of a preceding one. They have not tried to be original for the sake of being original. They have been original through the strength of their genius.

It has been said that, between a phrase of Haydn's and one of Mozart's, it is very difficult to discover an essential difference in its conception and its composition.

It is true that if one hears a phrase of Haydn's after one of Mozart's, one can confuse them, but, in fact, the two Masters are very different.

". . . the delicate and restless sensitiveness of Mozart's outpouring is totally different from the peaceful certainty and serene optimism of Haydn."[1]

True. It seems to me that we could describe Bach as being pre-Romantic rather than Haydn. Nevertheless there are moments when Haydn dodges in every direction and so surmounts the barriers of all

[1] Emile Vuillermoz: *Histoire de la Musique.* (Librairie Arthème Fayard, Paris.)

classification. As I told you just now, Haydn has a fantastic power of invention, and that is what makes his music a constant surprise. I insist: the real hour of Haydn has not yet arrived. We must remember that of his enormous production, only thirty per cent had been published some thirty years ago and, even then, only about a fifth of it was played.

Some people say that both Mozart and Haydn share the "rare privilege" of pleasing both the highbrow as well as the lowbrow.

The lowbrow will also like Bach, Schubert and so many others, if these Masters are performed as they should be. Do remember what I told you about what the workmen and clerks who formed the audiences of the *Associacio Obrera de Concerts* liked best!

Thanks to gramophone records the works of Haydn are becoming better known and, as you said, numerous music-lovers can hardly get over their astonishment at finding such treasures which were hidden until now.

I am very glad to hear it. It marks the beginning of a fair reparation. In music we have not finished "discovering" the great masters of the past!

Can you think of any decisive factors which contributed to this "revival" of Mozart and to the changes in approaching and performing his works?

In a way we can say that Vienna has followed up the Mozart tradition, and we might think that this "return" is due to the Austrian capital. But I do not think that is the case. (I have the impression that this movement took place in many countries, not to say in all countries.) It seems to me that if this "revival" had had its origin only in Vienna, it would have been more difficult for it to spread all over the place as we can see it has done. In my opinion, the real cause is to be found in the transformations which have taken place in music since the beginning of our century. In that period we first had the so-called "impressionist" school, followed by a general sinking into chaotic music. It follows that with the intuition of artists and listeners a natural reaction towards great music has led them to appreciate the "light" of Mozart.

Adolphe Boschot reckons that the "Wagnerian-fever", much more than Wagner himself, was an obstacle to the real understanding of Mozart.

It does not seem to me that Wagner interfered with the understanding of Mozart, because we find Wagner, in spite of all that has been said, easy to explain and to understand. It may have happened that, with the appearance of a figure as important as that of Wagner, some great names were provisionally put on one side, but that is not the case with Mozart, since he was not very well known or appreciated as he deserved *before* the infatuation with Wagner.

Around the beginning of our century we find the "rediscovery" of Mozart, which has only been intensified through the propagation of chaotic music, and the obvious necessity which follows to return to real beauty and greatness in music.

You have lived through the years when Mozart was neglected?

Of course I have! I can remember when one of his symphonies was used to fill up an empty space in a programme where the main dishes were Beethoven, Wagner, etc. He was thought of as a trinket, charming, delicious, yes—but a trinket all the same. Yet there were some real artists, like Saint-Saëns, I remember quite well, who were ready to grant him the great position he occupies now.

"It is not easy to define Mozart's genius. He escapes all definition."

Every genius escapes all definition. How can one define sublimity—or even the charm of a flower?

Someone wrote that Mozart remained graceful even when he painted something frightful.

The "grace" and "charm" of Mozart have become commonplaces. There are many mansions in the house of the master who also knows how to picture violence: how could a lyrical composer ignore them, when he has to characterise wicked personalities in music? And if the composer gives us an artistic and masterly reading of this character, what reproach can we bring against him?

Beethoven said about Don Giovanni *that a sacred art should not lower itself by dealing with scandalous material.*

As Beethoven grew older, his aspiration towards purity and fraternity became stronger. The theme of *Don Giovanni* must have displeased this noble moralist, but, I should say that in *Don Giovanni* only the Da Ponte libretto can be called scandalous.

Could one apply this adjective to the music?

In his letters and notes one can detect an intellectual strength. In Mozart's letters we often see traces of childishness.

This childishness must not disturb us. In Mozart there must have existed a continuous joy of musical creation. I have in mind my great friend, Granados, whose language was also free and without malice. The puerile expressions and remarks—even when they are voiced in crude forms, show in these people a kind of childish spirit, always at the mercy of the creative instinct. Try to imagine the topics of conversation and the jokes of Schubert when he met his friends in a

Viennese café. It is the spirit of relaxation, all superficial and without importance. It may be that when Mozart wrote some farcical things in his letters, or when Schubert burst into laughter with a glass of beer in his hand, that wonderful creations were elaborating in their subconscious minds, resulting in some of the most poetical works they have left for us.

There are no rough drafts of Mozart's works. The facility . . .

It is as I told you before, and I don't think we need elaborate. When Mozart took his pen in his hand, the work was already conceived in his mind. There are some great artists who create even when they are asleep.

"Within a special domain of musical expression, Mozart was certainly an innovator and a conqueror. In those days when the different sound of instruments did not come so much into consideration with the composers, Mozart showed himself very sensitive to the material of the orchestra at his disposal. His curiosity in this respect constituted a sort of anomaly. His predecessors and his contemporaries used an instrument in relation to its range and texture, but did not take much notice of its own quality of sound." (E. Vuillermoz.)

An innovator? This is not such a simple question. In Bach we already notice a preoccupation with the different sounds of different instruments. I would certainly say that Mozart was a genius who continued such innovation.

But is it not the privilege of Mozart, amongst all the lyrical composers, to have known how to make the most diverse personalities talk musically with the same ease and perfection?

I agree, and I think his lyrical genius deserves all possible praise.

Before Mozart, nobody, except Bach, had succeeded in mixing so perfectly "expression and beauty", says Boschot. "His six string quartets, dedicated to Haydn, divide the history of music into two sections."[1]

Even if this is not completely right, I accept the remarks, and what else?

"Mozart," says Boschot, "is accused of having a style of writing too much in one key. So much monotony; tonic, dominant, sub dominant, 1, 5, 4 . . . ! Instead of this so-called monotony, there is such a neat plan of keys in his compositions, such evidence and tranquil certitude, this is precisely what brings surprises and the power of all expressive effects. One accidental, one modulation, becomes exciting, just because of this limpidity and this tonal fixity."

[1] All the quotations from Adolphe Boschot are extracts from his book *Mozart*.

This opinion on the value of an "accidental" or a "modulation" is good, but the accusation of being too much in the same key falls to the ground by its own weight. In the art of modulation Mozart is a past master. His music is so varied and so far from a shadow of monotony. In his compositions we find a constant stream of varied rhythms, different character, nuances, modulations, everything applied in the most perfect and natural way. When the "tonal limpidity" appears it is always required by the musical sense of the composition.

Beethoven said: "The best work of Mozart remains The Magic Flute. Don Giovanni *has still the Italian touch."*

Some of *The Magic Flute* themes could also be of Italian origin. Just as Bach uses the Italian recitative in his *Passions*.

The Italian influence is also evident in Mozart. Is it possible that from the great works of Italian origin derives the rule that expression is to be found only in melody, so that "singing" is the essential element of music?

I agree with this last appreciation, but not with the assertion that "singing can only be found in the Italian School".

Don't we find reminiscences of bel canto *amongst the composers before Mozart?*

Do these reminiscences come straight from the Italians or are they a natural expression of melody which might equally come from other sources? In other words, were the Italians the first to fix the rules of melody?

Edwin Fischer[1] writes: "When the devil comes out in Beethoven, when we find a whole scene characterised by a few notes, we should not say: This is truly Beethoven, but: This is truly Mozart, since it is in Mozart's works that the great dramatic moments are first to be found in the most striking manner."

Possibly there are some instances when we could make such comparisons, but the works of Mozart and those of Beethoven belong to two very different worlds.

Wouldn't you transcribe some Mozart work for the 'cello and record it so that we may have some of his music played by you?

I never had the idea of doing such a transcription. (There is already a transcription for 'cello of a bassoon concerto.) I have often thought that Mozart, who wrote for so many instruments, must have written a 'cello concerto. But nowhere is there any mention of it. Since Haydn and Boccherini have given us works of such importance from

[1] All quotations from Edwin Fischer are extracted from his book, *Considérations sur la Musique*.

the technical point of view, it is difficult to understand why Mozart did not write a concerto for the 'cello. Sometimes I put the question to myself: did Mozart think that in his day 'cello technique was not sufficiently developed? But on the other hand, I imagine that Boccherini (who was before Mozart) must have been a great 'cellist, in view of the masterly technique revealed in his works.

Beethoven did not write a 'cello concerto, but he wrote a triple concerto in which the 'cello part is the most important. However, it proves that the 'cello was not played well enough in his day for Beethoven to use it as a solo instrument. With Brahms, who wrote the *Double Concerto*, the same thing must have happened—and yet when he heard the Dvořák concerto he said that if he had known one could produce such effects on a 'cello, he also would have written a concerto for it. All this tends to show that the development of the 'cello as a solo instrument is fairly recent. Bach is an exception, in that he foresaw, two hundred years ago, the future development of the instrument.

Some musician has written about Mozart: "His art took him to the highest spheres of spiritual maturity to which any human being could attain. That is why he is so difficult to perform if the simplicity of his style is to be preserved."

We should perform Mozart—as any other great composer—in the way we feel about his music, and we must do it in all earnestness and without prejudice. Possibly we may do the wrong thing; but it is better to be carried away by our feeling, than to get tied up with theories which would prevent us from experiencing it.

"A unanimous admiration has never been granted to Rameau, Bach, Mozart, Schubert, Wagner, Debussy and many other composers who have endowed music with discoveries more fertile and more original or positive than Beethoven has; however, this unanimity has sprung to life quite effortlessly round his name. For some years now, important musicians have shown signs of surprise at this anomaly, and hope that posterity will value with more precision and justice the contribution of a great musician whose character has been unwittingly misrepresented in literature. It is striking to realise that, in fact, Beethoven owes his dictatorship more to poets and novelists than to musicians." (Emile Vuillermoz.)[1]

Why use this word "dictatorship"? The immense radiance of Beethoven may have momentarily outshone the glory of other

[1] All quotations from Vuillermoz are from his book, *Histoire de la Musique*.

masters. This sort of thing has always happened. But time has always given to everyone the glory he deserves. As for the musicians' attitude towards Beethoven, what should we say about Schubert, who is so close to him? And of the devotion of Schumann and Liszt? And the "unswerving" veneration of Wagner? I don't understand why such opinions should be reproduced. In any case, the greatness of Beethoven does not lie in the amount of discoveries he made in music but in the significance and transcendency of his message. In my opinion, anything that has been said—truly or falsely—about him will not diminish the radiance of the light such a mind has brought us, and it will always be looked upon as one of the most glorious gifts humanity has received.

"*. . . The abyss that separates the commonplace passages which abound in the nine symphonies from the sublime thoughts that we find everywhere in the sonatas and the string quartets.*" (Emile Vuillermoz.)

All geniuses, in the course of their lives, have been through a process of development which is influenced by their personal experience. But in all genius, the germ is the thing to observe: and with Beethoven, perhaps more than with other great composers, this germ appears already in the first *Opus*. That is the most important fact to notice, as against analysing the process, which inevitably bears the marks of all stages every composer must go through.

It has been said that in the first Trios and Sonatas, the real Beethoven is already there.

Yes, the early Opuses already carry the germ of the *Ninth Symphony* and of the *Missa Solemnis*.

Opus I is the delicious Trio in E♭ major *which you played with Istomin and Fuchs this year* (1953) *in the Abbey of St. Michel de Cuxa?*

Yes, but Beethoven had written it when he was twenty-five. One can imagine the attempts and the gropings which must have preceded it, until he reached the mastery we already witness in this work.

Do you accept the famous division of Beethoven's works into "three manners"?

Yes, as long as we only wish to classify the period of some of his works, but not in order to draw irrelevant conclusions.

Would you say that the compositions of the third period are deeper and "musically superior" to the others?

Deeper, yes. The Beethoven of the later years seems to hover in a mysterious and sublime sphere. In any case, I would not dare to say that, purely as "works of art", the later works are superior to the early ones, not even to the earliest ones. One cannot fail to see that the *Opus I* is a masterpiece in the fullest meaning of the word.

Debussy criticised Beethoven for "describing" instead of "suggesting" or "insinuating", which, according to him, is the real rôle of music as an art.

One can "describe" or "suggest". What really matters is the result, not the method.

In one of the early string quartets of Beethoven we find the title Malinconia. Do you think that Beethoven might have been the first to describe in music this melancholy which became a sort of disease amongst artists affected by le mal du siècle?

As I pointed out to you before, we find that Bach has "described" all manner of feelings, including melancholy. And I think one could say the same thing about Mozart.

Don't you think we ought to establish the difference between sadness and melancholy in order to keep the latter for the romantics, who made it their own and "exhibited" it—with varying degrees of sincerity, I feel bound to say.

Maybe. Although sadness and melancholy are different, it would sometimes be very difficult to draw a line showing exactly where the two are separated. Especially with music, where one cannot put one's finger on any intellectual conception and where emotional reactions, with performers or listeners, differ endlessly.

All depends on our idea of romanticism. I see it first in Bach, if one thinks of romanticism as a strong expression of feeling. In Bach, all is expression, often bursting, overflowing.

And what about the romantic attitude to nature, not as scenery outside the artist, but as an element in which he is absorbed? Beethoven, who wrote "Nobody has loved nature as I have", may have been the beginner of this movement.

It also depends how we consider nature as an inspiration in music. Who can say precisely how certain Italian composers of the XVIIth century reacted to nature, or Bach, or Handel, and so many others? In music, it is more difficult than in literature to establish neat divisions between one tendency and another, for instance between classicism and romanticism. Of course the pathos of Beethoven emphasises certain aspects, but to go further and assert that these aspects have their musical origin in him is a big step which I am not ready to take.

Do you think that the quality of pathos in Beethoven comes from the "concentration of his soul"?

But with Mozart we also find, in spite of certain appearances, a "concentrated soul".

Arthur Honegger says: "What always puzzles the masses is that the great composer was deaf. One cannot deny that a great deal of the admiration devoted to Beethoven is due to his infirmity. To tell the truth, once we forget the tragic side of this situation, the fact remains that, as a creator, he could never hear the performance of his work, which must have raised many technical difficulties for him. However, I am tempted to say that this affliction forced him to 'wall' himself in, and helped him to concentrate with all his genius, and, in so doing to avoid the 'insipidity' and 'banalities' of those days." [1]

This deafness naturally affected Beethoven's character. However, I would say that the great strength of his mind already protected him from the usual banalities of life, which surrounded him just as they do each one of us.

How do you see Beethoven as a man?

Just as he appears in the documents we have about him, the testimony of his contemporaries and the descriptions of his biographers. I have not got a personal picture of him in my mind. Although I can say that I have seen Beethoven and have spoken to him . . . in a dream of course!

It was the Beethoven of the last period, a man stricken by a great sorrow, but a very serene sorrow.

When writers, not musicians, speak of Beethoven . . .

It all depends how they set about it. For instance, I very much like the biography by Edouard Herriot. On the other hand, without wishing to depreciate the value and the interest of Romain Rolland's writing, I fear that when he sometimes gets mixed up with very technical questions, he generally shows that he is not qualified for it.

It has been said that in Fidelio *the composer appears more like a poet than a lyrical author for the stage.*

Yes, everyone seems to think that Beethoven did not feel at ease with the stage. It may be true. Everyone to his own opinion. But can anyone deny the unforgettable impression *Fidelio* makes on the listener?

Wagner recounts in Mein Leben *that after the final rehearsal of the Ninth Symphony in Dresden in 1849, Bakunin said to him "that if all music were to be destroyed in the coming universal conflagration, we ought at the risk of our lives to unite to preserve this symphony".*

[1] Arthur Honegger: *Je suis compositeur.* (Editions du Conquistador, Paris.)

It does indeed deserve to survive eternally, but perhaps Bakunin was mainly thinking of the *Hymn of Brotherhood*, in the last movement.

Seid umschlungen, Millionen!—and then, when we hear this call in our own times—and think of the hydrogen bomb . . . ! In spite of all gruesome predictions and dangers we must not lose our faith. I have always believed the day would come when the *Ode to Joy* would be sung by all the peoples of the earth. I inscribed this thought in the Book of the League of Nations at Geneva.

Vincent d'Indy has said that Beethoven's Sonatas are dominated by the search for an idea. On the other hand, Furtwängler, having asserted that Beethoven is neither a poet, nor a moralist, nor a philosopher, but only a musician, goes on to say: "It appears that Beethoven, more than any other musician, tends to answer the question put by his ideas in the most purely musical form possible. . . . He does not go half-way to meet the poet. And that is why he is not lyrical like Schubert, or a dramatic musician like Wagner. If he appears to be less willing to reconcile words and music, it is not because he is less of a musician, but because he is more so, more exclusively a musician." [1]

First of all, I think that nobody can be "more exclusively a musician" than Schubert is. That Beethoven has answered his ideas by elaborating purely musical forms seems to be quite evident. But I must say that I don't see very clearly what Furtwängler means with all this—perhaps his words are a bit exaggerated. Otherwise, how could we explain the character of supreme exaltation we find in the *Hymn of Brotherhood* in the *Ninth Symphony* so intimately adapted to the central idea of Schiller's text? I only give this as an example.

Curiously enough Furtwängler says about the finale of the Ninth Symphony: *"This theme—a theme par excellence, a theme of the highest type, the discovery of a great musician if ever there was one, this theme could not be in anyway conceived in order to comment or expound one particular text. Just the opposite: it looks as if it were the poem which expounds the theme."*

This theme becomes the musical climax (exclusively musical) of this symphony, but I cannot agree with anyone who says that it was not inspired by the *Ode to Joy*. When I hear it, I get an impression which is almost religious, a sort of feeling of fraternity, and it penetrates me like a glorious musical rendering of the poetical humanitarianism of Schiller.

[1] All the quotations from Furtwängler are extracted from his book, *Entretiens sur la Musique*.

"With Beethoven great discoveries, especially the invention of themes and of details, are numerous. But that is not what his genius is made of, and those who see traces of hard work almost everywhere are not far from the truth. But his intuition goes much deeper, and that, in his best works, allows him to find a grouping of themes, made to complement each other by some inevitable law." (Wilhelm Furtwängler.)

Supposing Beethoven had one quality only; for instance, that of inventing great themes, but was lacking in the one Furtwängler talks about, he would not be the great composer he is. However, we find him complete because he possesses these two qualities amongst many others. As for the themes, it is true that we can find in his note-books all the transformations they underwent, which show the difficulties he encountered before these themes finally took shape. If we take the slow movement of the *Eroica Symphony*, we shall see how many phases it went through before its completion. Nothing of the kind happened with Mozart or Schubert, whose themes emerged entire and complete in themselves, at least, so it seems to me.

Beethoven, I feel sure, had to fight with his material, and his works did not reach perfection until they had undergone many transformations. These transformations sometimes consisted of changing one note only, as we see in the initial theme of the *Ninth Symphony* (which is in my possession) where the previously modified note corresponds with a similar chord, and where this transformation simply gives a different rhythmical aspect to the final version.

"In Bach we find that the whole piece with all its developments exists implicitly in the theme. In fact, Bach never wanders away from the material of his principal theme, even in a fugue where there are counter subjects, the style remains essentially monothematic. But in Beethoven, though the need for development in any theme is just as urgent, the way to it is not rigorously planned, as it is with Bach. The reason is that, with Beethoven, the development does not rest exclusively on the first theme. He has many, and through their contrast and interpenetration, the development proceeds on different lines." (Furtwängler.)

Yes! That is what we find in Bach and in Beethoven. The latter has felt the necessity of mixing up different themes. It can be compared to a tree-trunk from which start so many ramifications. And sometimes we find Beethoven producing all of a sudden a completely unexpected theme. One is tempted to ask "Where does it come from?" With Bach we find that, the requirements of musical expression being different, he does not proceed on the same lines. As we said before, Bach goes right down to the bottom of the initial theme, and exploits it deeply. Is the Beethoven form an innovation? Of course it is, but he achieves it simply by saying what he has to say without veil or artifice.

Hans von Bülow has said "The Well-Tempered Clavier is the Old Testament, Beethoven's Sonatas the New". Can we still say that?

Yes, but I would place *The Well-Tempered Clavier* in both the Old and the New Testaments. As I have told you before, I think that it is the foundation of all music.

André Coeuroy[1] says: "Individualism is the most striking attribute of Romanticism. The sort of individualism which leads some musicians to show not only their personality in their works, but even the vicissitudes of their existence. We find nothing in Bach, Mozart, or even in Beethoven, which might suggest that." I don't suppose you will agree with this?

It is not the whole question. What I don't see is how there could be such a cleavage between the works of a musician and the "vicissitudes of his existence". It is inevitable that one should affect the other at every stage. On the occasion of the departure of one of his great friends, Bach wrote a piece full of the sorrow of parting. We could find so many examples like this and in any case, what do we know of the feelings of the ideas and dreams which have inspired the compositions of these masters?

Talking of Schubert, someone has said that he had no purpose or doctrine. He is just "full of music".

Well, without being pedantic, he could translate his feelings into music in a way which proved what a great composer he was.

Some say that his life did not tally with his genius, others, that it was a great example of modesty!

Yes, his life is an example of simplicity and modesty. In Schubert we find a great artist, unassuming and unaffected. In fact, a rare example amongst artists of all periods!

"He writes a short work with perfection; the lieder, the waltz, the impromptu, the moment musical."

I agree, but what of the long works?

"In such cases Schubert does not follow the classical system of developing his themes. Romanticism comes into it in the sense that he will paint the same theme in different colours and change its harmony and its key. No other

---

[1] *La Musique des origines à nos jours.* (Librairie Larousse, Paris.)

composer of the Romantic school has been so prolific in the domain of harmonic change." (André Coeuroy.)[1] *This is an arguable opinion!*

Very arguable. And what do we say about Beethoven?

Is Schubert a symphonist? The Unfinished *very often played—the* C Major Symphony, *not so often. The others . . . ?*

We are beginning to understand the other symphonies. There was a time when people talked about the lengthiness of Schubert's works. It doesn't exist! One day in Vienna, at the house of Karl Wittenstein, I saw the old manuscript of Schubert's *Second Trio* for piano, viola and violoncello. On it I saw annotations and a cut made by Joachim—it just shows you how wrong great men can be! No cuts are required in Schubert. Joachim made the same mistake as Schumann, Gounod, Grieg and so many others in regard to some of Bach's works.

As for the string quintet with two violoncelli you have played . . .

So many times and always with the greatest admiration and the deepest emotion!

In Schubert do you feel that indefinable nostalgia of which he is supposed to have the secret?

If one had to enumerate all the things one can find in his music!

There is an inner sensitiveness which has nothing to do with the stage— although we have Rosamunde.

I prefer *Rosamunde* to hundreds of lyrical pieces written for the stage.

"In the piano works," says André Coeuroy, *"Schubert follows the sonata form which he does not try to change at all. But in the short pieces, with more freedom of form, he becomes more of a precursor and opens the way to the* Novelets *of Schumann, as well as to the* Songs Without Words *of Mendelssohn, the* Pèlerinages *of Liszt or the* Impromptus *of Chopin."*

There is some truth in this, although we must not forget that Beethoven was also a precursor in this form; in his *Bagatelles* he used a form which was best adapted to pure fantasy.

In lieders Schubert has not been equalled.

I agree! Not only do we admire the beauty of the melodies, but the accompaniments acquire an importance and an expressiveness which only a master could achieve.

"He does not try anything new in the construction of a work, but he uses the classical form to expound his own emotion." (André Coeuroy.)

[1] *Op. cit.*

Why should he invent anything new, if he found the usual form of the Sonata and the Symphony suitable to his own creation? He has given us in his mind certain things that are completely his own. When we hear a work of Schubert we never think that it resembles Beethoven or any other composer. It is "his own music" —entirely his own—and it can say things and move us as nothing else can.

You once performed the Mass in B♭ *with your orchestra and the* Orfeo Gracienc, *didn't you?*

Yes! It is a work which is very seldom done.

Like so many others of Schubert! Don't you think that posterity has been unjust to Schubert? Out of his immense production, only a small proportion appears on concert programmes.

Schubert is very much played in chamber music concerts. As for the Symphonies, they were neglected as were those of Mozart and Haydn—they were considered as minor works. But this state of affairs seems to be disappearing. But in any case, as time goes on, the more I find Schubert one of the purest poets of music.

"Schumann, who started to compose rather late, has remained a sort of artisan, exquisite and unique, but more at home in intimate music than in big works." (André Coeuroy.)

That may be . . . each artist is what he is.

"As soon as the piano intervenes in his symphonic music, the interest increases. Thus, the greatness of the Piano Concerto in A Minor." (André Coueroy.)

I don't agree with this remark; with the piano or without, it is the same great poet who speaks to us.

The Violin Concerto *which Schumann wrote at the request of Joachim, and which gave rise, a few years ago, to some stormy debates. . . .*

I don't know it, so I can't say anything.

Many biographers content themselves merely with noting the existence of the 'Cello Concerto.

It must be because they fail to see the interest and the value of this work. It is one of the finest works one can hear—from beginning to end the music is sublime.

"Schumann's themes are generally brief, rarely more than four bars, very often written in an ascending line which gives to the melody an interrogative character, very typical of Schumann's restlessness."

That is true!

Talking of Schumann, Furtwängler says "His flights faltered prematurely".

Many have spoken of his difficulty, even the impossibility for him in develop-
ing his themes. "The conciseness of his themes," says Coeuroy, "has brought
about the criticism of 'short inspiration'."

There is no question of "brief inspiration" with Schumann. I find
that in any of his compositions the inspiration ever weakens from beginning to end. Schumann is pre-eminently a person who acts under
the influence of some mystical inspiration, what the French call an
inspiré, and I mean it in its highest sense. The structural elements of his
works are those best fitted to his needs of expression, and it would be
out of place to speak of any incapacity for development. If his themes
are short it must be simply because this conciseness suited his inspiration
and not because Schumann could not or did not know how to develop
them.

René Dumesnil wrote: "Schumann's genius is one of the most varied that
has ever inspired a musician."

I absolutely agree!

"One day when Schumann tried to define his personality, he created for
himself a Symbolic second self, which seemed for him the only solution of a
psychological problem! Hence his reincarnation as the twin brothers and
enemies:—Eusebius and Florestan. Here was an indication of his great
perspicacity, which all his biographers have had to recognise.

"Schumann's dual personality consisted of:—an elegiac dreamer and
passionate apostle . . . all his life is dominated by this instinctive duality in
his artistic and philosophical tendencies. This inner instability, alas, ended
in the tragic paroxysm in which he lost his reason." (Vuillermoz.)

This opinion is interesting. In all great masters one can discover
not only a duality, but also a multiplicity of tendencies. If we wished to
go further in analysing Schumann's genius, we would find many other
elements and peculiarities to be investigated.

Talking of his lieders: "The melody itself is, as it were, supported by the
sense of poetry, to which Schumann responded eagerly, all the more, because
in his youth, he was surrounded by poetry, hence his sure and subtle know-
ledge of literature, which gives him an advantage on Schubert." (André
Coeuroy.)

What is true is that in his *lieders*, Schumann not only interpreted
the character of the text, but also took care of each word, which,
perhaps, Schubert did not do as much; with the latter, inspiration
generally worked in the atmosphere of the written text, in order to
transfer to the music the poetical idea, although we sometimes find
him following the magic of the words very closely. In any case it

would be idle to assert that Schumann is inferior or superior to Schubert.

What do you think of Schumann's opinion when he says, "Any modification in the works of the great composers, any omission or addition, should be completely barred as being detestable"?

It is the biggest affront that can be made to art.[1]

One can do a worse injury to art to allow a performance to be inexpressive and dead because of a so-called respect for some things as static as the printed notes and signs of music. Writing as we know it being a very incomplete means of expression, how could the composer indicate everything? Does Schumann (or any other composer) give all indications that are needed?

It just happens that a number of musicians say that instrumentation is Schumann's weak point, and there are conductors who take the liberty of modifying some details in the instrumentation of certain passages in some of his symphonic works. Personally, as I do not share this opinion, I have always respected the text of the original version when I conduct, but it is not for me to condemn those who sincerely think that their devotion to the music they perform imposes such minor alterations.

If we speak about Beethoven, should we condemn some corrections (as Wagner has himself made) in the instrumentation of the *Scherzo* of the *Ninth Symphony*? Cerainly not!

If we proceed from Schumann to his great friend Mendelssohn, why is it that his music has been so neglected for some time now?

It may be because he knows too much in comparison to the apprentices of our days.

The grace, the clarity and the distinction of Mendelssohn! Some people think he is the Murillo of music.

Yes, I have heard this comparison! But everyone can make comparisons. Personally, I prefer the musician to the painter!

I have read that the admiration of Mendelssohn for Schumann and Liszt was not entirely without reservations.

I do not know of his reservations about Schumann, but I have heard of those concerning Liszt. I wonder if they were not all more or less

---

[1] *As Casals asked in the chapter on Bach:* "Why did Schumann write piano accompaniments to the Six Suites for Solo Violin? These are completely foreign to Bach's music!" (*Translator's note.*)

dictated by questions of the various cliques then existing: Mendelssohn, Schumann and Brahms, and on the other hand, Wagner and Liszt.

Would you say that Mendelssohn is a romantic "without the excess or frenzy" of Romanticism?

Yes, a romantic who felt at ease within the mould of classicism and who was able to solve, with an elegance and imaginativeness peculiar to himself, the most difficult problems of form.

Did the style of Mendelssohn have repercussions on music in Germany and elsewhere?

Indeed it did. There was a time when every musician had to submit to the Mendelssohn fascination, so strong was the influence he had had. At that time all musicians—and I was one of them—had to understand Mendelssohn before appreciating Beethoven. He has certainly been neglected in recent years. But I feel sure he will come to his own again.

"Liszt was the first to insist on the complete independence of the fingers. When he played he did not use the wrist and the hand only, but also employed the articulations of the elbow and the shoulder, including the arms, which were thus set free; he crossed them over, leaping from bass to treble at a speed like that of a conjuring trick. Movements of the torso which, hitherto, had been kept rigid, were part of a technical scheme to distribute the flow of movement of the arms and fingers, even to the back of the pianist: his whole body expressed his emotion." (Emile Haraszti.)[1]

All great artists are innovators. Liszt's conception of the piano was to give it an orchestral character. He probably was not even conscious of making any discovery or of the movements of his body while he played. All he was aiming at was to treat the piano as if it were a powerful orchestra, and that was the cause of different movements and positions.

I have read that Liszt heard Paganini in Paris, and was so tremendously impressed that he spent a long time practising with the idea of making the piano do as much as Paganini did on the violin.

Yes, but before he went to Paris Liszt already had such personal ideas about the piano; his conception of the instrument had not come by learning or imitation; it was just his own. It is true that Paganini made a great impression on him, as he did on all those who heard him,

[1] *Liszt et la Musique Hongroise*, in *La musique des origines à nos jours*. (Librairie Larousse, Paris.)

and that happened because this great *virtuoso* used the resources of the violin as no one had before him.

Liszt must be the composer who has written the greatest number of transcriptions: apparently more than five hundred. Some people say they are not all equally good.

Some may be better than others, but they all show that they have been written by *the* master of the piano.

"*Of all his works, the twenty* Hungarian Rhapsodies *are the most vital examples of his Hungarian style. Perhaps it was under the influence of Chopin's Polonaises that he used the melodies of the dilettante composers of his period, popularised by the* tziganes." (Emile Haraszti.)

Of course Liszt knew the folklore of his country, but I do not consider him as a typical Hungarian. Although the *Rhapsodies* sound Hungarian, in their composition Liszt applies the same ideas as in his other piano works (always searching for orchestral effects). There is nothing especially Magyar in Liszt's writing as a whole.

Do you remember when you were in Hungary and asked Bartók and Kodály whether they thought that the Liszt of the Rhapsodies *had been their predecessor in the creation of a national music?*

I can't say I remember that. Whereas with Bartók and Kodály I feel that their music is impregnated by the savour of their soil, I don't find the same influence in Liszt; whether this happens on account of his universality, or of the circle he lived in, or his ideology, I can't say. He has shown in his *Rhapsodies* that he could assimilate the popular characteristics of his country, and it is strange to find a man, who when he wanted to could be entirely Hungarian, showing so little trace of it in his other works. On the other hand we find Chopin is Polish to the marrow of his bones. Liszt is the creator of the Symphonic Poem, although these works are not, really, programme music. However, one can say that Liszt started the idea of a programme in music; he discovered and developed a musical form based on first and second themes, episodes, etc. . . . from which emerged the Symphonic Poem.

I believe you admire Berlioz?

Yes, certainly. One is tempted now and then to use the adjective "fantastic" to describe his works, probably because we find in him an artist who has broken right away from accepted procedure. This gives a feverish, sometimes frenzied, quality to his music, which is nevertheless full of genius. *The Damnation of Faust* is a work I admire enormously.

On the question of Liszt and Wagner: "In Liszt we find that when he uses characteristic themes they play the same part as the leitmotiv *of Wagner.*

But who had the priority? We have not got sufficient data on this subject yet, but it seems obvious that the accidentals and unharmonics of Tristan *would never have been written without Liszt. . . ."*

In the correspondence between Liszt and Wagner, we can see how the man who wrote *Tristan* acknowledges his debt of gratitude to his friend and benefactor. The Symphonic Poems of Liszt are, in a way, *Wagner avant la lettre . . ."even if one admits that Liszt's chromaticism, when it started, had a flavour of Chopin (although Liszt went much further than Chopin in his harmonic progressions)."*

I never found any trace of Chopin in Wagner. It is Liszt and not Chopin who influenced Wagner's chromaticism.

". . . Liszt was a forerunner in the field of revolutionary harmony. In Berlin, people were violently against these harmonies, which they described as 'dissonance' and 'musical terrorism'."

In Liszt, as in Wagner, there is no "musical terrorism". All can be explained, and all is linked together. "Terrorism" came later. . . .

"It was the piano which helped Liszt to develop his harmonic richness, which in its chromatic flights sometimes produces the most daring effects. Chopin and Schumann also owe the profusion of their harmonies to the piano." (Emile Haraszti.)

Daring effects? Yes, but not in any way strange: even easy to understand. In the same way Schumann's harmonic structure is perfectly easy to understand: he, himself, invented his own chomaticism. Chromaticism and the profusion of modulations can already be found in Schubert. I don't think that it was the piano that was responsible for the developments of chromaticism in these composers, but only the music they wanted to write.

I have read that in 1860 Brahms, Joachim and others published a manifesto against the "music of the future" which was aimed at Wagner as much as at Liszt.

The divergences which existed between these two groups were very regrettable. Fortunately, when great masters are involved, time always seems to obliterate such details while consolidating their prestige. Future generations will remember Wagner, Liszt and Brahms and forget the rivalries and the polemics of that time.

You always speak with great admiration of Liszt's generosity and of the disinterested protection he extended to so many of his friends. It has been said that Weimar marked a date in the history of music.

Not only Weimar: it is the radiance of his musical achievement and of his fabulous personality which will place Liszt very high in the history of music. The universality and the generosity of his genius caused him to be interested in all creations and musical manifestations of his period. (There is an exception which must be recorded: Liszt, who was an enthusiast of Wagner, did not recognise the high value of Brahms' music.)

As he got older he still had a great desire to help young composers. It was through him that Saint-Saëns' Samson and Delilah was produced at Weimar.

I well remember the veneration Saint-Saëns had for Liszt. And, I presume, a great deal of gratitude.

I remember your telling me one day that you had been able to trace all the contemporaries of Liszt you have known, the extraordinary and lively persistence of the great impression which he made on them.

Yes, indeed. I could verify this with all the former pupils of Liszt who have been my friends—all great pianists. Busoni, Siloti, d'Albert, Sauer, etc. For example, Siloti, who was a perfectly normal person, would sometimes say to me in a most natural way: "I am very happy today. During the night Liszt told me this and that," and his wife shared his enthusiasm. I said: "Bravo!" What else could I have said? It would have been cruel to start arguing with him on the subject.

Alexander Borodin, after a stay in Weimar, wrote: "Liszt never imposes his method on his pupils, neither does he make detailed observations regarding the position of the hands or the touch; he allows the greatest liberty as to the means used to obtain the desired result."

Then what did he do? How did he teach?

Did Siloti not tell you?

No, it may seem incredible, but he never spoke of the ways in which Liszt taught. I could see that it was a subject he did not want to discuss.

What about the other pupils of Liszt whom you have known, Busoni, Sauer and others?

They did not speak to me about it either. Yet all my conversations with Siloti invariably ended by talking of Liszt. My friend gave the impression that it was the Master himself who was playing. (As a matter of fact he had the same figure, the same face, the same hands and the same wart on the cheek—a perfect double in fact.) Busoni's way of playing was different. Of course with pupils of this kind, one can understand why it was not necessary for the master of the piano to waste his energy in teaching technique only. Nevertheless I should

Piano and pipe

Casals with a
young Chinese
pupil

Casals, Prades, 1949

very much like to know of what exactly his lessons consisted. It was not only his pupils, everybody was subjugated by his personality. Siloti told me that at a gathering with Kings and Princes, it was Liszt who was the real king.

What about the concert that Anton Rubinstein . . .

. . . gave one day near Weimar? Yes, Siloti told me about it. Liszt had advised his pupils to go and hear the celebrated pianist, and report to him afterwards. Next day they all came to see Liszt and told him with enthusiasm how they had enjoyed the concert. At that time Liszt had given up playing in public, but having listened attentively to his pupils' descriptions of the concert, he got up, went to his upright piano, and without saying anything performed the whole programme of Rubinstein! "How wonderful it was . . . even more than wonderful," Siloti said to me. . . .

Enesco said that "people have not yet forgiven Liszt for being a great pianist and a great composer at the same time".[1] I wonder what causes this suspicion of "virtuoso's music" amongst music-lovers?

Unfortunately it certainly exists. (Enesco himself, and many others, have been victims of this attitude.) It seems to me that the opposite would be more logical, since the high value of a performer should awake more interest in his compositions. What can we do about it? I have thought of Liszt as a great *virtuoso* and I have always regarded his music as being the work of a great master.

Liszt wrote about Chopin: "It is no use writing tempo rubato, *it does not teach anything to those who know nothing." Later on, Chopin ceased to add this indication to his music, as he realised that, given enough intelligence, the player would see the need for "irregularity" himself.[2]*

But of course! Only today, when I was playing one of Bach's *Partitas* on the piano, I thought to myself, as I always do: how is it that "purists" don't realise that following written notes *à la lettre* is a mistaken course, quite contrary to the music itself? The written note is like a strait-jacket, whereas music, like life itself, is constant movement, continuous spontaneity, free from any restriction. How can great artists confine themselves to the rigidity of written signs? Let us imagine the human language shown in values, and that linguistic "purists" compelled themselves to follow the rigidity of these values. What would be the result?

[1] All quotations from Georges Enesco are from his *Entretiens radiophoniques avec Bernard Gavoty*.
[2] Franz Liszt: *Sur Chopin*.

Cortot writes[1] that in Chopin's correspondence one finds "few suggestions which, for many people, would have put the technical performance on a plane of secondary importance, the imagination rather than the fingers at the service of the inner significance of sonority".

But Chopin was particularly careful with the indications of dynamics. In that he was very different from Granados, who used to say that anyone playing his works only had to feel and decide the tempo for himself. This way of writing put me in an awkward position in New York before the first performance of *Goyescas*. The conductor and the American musicians kept on asking me exactly how this and that should be played. And when I translated their questions to Granados he said, "But tell them to play as it seems right to them!"

What do you think of Chopin's works for the 'cello?

There is a *Sonata* and a *Polonaise*. They are quite well written for the 'cello. Chopin is not a composer who believes in writing easy instrumental parts for performers, an attitude I approve of, since it is the best way to improve instrumental technique.

And what of the famous Nocturne *you played when you were young?*

Half a century ago I used to play this transcription as an encore. Everywhere I was asked to play it, and as soon as I had played the last work on my programme the audience would shout "the Chopin *Nocturne!*" I gave in against my will. I soon decided not to play it any more, in order to avoid becoming known as the musician of the Chopin *Nocturne.* . . .

An old gramophone record of this transcription has just reached me—and I must say, that as I listen to it, I cannot repress a certain emotion when confronted by this nostalgic reminder of my long distant youth.

Heinrich Heine said about Chopin: "Poland gave him his chivalrous character and his 'historical' melancholy, France, his graceful elegance, Germany his dreamy profundity. . . . But now we don't think of him as Polish, French or German, he has a higher origin: he comes from the country of Mozart, Raphael and Goethe. His real home is in the birthplace of poetry.

I don't agree. I find his music essentially Polish; if you select any of his subjects and look for the origin of his inspiration, you'll find it can only come from his native land. I just cannot see what there is in Chopin that could be French or German.

.   .   .

[1] Alfred Cortot: *Aspects de Chopin.* (Editions Albin Michel, Paris.)

When you were studying in Barcelona, did you hear any opera of Wagner?

I cannot remember exactly, but I don't think I did until later on.

There were some musicians and music-lovers at that time who said that Wagner "killed" melody and also that he gave the wind instruments an importance out of all proportion.

Right from the beginning I thought that Wagner's music was great and that he used very natural means of expression which were easy to understand.

Were you impressed by all his symbolism, his philosophy, and other considerations that were outside the realm of music?

No. I was not interested in those: it was the music which impressed me straight away.

Have you been to Bayreuth?

Yes, I think about 1907.

What is your recollection of it?

I thought the actors were not very good and not up to their task.

Did you meet Cosima in Bayreuth?

No, but later on I met her daughter, the Countess of Gravina.

The name of Hans Richter is inseparable from the Wagner story. When you used to talk to him in Manchester, did you find that he had remained faithful to the memory of his Master, in spite of all he had to go through with him?

Yes, years did not seem to have obliterated any of it.

Your friend, Ysaye, having heard Tristan for the first time, speaks of an "annihilation in rapture". When he got home, having taken his shoes off he threw them on the fire, at the thought that in this life one had to give up ecstasy in order to attend to things as dull as unlacing one's shoes.

I did not throw my shoes in the fire after I heard *Tristan*, but I remember how deeply moved I was, I am sure quite as much as my dear friend Ysaye. There must have been very few musicians of my generation who did not fall under the spell of *Tristan*.

In France, it was Lamoureux who first produced Wagner on the stage (in Paris) in spite of all the protests expressed in an unfortunate pamphlet called "Une Capitulation".

Lamoureux's admiration for Wagner made him put aside all other considerations. He firmly believed that, in spite of a very justifiable resentment, his countrymen should not be deprived of hearing the work of a musical genius. When in 1899 *Tristan* was given in Paris for the first time there was no fear of any scandal, for Wagner's cause had already been won in France. But when Lamoureux first produced *Lohengrin* a real battle took place in the theatre, during which shots were fired.

Tell me: I imagine you must have had a great admiration for Hans von Bülow.

Of course I had. And that reminds me of a very interesting conversation I had at a party in Venice with the Countess of Gravina (who, as you know, went with her mother when she left her first husband.) I said to the Countess that I very much wanted to possess an autographed manuscript of her father's music. She said, "What a pity, I have nothing to give you: I had a leaf from the sketch of the *Twilight of the Gods* but I gave it away to someone quite recently. (Wagner in those days was already looked upon as a semi-God and the Countess obviously thought I was referring to her mother's second husband.) "Forgive me, Madam," I said, stressing my answer, "it is an autograph of *your father* I wanted to have." She was most surprised and said, "No one has ever asked me for such a thing."

Some critic has written that some eighty years after Wagner's death "the only works he is remembered by are a few grand operas, which were those he least cared for".

As far as I am concerned, what interests me in any opera is the music, and that of Wagner is always the music of a great master. (The day before yesterday I was listening to the second act of *Lohengrin* on the wireless. How beautiful it is, and how pale some of our contemporary pieces sound, as compared to it.) The "drama" in the libretto of an opera is to me almost without importance, just as are the symbolical and philosophical allusions it tries to convey.

With a certain amount of irony Schönberg once said, talking of post-Wagnerian operas: "A symphony for full orchestra with accompanying voice." According to Schönberg, Wagner managed to keep some dramatic structure together in spite of the symphonic tendency he followed, but he says that this structure tended to disappear in Wagner's successors.

I must own that I have not followed the development of Opera since Wagner. (It would have been a very different thing if, for instance, it had been a question of Mozart's operas.) Yet I must say I have been very interested in Richard Strauss' operas. I think they are the most important ones of our period.

Darius Milhaud thinks that the works of Wagner were the prelude to the Hitlerian tragedy.

Up to a point, it is possible. But if we investigate further perhaps we ought to talk of Brahms and even of Mozart who, after all, was the creator of German opera. Did I ever tell you what happened to Brahms when he was in Copenhagen?

No.

Brahms went there to conduct some of his own works, and he was taken to see the Thorwalsden Museum, which is an object of national pride for the Danes. Do you know what Brahms remarked? "Why are these sculptures here? They ought to be in Berlin." This caused such indignation that Brahms had to go away without conducting the advertised concerts. It is often natural to find national feeling in some work of art; the danger is when this feeling is used to exalt the greed for domination.

Do you remember your visit to Tribschen with Emil Ludwig in 1945?

Yes, I remember it very well. My friend, who had no sympathy at all for Wagner, said to me, pointing to a copy of the magnificent portrait of Wagner by Renoir (the original of which belongs to Cortot), "Look at him, the old comedian."

Nietzsche also, after his great quarrel with Wagner, said he was very much of a comedian.

Yes, but before the rupture, Nietzsche had been under the spell of his friend and he had spoken in the highest terms of the reforms in lyric drama started by Wagner.

When you were at Tribschen you sat at Wagner's piano to play the Prelude of Tristan.

Yes, and I was very surprised to find Wagner's piano completely out of tune. . . .

The way Ludwig described this visit seems to show that you shared his antipathy for Wagner as a man.

No. I think one should show some tolerance; the vanity and the terrible bad temper of Wagner must have caused some very disagreeable scenes, but, in order to judge him, one should first remember the atmosphere in which artists of that period lived. In any case, the works which survive a great artist are what matter.

It has been said that great musicians like Bruckner and Mahler have been eclipsed by the amazing radiance of Wagner.

It is true.

Apparently nowadays, through long-playing records which have been made, their works are getting much more known outside Germany.

I am glad to hear it. As I told you before, I do believe that great works of art come to be recognised in time. In the case of Bruckner, it was even touching to see his modesty. Do you know that he used to hide himself in order to see Wagner in the distance as he came out of the theatre? From what one of his pupils told me, Bruckner's nature was so angelic that he went into a trance while he played the organ.

You once told me that your first contact with Brahms' music had been an overwhelming experience.

Yes, it is very true. I was a child then and no one had told me anything about him. I did not have to think twice before I realised I was hearing the music of an exceptional master.

"*He forces his romantic extravagances into a mould of strict classicism. He only seems to be at ease with the most rigorous counterpoint.*" (René Dumesnil.)[1]

If, in order to express what he had in him, he chose a "strict classicism" and with it wrote great music, there is nothing to criticise. Brahms had enough genius and craftsmanship to choose the means which best suited his musical conceptions. Why not accept a composer's ways of saying what he has to say, as long as they lead to great artistic achievements?

About Brahms' music, Darius Milhaud said, not very long ago, "Bogus greatness, long drawn out."

No, Milhaud is wrong. Brahms is a great composer amongst the great ones.

"*Whoever likes or dislikes Brahms cannot avoid his great personality, which is precisely the reason why he is accepted or rejected; his music calls at once for adherence or refusal. There is no middle way.*" (René Dumesnil.)

If one is sensitive and not perverse, one can only reject what is bad, ugly or stupid. Are there any trustworthy or truthful people who could apply these adjectives to Brahms' music? Therefore, those people Mr. Dumesnil has in mind in his article have not got the right to intervene in the cause of the composer. Brahms' position in France should be made clear once and for all. Mr. Dumesnil could do that very well. He knows that the French public would like to hear Brahms, but that a number of musicians and critics always run him down and try to stop further performances out of pure prejudice. The proof of this prejudice of the critics and composers towards Brahms' music, is contained in the false accusation that this music is too Germanic. (The same might apply to Mahler, Bruckner, Reger, etc.) Pierre Lalo,

[1] *Le Monde*; Paris, 5th August, 1953.

the celebrated critic, is largely responsible for this state of affairs, which spread from France to countries like Belgium, Switzerland (the Romande part), Italy and Spain. It may be due to incomprehension on his part, but I should say it is mostly dictated by bad faith, which is sad to relate. I have known a time, in Paris, when it was impossible to speak of Brahms to Debussy or Ravel, and even to Fauré. It hurts me to think of it. I can remember an article in *Figaro* signed by Alfred Bruneau after a performance of the Brahms Violin Concerto at a concert of the Colonne Orchestra. He only wrote: "Mr. Carl Flesch played the long and heavy concerto of Brahms."

Did Fauré also dislike Brahms?

Fauré always asked me to sit on the jury for the yearly 'cello competition when I was in Paris. One year the candidates had to play a Brahms piece, and I have not forgotten the remarks Fauré made to me on the music!

Some people have said that the misunderstanding of Brahms' music in France could be compared to the same misunderstanding of Fauré's music in Germany. Did you play Fauré in Germany during your tours in that country?

Yes, I have played Fauré in Germany, Austria and in the German part of Switzerland.

And how did the public take it?

Always very favourably, although I must own that Fauré is almost unknown and little played in Germany.

"*Brahms was criticised for having written his* Requiem *in a 'dead' language, which is not even the language of Beethoven or Mozart, but that of the pre-classic period. What we want to know is whether Brahms, having gone to this 'Fountain of Youth', reappeared younger or older. The answer to this is a question of taste. But it is impossible, without being unfair, to accuse him of having dived into it.*" (René Dumesnil.)

He "dived" into it willingly and that's all. The question is: Is the *Requiem* a great work?

I have read in Brahms' correspondence: "If we cannot write with as much beauty as Mozart and Haydn, at least let us write with as much purity in the counterpoint and harmony."

That is splendid. There is advice I would gladly give to any young composer.

Is it true that when Brahms wrote his Violin Concerto *and his* Double Concerto *he got his great friend Joachim to give him advice on the technical side?*

Yes. Brahms followed some of Joachim's advice, but not all. (I have read their correspondence on the subject.) For instance, in the bowing in the theme of the *Finale* of the *Double Concerto*, Brahms did not agree (and quite rightly) with Joachim's indications, since they did not fit in with the character Brahms had given to this movement.

This Concerto is, I believe, dedicated to Joachim and Hausmann.

Yes. Joachim having parted from his wife, Brahms took her side, with the result that their friendship was broken. One can guess the consternation this rupture caused amongst their mutual friends, especially Hausmann and Wirth. Eventually these two managed to effect a reconciliation between Brahms and Joachim. This was the reason why Brahms wrote the *Double Concerto*, to show his gratitude. It is a masterly work. I possess, at Sant Salvador, a photograph dedicated by Brahms to Joachim and Hausmann in memory of this occasion.

Ysaye, when talking of the Violin Concerto, *said: ". . . the technical knowledge is what makes it so interesting in every way". On the other hand, when talking of the Beethoven Violin Concerto, Ysaye wrote: "Do not let us forget that the work, which is the object of this study, is primarily lyrical and the raison d'être of the violin (its singing quality) is at the bottom of it all, whereas in the Brahms Concerto it is outrageously lacking."*[1]

Did Ysaye say that?

Yes.

It is hard to believe. And also, does this singing quality of the violin ever stop in the Brahms Concerto! Furthermore, you ought to have heard how Ysaye played it.

The large symphonic output of Brahms can only be considered as a continuation, not as progress.

But what is progress in art? That is a question I'd like to put, and I should like to have some pertinent answers.

On one occasion Vincent d'Indy (who had previously sent one of his compositions to Brahms) went to see him and was not received. Brahms easily lost his temper and often gave slashing answers. Did I ever tell you what he said to a 'cellist?

No.

It was during a performance of the second *Sonata in F*, with Brahms playing the piano part (which has very turbulent accents at the beginning). The 'cellist said to him: "Master I cannot hear myself," to

[1] A. Ysaye: *Eugène Ysaye—Sa vie, Son oeuvre, Son influence, d'après les documents recueillis par son fils. Preface de Menuhin.* (Les deux Sirènes, Paris.) P. 393.

which Brahms, who probably had reason to complain of the 'cellist's playing, replied: "How lucky you are!"

There is an opinion on Brahms given by a German critic which is very different from that of Vincent d'Indy: "What distinguishes Brahms from a number of small composers is the fact that he brought new ideas to the old forms and has also disciplined and brought under control the forces of fantasy and imagination, thus bringing together the contradictory forms of classicism and romanticism." (Miller-Blattau.)

Yes, this seems to me fairly true. Brahms is given to great emotion and he never sinks to dreary academism. He never even dreamt of being an innovator, but all the same he has been one by giving to his music the natural imprint, the soft and deep light of his personality. I should have liked to have known him. Some of his friends who are also mine have told me of what I missed.

VIII

Music of Yesterday and Today (ii)

Now I would like to question you about some musicians you have known personally. You must have seen Albeniz again after he had heard you at the Café Tost and offered to take you to England?

Of course! A few years later I had occasion to see Albeniz frequently.

I have read somewhere that Count de Morphy also took an interest in Albeniz. He sent him to study the piano at the Brussels Conservatoire when he was fifteen.

Yes. Did I never tell you how Count de Morphy met Albeniz? The Count was travelling by train with his wife and daughter when he heard noises under the seat. Leaning down, he discovered a boy of ten or twelve, hiding. It was Albeniz. "Who are you?" said the Count. "I am a great artist," answered the boy . . . The childhood and adolescence of this great musician was a series of romantic adventures!

Tell me about Albeniz as a pianist. I was told that he did not play in public after 1892.

I only heard him play his own works, but I always thought he was a remarkable pianist. His hands, which were rather small, had an astonishing strength and suppleness. I remember calling on him at the Continental Hotel in Barcelona when he was wearing just a pair of trousers and smoking his usual cigar. He was finishing some composition which he immediately played to me on the piano. I had heard him before in Madrid at Count de Morphy's house and in Paris, where he lived near my *Villa Molitor*.

Do you think that Pedrell had much influence on Albeniz and on Granados?

Not the slightest. When very young Granados had been a pupil of Pedrell, and later on of Massenet in Paris, but I can definitely say that the counsels of both teachers had very little effect on my friend. One can say about Granados, and also about this other Catalan composer, Juli Garreta, that they were both completely self-taught. As for Albeniz, I am sure that his conversations with Pedrell were of relatively little use to him as a composer. Pedrell was not the man to teach musical structure, and, on the other hand, Albeniz was essentially an improvisor and was much more sensitive to the colour and atmosphere of Spanish scenery than anxious to follow didactic rules.

After Albeniz died, Pedrell wrote an article for La Vanguardia *of Barcelona in which he quoted what he had once said to Albeniz: "Down with rules! Burn all the harmony text-books, the counterpoint ones also, and those on composition and instrumentation which have not been written for you and would stifle your natural genius."*

Yes, Albeniz was like that, and one cannot expect to teach anything to such temperamental people. But, some years later, when he went to live in Paris, he came under the influence of his friends of the *Schola Cantorum*, d'Indy, Bordes, etc., and this influence is reflected in the architectural structure of the works he wrote in that period.

I knew Pedrell very well. He and Count de Morphy were the first who tried to create an authentically Spanish opera. A remarkable scholar, Pedrell has written the most authoritative books on the popular Spanish music of the XVIth and XVIIth centuries. He rediscovered the treasures of folk music forgotten in the XIXth century, and he advised young musicians to use such material as inspiration for their compositions. By and large, his contribution to and his influence on the musical renaissance of our country has been of a very positive and beneficial kind.

"I am a Moor," said Albeniz.

It is so! And it is curious to see how far a Catalan can become like a Moor. (That reminds me that one of my friends told me that the best *flamenco* singers are the Catalans who sing in the cafés of Barcelona.) Pedrell, Granados, Garreta and de Falla's mother were also Catalans. Granados, in spite of the typically Spanish element in all his works, was the first composer, and the most remarkable one, to write music with a real Catalan flavour without making direct use of our traditional folklore.

Do you think Albeniz and Granados were "fascinated" by Wagner, as one might think on hearing Merlin *by Albeniz or* Liliana *by Granados?*[1]

What lyrical composer of that period was not "fascinated" by Wagner? But, except for a few traces of a general character, one cannot detect any real influence of Wagner in the compositions of Albeniz, and even less in those of Granados. I should like to know what has become of the original manuscripts of most of Granados' operas. (The MS. of *Goyescas*, which was bought by my friend Mr. Huntington, is now in the Hispanic Museum in New York.)

[1] Henri Collet: *Albeniz et Granados*. (Librairie Plon, Paris.)

Henri Collet thinks that the Spanish composers who came after Albeniz and Granados have not surpassed Iberia and Goyescas.

Certainly not as far as personal genius and true inspiration are concerned.

Some people have said of Albeniz, that he could have been called the "Spanish Liszt", for he was always ready to devote himself to somebody or to some idea.

Yes, it is perfectly true. His kindness and his generosity were proverbial. The door of his house was open to friends and strangers alike. I remember the last time I saw him at Cambo, in the French Basque country, where I went when I heard he was very ill. He was suffering acutely but never complained. He only talked about his wife and his daughter. "They are both angels," he said to me. And he was crying at the thought. Albeniz was an artist with a beautiful and noble nature.

Did Granados belong to a quartet with Crickboom?

Yes, and so did I. I think I told you that Granados and I gave many concerts together.

What was he like as a pianist?

He made me think of Chopin. Chopin as I imagined he was: nervy, delicate, listless, ailing, not a great worker but a born pianist. He could tackle any of the big works written for the piano, and would improvise passages to avoid working at them, without the slightest compunction.

In the trio, Albeniz-Granados-Falla, which place would you assign to Granados?

First I must tell you that the works of the three of them show a display of a very varied nature which makes up a real Spanish School in the midst of "universal" music.

Granados is the most authentic creator. He does not go to the sources of folklore for inspiration—although his themes are very characteristically popular, they are his own personal creation. Neither does Albeniz use folk tunes, and yet a number of his themes sound as if they had been based on popular songs, which makes it perhaps a little less original. One could say the same about Falla, whose originality lies especially in the "dressing up" and his rich variety of harmonies. So, of these three composers Granados is incontestably the greatest, the most original and the most delicately poetical. On the other hand, Falla is the most learned and the one who dominates most the technique of composition. And after him we must put Albeniz, and give third place to Granados who was, as I told you, a completely self-taught composer.

Granados has been compared to Schumann because of his melancholy quality.

No, he had a most seductive and childlike gaiety which overcame the melancholy. Of course his music has (like all good music) an endless variety of mood. To my mind he is more like Schubert because of his spontaneous inspiration. Granados is "our" Schubert, our great poet.

What about his Tonadillas?

They are absolutely delicious. As I told you before: Granados goes back to the traditional *tonadilleros*, gets inspired by Goya, revives the *majos* and the *majas* of Madrid, and writes music sparkling with local colour. These *Tonadillas* are complete creations in which the personality and genius of the composer are expressed. I would add that I have never met a better interpreter of his vocal music than Conchita Badia, a Catalan pupil of his.

You were in New York when they presented the Goyescas *for the first time, I believe?*

Yes, I took part in their preparation and assisted at all the rehearsals. Granados was there, sitting in a corner, like a frightened child who does not dare say anything.

The first performance of *Goyescas* at the Metropolitan stands out as a date never to be forgotten. I have never witnessed such an explosion of enthusiasm in the theatre. The audience not only applauded like mad but were crying at the same time. This audience was mostly composed of the Spanish and South American colony in New York, and they were therefore able to understand the real character of the work.

I have read that when Granados was invited by the President to play at the White House in Washington he missed the boat on which he was travelling back to Europe.

Yes, it is true. Later he went back to England, and from there he and his wife boarded the Cross-Channel boat, the *Sussex*, which was torpedoed without warning by a German submarine. This was a terrible loss for Spanish music and for music in general.

You were also a friend of Manuel de Falla.

Yes. He was a most charming man and an Andalusian to his fingertips.

Robert Bernard writes:[1] "*As opposed to the rich and romantic lyricism of*

[1] *L'Ecole Espagnole*, in *La Musique des Origines à nos jours*. (Librairie Larousse, Paris.)

Albeniz and Granados, Falla is a classic with an acute perfection of form, supported by a supremely aristocratic musicality."

This is true.

And what of your admiration for Juli Garreta?

The fact is that I don't know of any other case we could compare to that of Garreta, the case of a self-taught man who dealt with the greatest musical forms: sonatas, quartets, symphonies, with the incredible ease this Catalan composer had at his command. (You will note that neither Albeniz nor Granados ever tackled this class of composition.) After all, Granados had some teachers, even though he didn't get much out of them, whereas Garreta remained entirely self-taught, living all his life as a clockmaker in the small town of Sant Feliu de Guixols. In his *sardanas* and symphonic works you can find some music of the highest order. This "wild flower", which never received any cultivation, was a true miracle. There was in Garreta the germ of a great master, a germ which could not develop properly without the studies, the guidance and the propitious surroundings so necessary for the flowering of such a talent, the sort of "larva" which develops into a Beethoven or a Brahms.

Albeniz used to say, that some foreign composers, believing they had written certain of their works with a real Spanish flavour, had, in fact, just produced pieces like Polonaises. This opinion, all the same, could not apply to the Capriccio Espagnol *by Rimsky-Korsakov?*

Certainly not! This work of Rimsky-Korsakov, although its construction is basically Russian, seems to me an admirable and extraordinary interpretation of the Spanish spirit as seen through the eyes of the Slav.

Furthermore it is rather surprising to find the interest Russian composers have in Spanish subjects, considering the distance and the difference between the two countries. We find Glinka, the real founder of truly Russian music, writing works inspired by Spain.

Cesar Cui found that the Danses Espagnoles *of Granados were similar to Russian dances. Is there any parallel between the musical products of these two separate poles of Europe?*

The resemblance is evident. Both countries have composers using popular tunes and folk-songs arranged and harmonised according to the artistic procedure of each country and each composer. But this does not solve the whole question. The Russians, being intensely fond of colour, have naturally been attracted by Spanish music. Of course Spanish music has also attracted the French, but in a very different way. The French have approached it with more intellect, whereas the Russians feel an instinctive thirst, deep and at the same time wild, for colour. That is what produced their ballets.

(I remember how passionate Glazunov became when he talked to me about Spanish music, although he was generally very calm—and he liked to recall how Glinka had already realised all the potentiality of our music for theirs.)

You have a great admiration for Russian composers?

Yes, and I can't explain the rapid flowering of Russian music. I speak, of course, of great music, apart from the traditional folklore which exists everywhere. But the process of formation, which lasted for centuries in other countries, seems to have borne fruit very rapidly in Russia.

Numerous musicians think Richard Strauss is the greatest composer of the XXth century.

That is possible. In any case I admire him enormously. In all his work you find such clarity and precision; his way of treating and bringing out instrumental colour is positively extraordinary and I doubt anyone having surpassed him in that direction.

If it were not for your moral convictions, which keep you in Prades, you could play the Don Quixote *of Strauss to commemorate the fiftieth anniversary of the first hearing of this work in New York, in 1904, when you were the soloist.*

It is true. Alas, I must give up so many commemorations!

What do you think of impressionism?

To my mind musical impressionism, of which Debussy and Ravel are undoubtedly the leaders, is a decadent deviation from the stream of great music. Not that I deny the value of what these two composers have created: their new artistic formula is of great interest and denotes an exquisite poetical charm and is very suggestive. If one wanted to put a label on impressionism (if labels could prove anything) one could write on it "decorative music". Debussy's melodic line is far from being remarkable: it is through his harmonic invention that he has given to his works the interest and charm of which I was speaking.

You knew Ravel when he was very young?

Yes. It was at the time when we all visited Mrs. Ram. In those days Ravel was still a student attending Fauré's composition classes at the Conservatoire. He asked me one day to listen to one of his latest compositions. It was the *Pavane pour une Infante Défunte*. I told him that (as I thought) it was a masterly little work. He was surprised, as I remember it, and, of course, as I told you, he was still a student.

Enesco used to ask: "Who is not touched by the charm of Ravel or Debussy? But, besides this charm, I should like some broader and more spacious music" (I cannot vouch that these are his actual words, but it was what he meant).

I quite agree with Enesco.

And what about Fauré?

Fauré may have contributed to the impressionist school of music with his great delicacy and his capacity for harmonic invention, but he derives from the central growth of art. To use a simile, we could think of Fauré as coming from the trunk of great music, while Debussy and Ravel are only offshoots of a branch.

I have heard it said that Fauré had the rare privilege of being "the man of his work".

Yes, both as a man and as a composer we find in him a deep and exquisite nature.

Talking of Fauré's originality where harmonies are concerned, Vuillermoz writes: "Counterpoint as a means of writing reached the highest point of perfection with Bach. His masterly virtuosity in applying the practically unalterable rules of counterpoint was not transmissible and could not be used by his followers: but novelties in the domain of harmony, on the other hand, can still enrich music and are eagerly sought after."

Personally, I don't think that contrapuntal devices have been exhausted. Although the procedure is the same as before, some combinations of counterpoint can present individuality and even novelty according to the personality and creative power of the composer. Indubitably, if anyone says that Bach has been the greatest master of polyphony and counterpoint, it cannot be denied.

"Some works of Fauré appear to be the quintessence of refinement in musical language before its corruption." (Max d'Ollone.)[1]

This is true.

The broadminded attitude of Fauré towards his pupils has been praised and recognised as beneficial to the teaching of composition when it produces such varied names as Ravel, Enesco, Florent Schmitt, Nadia Boulanger, and others.

There is no doubt about the excellence of Fauré's teaching, but pupils with a spark of genius, like Enesco and Florent Schmitt, have

[1] *Le Langage Musical.* (La Palatine, Paris—Geneva.)

not been "formed" by their master, however great he was—genius forms itself, and professors, however eminent, contribute only to a very modest extent to their development.

Would you say that, when teaching an instrument, the personality of the pupil should be respected?

Personally, I have rarely approved of the way pupils played when I heard them for the first time (even in the case of a very gifted pupil). As far as I am concerned, I think there is only one kind of technique which is of any value, that which is exclusively at the service of music. Never have I been able to say to someone who came to ask for advice and guidance, "I need not say anything since all you do is perfect." Of course I have always been glad when I liked the personality of a new pupil, but as a rule I am bound to say to him: "You are far from having reached the top" or "You have not yet got a complete conception of your art as far as music and technique are concerned. My rôle is to correct what needs correcting; I can't accept any initiative which I think unsound and can only teach you in my own way. You must realise this if you wish to work with me. Later on, of course, your personal reactions will become entirely your own responsibility."

Did you know Schönberg well?

Yes, I was in touch with him, I followed his evolution and, through conversations I had with him, I know what his anxieties and aspirations were. I know where he stands, and when I hear that he and some modern composers are put together in the same category I say: No, there is a mistake. In Schönberg we have a man who deliberately chose the path of research with complete sincerity towards himself. Some people thought that, because he was successful, he allowed himself to write insignificant works in the belief that they would naturally be applauded by people who were unable to understand his compositions, but wanted to look as if they did.

Schönberg was not like that: he had musical genius and he revered all composers who deserved it. (What would some of the iconoclasts of our time say if they had heard him say, as I have, how well he understood and admired even a composer like Donizetti?)

With the prophetic instinct of his race and his profound devotion to music he wished to explore unknown spheres, like atonality,[1] with

---

[1] As a matter of fact, Henry Purcell used atonality in some of his *Fantasias in Four Parts* (*No. 4*) which he wrote in 1680. (*Translator's note.*)

the object of finding out what could be done with it. His attitude was one of self-sacrifice—it consisted of putting on one side the "known" methods (in which he excelled) in order to penetrate into the "unknown". His goal was not to break with the past, but to increase the treasures of music with the new possibilities produced by his researches.

What was he like as a person?

Oh, delightful! Very simple, full of charm and possessing a brilliant intelligence.

You have played a 'Cello Concerto of his?

Not in public. I'll explain to you what happened. On the occasion of a music festival in Vienna, Schönberg had found the Figured Bass of an unpublished Concerto by G. M. Monn (a remarkable and unknown composer of the XVIIth century). Schönberg's work on it was masterly and I played this Concerto a good many times, especially in Vienna where it was given its first performance. Then Schönberg discovered another work of Monn from which he borrowed the themes, and made a 'Cello Concerto of it after he had added a good deal himself. He sent it to me with a dedication and I thought it was a highly interesting work. I worked on it for some two years; just as I was on the point of playing the Concerto, the music publishers, Schirmer of New York, who had acquired the rights of the work, told me that I would have to pay one hundred dollars for each performance. I said I did not agree, and on hearing my answer they reduced it to fifty dollars. This haggling made me feel so sick that I said I would have nothing to do with it. (Schönberg, having heard of this, wrote me a letter in which he begged me not to accept Schirmer's terms.)

Feuermann played this Concerto for the first time and in spite of the remarkable performance he gave, the work had no success at all. I never heard any more about this Concerto except when a 'cellist called Bartsh played it on Paris Radio. It is a pity that it has not become known, as I think it is a masterly work.

What do you think of the result of Schönberg's innovations?

By and large I think that some of his ideas will help in the normal (but not purely cerebral) development of music. But, on the other hand, I think that some of his innovations will prove fruitless. I remember one day in Vienna when Schönberg talked to me of his plans. In spite of all his enthusiasm, I could not escape the vision of the abyss which was opening beneath his feet!

I have read that some of the former pupils of Schönberg and Alban Berg said: "The twelve-tone system cannot form a school. It is only a valueless doctrine in itself, in which Schönberg has experimented on his own account, and when passing it on to his pupils he always warned them against taking it too seriously."

Of course it is natural to find pupils following the teaching of their master, even taking it too seriously. They cannot all have as much talent as Schönberg had, nor his great sincerity when experimenting. And have we not seen already how ridiculous some people can be when they are afraid of looking old-fashioned?

Our compatriot Roberto Gerhard, when he came back to Barcelona after a stay in Vienna, had been so influenced by the innovations of Schönberg that he wrote exclusively in that style. He managed to express his talent, but it became sterile since (as I think) any music which is not expressive has no reason to exist. I told him, "You are walking in a maze and you must do everything you can to get out of it." Later on, Gerhard changed his way of writing, but in his latest works, which are of a different kind as far as structure and style are concerned, one can detect the mark of Schönberg. I feel sure that this period under Schönberg, and the experience he had through it, have been useful to him. Any kind of new ideas are profitable to those who have something to say.

Did you know Alban Berg?

No.

Have you seen Wozzeck?

I only heard a recording of it on the radio.

What impression did this work make on you?

That of a master who moves in a world that is not mine.

Do you think of atonality as fundamentally wrong?

Not wrong in principle. I have used it myself to describe some kind of musical vision, especially in my *Sardana* for 'celli.[1] But before and after these descriptive passages, I have written some real music.

[1] "*Pablo Casals has composed six* Sardanas, *one of them being written for an ensemble of, at least, thirty-two 'celli, divided into eight principal parts. The middle part of the symphonic work combines the air of the* Castell *in D Major, with an imitation on the drums of a Gregorian chant in F Major and a processional march in B♭ Major. It is meant as a sound picture of the noise at a local feast, in a southern town flooded with light. Clever imitations and dynamic gradations prevent this surplus of melody, harmony and rhythm, from degenerating into chaos. Eventually it all clears up and a new melody emerges. It ends with a final theme, which starts quietly and gradually gets more spirited, recalling previous themes. It was written in 1930 to celebrate the annual Feast of Vila-franca del Panades, on September 4th, and the rumbling noise of the processions, the fair, the military bands,* Sardanas *dancing and* Castells (human mountains) *produce a wonderful impression.*" (Rudolf von Tobel, *op. C.*)

(Vincent d'Indy wrote to me about my *Sardana* for 'celli[1] congratulating me and explaining that he agreed with my way of using atonality. At the end of his letter he quoted a bit of the *Sardana* that he specially liked.) A composer has a right to use any means, even atonality, at a given time. We find Bach, Chopin and Wagner using it as a means to create an impression. But can music be reduced to a series of impressions as our modern composers try to do? It has no sense. It is absurd to turn atonality into a system.

René Leibowitz, one of the most ardent followers of Schönberg, has written on the connection between the chromaticism of Wagner and atonality: "The chord D-F-A-C (2nd degree of C Major, for instance), can be altered chromatically and become D♯-F♯-A♭-C♯. Of course, this altered chord can still be explained by the system of superimposed thirds but, in fact, it consists of only one third (D♯-F♯), a second, (F♯-A♭ (=G♯)) and a fourth (G♯ (=A♭) C♯). One can also (and one had to do it constantly in the Wagnerian period) give to this chord a definite tonal function by calling it really the second degree of C. Chromatically one can always explain everything. This chord we talk about becomes one based on the 1st degree of C, if the D♯ goes up to E, the F♯ to G, and the A♭ (if the C♯, thought of enharmonically as D♭, comes down to C) comes down to G. But one can also avoid giving any functional explanation of a precise character, which is exactly what Wagner does so often. It leaves a feeling of doubt. Another chord as vague as the first follows, and so on. A series of chords of that kind creates a complete confusion of keys. If we add to this a melody without any 'fixed' points (the sort of perpetual melody Wagner dreamt of), some moving and varied voices in the middle register, and an irregular rhythm, we can see clearly that if tonality exists in Wagner, it will end by being swamped under the weight of such complex polyphony."[2]

I cannot see why tonality must "end by being swamped", and I cannot see either why the systematic use of atonality should have been an inevitable consequence of Wagner's chromaticism. Schönberg himself confessed to me his intention of exploring this unknown region to see what it had to offer. But I am afraid his followers did not all

---

[1] The Sardana for Violoncelli *is dedicated to the London 'Cello Club (Herbert Walenn, London Violoncello School) where it was played; as well as in Barcelona in 1934, as a homage to Pau Casals, with sixty-five 'cellists, in Zürich in 1946 and 1951, on the occasion of Casals' seventieth and seventy-fifth birthdays, with the participation of ninety and one hundred and twenty 'cellists respectively, and in Paris in October 1952, at the Palais de Chaillot with eighty French 'cellists, including Maurice Maréchal, Paul Bazelaire, André Navarra, etc.*

[2] *Schönberg et son Ecole. (J. B. Janin, Paris.)*

show the same restraint and high musical conscience. They went deeper into the annihilation of all music. They didn't even do it with sincerity! More often than not there is only complete hypocrisy; that is, striving for effect.

"*Some people saw a sort of innovation in the Chromaticism of* Tristan. . . . *But they forgot that Wagner when he wrote* Tristan *did not mean to write 'something new' or to enlarge the harmonic language, or to 'make progress', but only to find the means of expression necessary to his poetic vision and the harmonies he wanted for the atmosphere of* Tristan." (Wilhelm Furtwängler.)

I am of the same opinion.

"*On the whole Furtwängler seems to be against the composers who try to expand the possibilities of the musical language. He asserts that the great composers of the past never thought of 'doing something new' in the language of music, but have in fact done so without meaning to, simply by trying to say sincerely what they had to say. This is not so: the corner-stone of all 'tonal' music is precisely the one that was composed uniquely to demonstrate the advantages and possibilities of this music*—The Well-Tempered Clavier *by Bach, the work which has set the seal on tonal music in such a majestic way.*" (Antoine Golea, *Journal Musical Français*, June 1953.)

This assertion of M. Golea is not well founded. As we all know, Bach, in *The Well-Tempered Clavier*, wished to show his contemporaries all the possibilities contained in tonality, some of which had not been used in his day. Does Bach look like an innovator in this work? He does, but in doing so he uses only a natural musical language. Innovation is one thing, annihilation is another. I advise those who wish to "demonstrate the advantages and possibilities" of "contemporary music" to start by writing comprehensively because, unless they do, one cannot begin to talk about music.

Furtwängler says that contemporary music "has a limited number of listeners but nevertheless these are passionately convinced ones".

It must be an artificial passion since there is so often in this music nothing to understand. These "passionate" people form a minority, which does not understand either. After all, they are not made differently from us, are they? Look, I am going to play to you a section from a 'Cello Sonata written by a contemporary composer (who, I am glad to say, has given us other proofs of his talent).

(*Casals takes his 'cello and begins to play a series of mewings and scratches. I must say that to watch him with his pipe in his mouth, his face showing perplexity as if he was waiting for something which does not happen, is a very funny sight.)*

Can anyone honestly pretend that this music (?) would create any emotion in the listener or even mean anything at all?

Francis Poulenc has said: "What the Ninth Symphony *did to stir up the people of the XIXth century,* The Sacre du Printemps *does already for those of the XXth century."*

This time I completely disagree with my friend Poulenc. Although I acknowledge the talent of Stravinsky and the interest of the *Sacre du Printemps,* I think that to compare these two works is nothing short of blasphemy.

Do you like The Firebird, Petrouchka, *the Stravinsky of the early period?*

Very much. But what he has given us recently is not the real Stravinsky. It seems to deal only with cerebral problems which exclude all feeling. The real Stravinsky is melodious, colourful, beautifully sensitive. Unfortunately all these qualities seem to have disappeared and that is very regrettable.

When Stravinsky says he loathes what he describes as musique-réligion and adds that we ought to like music for itself and not for the emotions it provokes . . .

What is exactly the meaning of "liking music for itself"?

Stravinsky writes in his Poétique Musicale: *"I am beginning to think together with the general public that melody should keep its place at the summit of the hierarchy of all elements which constitute music."*

Bravo! I rejoice to hear this.

You told me once that one could establish a parallel between Picasso and Stravinsky.

Yes.

Picasso has said: "All my pictures are only experiments."

For centuries the masters of music have kept their experiments to themselves and thought that they should only give to listeners the works which they had felt, thought over and allowed to mature.

One cannot stop evolution in the Arts.

We should not confuse natural evolution with a complete rupture with the past. A musician can get rid of restraints and find his own way without breaking, in a fit of temper, with all the ties which connect him with the experiments of his predecessors. Evolution following a normal course has always existed, and always will exist.

"We used to think that when an artist had originality it was revealed

without effort on his part. We found that the pleasure of the unexpected was born of those occasions when we were denied the pleasure of the expected. The variety, the very modifications a musician brought to the construction and the language used, were worked out within the accepted framework. But, in most present-day compositions, since the listener is unable to anticipate anything while the music is going on, the sensation of the unexpected has disappeared." (Max d'Ollone.)

It is true. The exaggerated desire for originality leads to worse aberrations. Each one of us possesses as much originality as the most modest creation of nature. How many leaves are on this tree in the garden, and yet there are not two alike! If you see a friend coming in the distance you will know him by his gait; there is no need for him to gesticulate in any fancy way in order that you may know who it is. Why? Just because he has his own characteristics, his originality in fact. In music it is easy to gesticulate and talk nonsense, in order to appear original; the difficulty is to put one's own mark on a composition while using the accepted language which is comprehensible to all.

"So one can see that in the best works of the classical and modern schools, the alternate use of consonance and dissonance (which is the equivalent of repose and movement), the question and the answer, the desire and the satisfaction, was a normal procedure, not only in the psychological and intellectual sense, but also in the physical sense." (Max d'Ollone.)

Of course. Everything can be explained, but this cannot be done unless we stop a moment to think about it. An explanation of what has been is necessary in order to understand what is to come. In music, without alternate movement and repose, which corresponds to the difference between tension and relaxation in physiological life, there would only be confusion at the start turning into chaos afterwards.

"We seem to be getting near the time when people will look with some astonishment at the selfishness of those composers who scorn the idea of pleasing and moving their listeners, and are concerned only with the praise of a small clique, and their own inaccessible little egos. Music will have to become conscious again of its possibilities and of the part it should play in society in order to survive. As the language of feeling, of humanity, accessible to all, it will live as long as the world. But as a pastime for the few and as a stimulant for jaded, nervy people, its days are numbered." (Max d'Ollone.)

This is very well said. Composers can use any material as long as they make a coherent whole of it, a whole which will express true life in music. What is inadmissible is to despise all feeling and to confine oneself to laboratory experiments and the speculations of the brain.

At the basis of this attitude, which is that of most "contemporary music", one can perceive vanity and impotence. I am the first to wish for the appearance of new flowers, but not of new monstrosities. I have said it for so long: if we are persistently faced by blunders, we must have the courage to say "no"!

At the end of his life Ysaye wrote to his son Antoine: "I can only see chaos in the products of today—sometimes I have the impression of a monstrous joke played by gifted but negative people. Art, which I thought of as a unique and ever unfinished monument to which each generation, each school is bringing its contribution, looks as if it had come to a dead end. I suffer for my inability to believe any more in the strength and truth of youth, and that is why I have come to ask you this question, for deep in my inner self I hope I am wrong. I cannot systematically reject all new compositions without wishing to find out what they mean. Such an attitude would be the betrayal of myself and would destroy the meaning of all my own struggle."

These words accord so well with the noble personality of Ysaye, always so open and generous towards most of the composers of his day—César Franck, Fauré, Debussy, Chausson, and others. I also have known the perplexity Ysaye talks of, but have eventually come to a definite attitude: I will have nothing to do with what is called "contemporary music".

C. M Widor said, as he was listening to a very dissonant work of his young pupil Darius Milhaud, "The worst of it is that one gets used to it."

I don't know which of Milhaud's works this was. But there are certain things I shall never get used to.

Some of the works now recognised have taken a long time to become understood.

If familiarity is necessary for comprehension the chaotic music I speak of would have had plenty of time to establish itself. The reason why the public does not wish to hear this music is not because it is new. What they feel is that it is lacking in human warmth.

Busoni thought that we ought not to consider as important the qualities of timbre, sonority or colour in music, and that our senses should not interfere with our musical pleasure which is of a purely cerebral and intellectual kind. Paul Hindemith said, "You must think of the piano as a percussion instrument and treat it as such."

I knew Busoni, I know Hindemith, and I cannot understand that men of such value can have said such things.

What do you think of composers who had reintroduced the Greek modes in modern works?

I don't see anything wrong in this, any more than in any other experiments which will enlarge the field of music. I have often thought, for instance, that composers should get to know Hindu music because of the richness and invention of its popular songs. We have already seen what has been done by incorporating negro spirituals and Chinese folk-songs. On the whole one cannot say that it has had much influence on universal music, but I think that the insertion of some Hindu music would have some happy results on the very development of what we consider is a superior art.

What can we expect by the use of new intervals like quarter-, third-, and tenth-tones?

I don't think that research on those lines can lead to any valuable results.

And what do you think of the "concrete" music we sometimes hear on the radio? This kind of music is always recorded and does not need to be performed. Using only some special instruments the authors will produce the sound of wind from high altitudes, as well as the noise of an engine running at full speed, or steps on stairs, or the noises inside a dentist's room.

I don't know any of these specimens, but I can say that they don't constitute music. Although I like to hear a furious wind and see trees bending under a violent squall, I have never thought of applying the qualification "musical" to the sensations I receive on these occasions. Different manifestations of nature can inspire a composer, and he may even try to reproduce them (there are countless examples); but in themselves they never constitute real music. We can observe the same difference between the natural beauty of a landscape and the artistic beauty of the same landscape seen through the eyes of a painter.

The public often goes wrong . . . although Toscanini insists that the great public is almost always right.

In the average concert the audience is made up of people who may or may not be capable of pronouncing a sound judgment. But I can't deny that, taken collectively, this audience is endowed with penetration and intuition. The test of public performance has become more necessary than ever. It constitutes a safeguard against unwelcome experiments which, in fact, the public refuses to accept.

"A young composer's symphony," says Honegger, "has all the disadvantages in relation to any great classical symphony." (Disadvantages about being performed at all, of course.)

That is obvious. I have always believed in the necessity of institutions, subsidised by the State, where new works could be heard at free concerts. The public would have the chance of getting in touch with new composers. As long as the latter did not think it their duty only to demonstrate extravagant styles of music in their works; that would inevitably make the public want to go and hear a Beethoven Symphony instead. How could it be otherwise?

Atonal music, people say, is a reflection of the uncertainty of the chaotic period in which we live.

Art should be used as a means of keeping alive the cult of an ideal, instead of for the propagation of morbid tendencies towards disintegration. Why should an artist be obsessed by the uncertainties of our time, instead of reacting against them by showing his faith in those human values which have survived so many collective catastrophies? The artist, as a man, will always find occasions to intervene, if he thinks he should intervene, in the conflicts of his time. But art cannot be the slave of these conflicts. However dark our times may seem, art should bring a message of hope.

Prokoviev said: "I have been trying to find a melodious and clear language without renouncing the harmonic and melodic shapes universally acknowledged. And this is where the difficulty comes in: to write music with a new clarity."[1]

The great masters have used the recognised harmonic system, but they have done it with such art and individual genius that their works always seem new. In Bach and Mozart I can easily perceive a "new clarity". I think that Prokoviev and Bartók are both extraordinarily gifted musicians. Some of their compositions will certainly survive triumphantly the test of time. The rest of their work I am not so sure about.

And Hindemith?

I have not seen Hindemith since 1932, when I played with him, Schnabel and Huberman in Vienna at some chamber music concerts I shall never forget. Never mind what his theories were, he has left unmistakable proofs of his remarkable talent as a composer.

A critic wrote about one of his last works, Nobilissima Visione, *that Hindemith had used again "a language which speaks to the heart".*

All to the good.

What of Milhaud?

Milhaud has a great gift for composition and has given us some magnificent works. It is a pity that he also thought he had to be

---

[1] Cf. I. Nestiev: *Prokofiev. Traduction de Rostilav Hofmann.* (Editions du Chêne, Paris.)

"modern" at all costs. I have a most touching letter from Milhaud in which he tells me of the impression I made on him the first time he heard me, when he was very young.

Honegger?

It seems to me that he is one of the contemporary composers of greatest musical value. (I think that the best composer of our time is Ernest Bloch.) In spite of his "modernism" Honegger refrained from going beyond certain limits. He has been influenced by modern tendencies but has known how to choose some innovations and reject others, while remaining faithful to what we may define as a musical idea, the thing that so many contemporary musicians have just abolished.

Musicians as modern as Honegger and Hindemith have said about dodecaphonism: "This serial system prides itself on having very strict rules. These people look to me like convicts, who having shaken off their chains, voluntarily tie up their feet with weights in order to run quicker! . . ." (Honegger.) "One can invent as many arbitrary rules of this kind as one chooses. But if one chooses to use them to produce a new style of musical composition, I think one could find other rules less narrow and more interesting. The idea of dodecaphonism seems to me more theoretic than all the pedantries of the professors of traditional harmony." (Hindemith.)

I am delighted to hear that Honegger and Hindemith say those things. What is necessary is that composers understand the art of expressing oneself musically. Those who have nothing to say should do something else. And those who truly feel a deep necessity to compose should do so in ways which may be new but which must in any case be simple and comprehensible. I insist: it is not the procedure that matters, but the result. In the long run, time will choose, and give to everyone the place he deserves.

Simplicity in forms of expression has never been prejudicial to a sincere creator, for he always knows that originality is above all a gift. I have heard a lot of music in the course of my long career, but every time I hear Haydn I have the impression that I hear some newly discovered thing. Great music, if well performed, is sufficiently rich to keep intact the sense of novelty and to increase the desire to hear it again.

How far we are from the time when Bach wrote those wonderful Cantatas just for the congregation of St. Thomas's Church! And we are even further from the humility of the Great Cantor, who after the Sunday service put away the Cantata in a drawer. . . . In our day there seems to be a cleavage between the artist and the collective sensibility. To "get in touch", to "communicate", has become very difficult, if not impossible. Isn't that the blind alley into which not only music, but contemporary art generally, has got? Nowadays if an artist composed like Bach, painted like Velasquez, or wrote like Shakespeare, he would be told that his works gave an impression of having been "seen before", or "heard before". On the other hand, if this artist is obsessed by the desire for novelty, he takes the risk of running into chaos, or at the best his work will only be understood by a minority. Can you think of any way out?

In our day an artist cannot compose like Bach, paint like Velasquez, or write like Shakespeare; even if he tried he would not succeed. (Of course we are not talking of common imitators, they are not worth thinking about.) The work of Art carries with it the personal conceptions of the artist, and those are never the same in different artists.

You have used a word, in talking of Bach, which is of prime importance and explains so many things: "humility". All great creators know that life and art don't begin with them, and in this we find the greatness of their humility—they are more intent on moving us than on surprising us. Contemporary music shows a regrettable tendency to exclude anything human or natural, and especially anything which might be pure emotion. What sort of communication can be established with others if one has such an attitude? Without sinking into melodrama or sentimentality an artist can find many ways to be great and human.

Honegger is very pessimistic on the future of music: "At present, what plays the most important part in compositions is the use of rhythmical shock in contrast to voluptuous melody. At the present rate we shall have by the end of this century an elementary, barbarous music which will combine elemental melody with brutally scanned rhythm. This will admirably suit the deformed ear of the music-lover of the year 2000!"

I do not share these pessimistic views. Aesthetically, the receptive faculties do not disappear any more than the discriminative moral faculties. There are periods of crisis and straying, but man finds again the notion of things that are beautiful and pure.

Furtwängler says: "Technical questions like tonality and atonality, historical considerations, are all secondary in relation to this other question: in which proportion does the music of today represent adequately what we are?

How much of ourselves do we find in this music? This question is positively a question of conscience: it would determine the truth of our musical expression and the authenticity of our existence as musicians."

These words seem to hit the nail on the head. The criterion of conscience is what will prevail in the end, because the great things of humanity will never change and what we shall always find in artistic creation is the man, the man in flesh and blood and not an abstract creature. Today we still like what is beautiful, even if the works are thousands of years old, like Chinese and Indian poetry. They have the same reason for existing as our true music has. Their life is the same today as in *all eternity.*

IX

On Interpretation

What of the personality of the artist in interpretation?

Everyone is different, and each of us must apply to this work all the drive and deep impulse of his nature. We have only to look round us to realise how all bodies are organised and to notice the harmonious variety of anything which has a life of its own.

An artist must be strong enough to feel independent of everything that has been done, and of everything he has learned, and he must convince himself that to "feel independent" of any routine or tradition is his main duty and purpose.

He goes the wrong way who does not question himself or listen to the "voice" of his artistic nature—provided that he has such a nature, of course. What *does* matter is what we feel, and that is what we have to express. With Bach, for instance, I knew that my duty was to reject strongly the examples and the traditions around me, and to persevere in search of my own way of feeling these works.

Can it be said that there is a style for Bach, a style for Beethoven?

I was talking with a great friend of mine and a great musician about this very question quite recently. It was apropos of a Mozart work. Some people think that there is a style for Bach, another for Mozart, and that it is necessary to go into research to build up the true style and bring it to life. Obviously each great composer should have his own style since the greatest power for creation, life itself, shows us what particularities there are in the humblest creature in existence. Therefore, why shouldn't a great master have a style? Now then, the performer looking at the score in front of him has got to reconstitute, not a so-called objectivity, but all the different phases which the author's mind went through when creating this work, and in doing so, observe the reactions which they produce deep down in his own mind.

How curious this fetish of objectivity is! And is it not responsible for so many bad performances? There are so many excellent instrumentalists who are completely obsessed by the printed note, whereas it has a very limited power to express what the music actually means. Great masters may have been as conscientious as you like when writing their scores, but they are always guided in their writing by a state of mind we call, in turn, feeling, passion, dreams.

All this infinite variety cannot very well be translated just by the writing of notes, and yet it is through these notes that we must reconstruct all the author's state of mind! Are there any set rules for this re-creating process? I cannot think of any.

On the subject of "the fear of giving way to romanticism", Furtwängler says: ". . . if a musician is capable of abandonment and passion he will not be afraid of appearing romantic and sentimental, nor will he have to avoid emotion in order to avoid its pitfalls. . . . This fear of sensibility, this fear of oneself, is farcical, as if "making music" had, for a musician, any other sense than having confidence in himself instead of the fear of oneself."

Can the artist who has confidence in himself do anything but let himself go? There is nothing worse than being held back by fear. The value of the performer's work consists of getting as near as he can to the deepest meaning of the music he performs, which, in a big work, offers him such a rich complexity of expression, and which the written signs of the "printed note" can only partly suggest.

Willingly or not, the performer is an interpreter and can only render the work through his own self.

On some occasions I have heard you say that just as a, b, c, etc., do not make a word, by the same reasoning the written signs of music are powerless in making "music".

Can anyone doubt it? We cannot *see* the musical idea which gave birth to a composition, but our talent and imagination, coupled with constant work, will help to reveal it to us individually and not objectively, for the understanding of everyone. Sometimes, looking at a score, I say to myself: "What marvellous music. But I must *make* it so." The performance must give to the work the full meaning of its existence and translate this ideal existence into reality.

May I be allowed to quote another opinion of Furtwängler? "First the actual notation: through it the performer gets to know the work: he traces backwards the steps of the composer, who gave life to his music before putting it down on paper while he wrote it down. The heart and the marrow of this music is therefore like an improvisation which he tries to write down. Whereas, to the performer, the work appears like something exactly the opposite of an improvisation, as a thing written with fixed signs and unalterable shape. Next the performer must guess the meaning and work out the mystery of this music in order to get to the work itself, which it is his business to bring to life."

Magnificent! What is necessary is to bring to life what is written, to infuse life, instead of avoiding it with timidity. No theory, however learned it may be, nor any edition, however covered with annotations from the editor, can ever replace this interpretation: the heart of a melody can never be put down on paper.

I have noticed how often you use the words "life" and "living" when talking of interpretation.

This is because, on the one hand, I consider life as our great adviser and, on the other, for an artist, and especially for a performer, the essential problem is to produce a vital creation. We must reject all things that are not clear or may be artificial. By no means should one consider this rule as an invitation to sloth; quite the contrary! Often we find that nothing is more difficult than to rediscover the marvellous simplicity of live shapes. First they must find an echo in our minds; after which we must pursue the work of investigation and elucidation of the different problems. An endless work. Years of study have confirmed the importance of this work. Every day I discover new things.

Even in the works you have studied and played for the last sixty years, such as the Bach Suites?

Yes, even in those, and especially in those. Only a few days ago I realized that I was making a mistake in one of the Suites.

There are artists who, not daring to let themselves go, will give way to something worse: routine (sometimes under a false pretence of looking for technical perfection). But, at the end of routine, we find a mechanical, congealed performance, the opposite of all art.

The interpretation of a work must be something organic, not mechanical, something which makes you know how to vary all repeated passages, how to establish a gradation of detail in the general unity of the work, how not to be put off by some small rhythmical liberties which the music demands, and, finally, how to remember two very simple things: first that the natural origin of melody was vocal, secondly that true rhythms come from the natural movements of man, steps and dance.

Is there any danger of the artist overreaching himself?

Not for the real artist. His intelligence and his good taste will guard him against taking too much liberty. Besides, this liberty is the opposite of any arbitrary initiative, since it should be the product of pains-

taking and constantly renewed study of the work. What an abundance
of varieties, possibilities and nuances is to be found in the music of the
great masters! Only a suggestion of all this can be detected in the
written score. Signs don't change, of course, and yet they may every
day reveal new things to the sensitive performer. The more he studies
them, the more marvels he discovers. It is not a question of being
original at all costs, in the bad meaning of the word; if the artist
wanted to show off an artificial originality having no connection with
the language the composer has used to communicate his thoughts, it
would be heresy. It is precisely his devotion and humility towards the
music which will allow him to get a glimpse of the heights where
hovers the creative spirit.

An eminent musician has written about rubato: *"This temporary
rhythmical liberty always reveals (rather like a barometer) the truth—or the
falsehood—of the musical impulses felt (or fabricated) by the conductor,
player or singer."*

Any performer who has not got a high conception of the work he
has to play will probably use means which will not help his interpretation. It is all a question of equilibrium being maintained by good
taste. The *rubato* in itself is such a natural means of expression, that we
could almost think of music as being a perpetual *rubato*. It is just the
same when we speak: even without noticing it, how many times do
we accelerate or retard the rhythm of our words to make them more
expressive?

*Rudolf von Tobel says that according to you "no composer is grateful
when, against our feeling and our convictions, we persist in following the text
like a slave".*[1]

Composers are very grateful when the performer succeeds in
realising through intuition their truest and deepest intentions, instead
of following blindly the written text, and this really proves how insufficient and vague are the indications they can give us. Further, I
have noticed that Saint-Saëns, Moor, Granados and many others did
not perform their works twice in the same way; neither did they
observe strictly the indications they themselves had written.

*"It is a fallacy to say that the performer, over and above his study of the
music, should reconstruct the concrete intention of the author in his performance. The intention of the composer can only be indeterminate in regard
to the realities of performance. When he listens to the execution of his work,
the composer rediscovers it through this performance, and by definition the*

[1] All quotations from von Tobel are taken from his book, *Pablo Casals.*

only performance that will be valuable to him is also the one which has given to his composition its greatest vitality."[1]

A composer will always dislike any performance of his works at the hands of a mediocre player. Nevertheless, this same composer will not only accept different versions of his work, but will enjoy the variety when it is produced by real artists. I don't think Beethoven thought otherwise on the subject of different performances of one of his works, as long as they showed zest for life and the freshness of novelty which, I repeat, only a real artist can infuse into a performance.

Ravel used to say, "Just play what is written."

What nonsense!

Did Ravel hear you play his Trio with Cortot and Thibaud?

Yes, and he seemed satisfied although we interpreted his indications in our own way.

Didn't he show any enthusiasm?

Oh, Ravel never showed any enthusiasm! As soon as he became a celebrity, performers did not matter much to him. He did not go to concerts and was not interested in a good performance. (The only thing that preoccupied him was, naturally enough, his work as a composer.) Having known him since he was very young, as I told you before, I felt a sort of pity when I discovered some aspects of his nature.

Ysaye would say, when he talked about Anton Rubinstein playing Chopin's Funeral March: "I have often thought, and I am not the only one of this opinion, that the performance had more value than the work itself. Rubinstein remade it, completed it, added something that was missing. He turned it into one of those poems which stir the most intransigent soul."

Yes, I also think that sometimes, even fairly frequently, an interpretation can be better than the work itself.

There are some examples where a performer has for ever attached the seal of his personality to a certain work. We can all think of your interpretation of the Bach Suites. Ysaye wrote about the Beethoven Violin Concerto played by Joachim: "It is forty years since the Hungarian Master played this work, which had not been much noticed before, but he played it so beautifully that his name seems to be coupled with the work ever since. It is he, if I may say so, who has made a masterpiece of it. If he had not produced this ideal rendering of the work, it is possible that it would have been put aside and forgotten. But no, he has revitalized it, enlarged it, transformed it! ..."

[1] Gisele Brelet: *L'interpretation Créatrice.* (Presse Universitaires de France, Paris.)

Fifty years after it was written, Joachim reinstated this Concerto. The violinists of Beethoven's day either did not attach much importance to it or else thought it was too difficult. The imprint of Joachim's rendering of the work has not disappeared yet. I heard the great violinist play it. Although I did not agree with all he did, I remember there were in his performance many moments of the highest order, which I thought were perfectly adapted to the spirit and character of the work.

Ysaye goes further. He adds that in the performance of Joachim "everyone can see the way, and follow it to the end, without losing his personality, or becoming too dependent, or moulding his individuality to that of Joachim. His rendering being the mirror of Beethoven's thoughts, it is permissible to be impregnated by it, even advisable not to try anything else, in the certainty that here is the truth and the light which illuminates, and will always illuminate, the road for those who want to follow it."

And how could one do that? Joachim's performance having gone, how can we avoid the different performances which followed his and will continue to do so? How can one avoid different renderings? In spite of Joachim's example, Ysaye himself had a very personal conception of the work, which did not at all resemble that of the great Hungarian Master. . . .

While you perform do you feel a sort of dual personality?

Yes, as you go from the physical part, which the artist must use, to the musical creation, another part of our being comes in. I spoke to Bergson about this.

You mean about the respective parts the intelligence and the instinct take during a performance. . . .

The sort of intelligence which is too self-sufficient might do harm instead of good. When all is said it is instinct which not only creates but directs the performance.

Mozart and Schubert are two exceptional cases of intuition whose works rise above the limitations of the intellect.

Of course, in music, as in everything, technical exercises bring facility and stimulate deep research. However, although intelligence is a powerful auxiliary, intuition remains the deciding factor. There are many intelligent people who think constantly and, as a result, get into a muddle. I have had two extremely intelligent friends who, through a constant fever of thinking, often ended in complete confusion.

Do you think of yourself as an intuitive?

Yes, all I do is based on intuition.

But you don't stop there; you just go on with hard work.

Intelligence helps the process of development and the progressive integration of perceived forms, but it must be nourished and directed by intuition. The fruitful blending of these two qualities depends on the amount of each of them.

When you arrived today I was studying a Bach Recitative. I worked at it for a few weeks, first on the piano then on the 'cello. Complete understanding through intuition does not come to me at once. I feel that I shall achieve understanding of the work as I wish, but I have not yet comprehended it completely. As to my faith in the final result, I could not say if it comes from faith in my instinct, or if I think my intelligence sufficient to capture the forms I have perceived through musical instinct.

You are now seventy-seven, and, in your solitude in Prades, you still spend weeks studying a recitative. . . .

I have always done it, and it is not because I have learned something through studying that I should stop doing it.[1] A member of my family said to me, talking about this recitative, "How do you manage to be so patient?" And I answered: "Why not? It is so difficult to find out the proper shape of all these notes, and their connection with each other and with the ensemble of it. To sort it all out is an immense work. However, you can now notice how different it is from when I began." One cannot undertake the performance of a great work without first sorting out its principal trends, its architectural sense and the relation between the different elements which make up its structure. What we must look for is the meaning of the music: that is only to be found when the performer approaches it with honesty and humility.

Does that mean that the truth of the music can vary?

Of course, if every time it varies it tends to greater simplicity and its meaning becomes more apparent. The artist is responsible for the music he performs. He must experience it and create it again. It is necessary to insist that the greatest respect he can pay to the music consists of giving it life. That is the first commandment.

---

[1] *Bruno Walter relates (in* Theme and Variations, *Alfred Knopf, New York) that once in London, when Casals was to play the Schumann Concerto with him, on arriving at the Hall for the last rehearsal he found Casals practising exercises in the artists' room. As he apologised for arriving so early, Casals just said "all right" and went on playing. During the rehearsals, says Walter, Casals played the Concerto with a saintly devotion and perfection. When, in the evening, he came again to the Queen's Hall, he found that Casals was conscientiously playing his exercises again, and he listened to them for about fifteen minutes.*

A celebrated violinist who belongs to a younger generation than yours, Yehudi Menuhin, has written this about interpretation: "The task for the performer consists in establishing an equilibrium between the composition and his own conscience. He tries his very best to reproduce the essence of what the composer has formed in his mind. At all costs he must keep in touch with the author's conception, and yet the possibility of this conception being revived depends entirely on the reality of his own conviction and of his own emotions."

This is very true. When Menuhin was very young and was being taught by Enesco, the latter invited me to go and hear his pupil play a Bach *Partita* at a concert in Paris. I remember sitting in a box with the Menuhin family. After the concert Enesco took me aside to find out what my opinion was. I told him I thought that his pupil was extremely gifted and had a perfect technique, but I also told him what to my mind was missing in his performance of the *Partita*, namely, that it was not fully alive. To which Enesco replied, "The reason is that in Bach's day one did not do that sort of thing." Confronted by this assertion I thought it would be useless to pursue the argument. In spite of the admiration I have for this very great artist and a friendship so dear to me, I was sorry to find him tied up with this idea, which I consider as a traditionalist prejudice. In Bach's time, people did not use *spiccato* bowing of course; but why not use it now if the music demands it? To my mind no expressive accent in music should be excluded any more than, in speaking, one should eliminate any means of reinforcing the expression and helping the nuances.

Ludwig questioned you on the decisive rôle of inspiration, to which you answered: "This is an error. Unless one keeps watch over one's feelings they can't be properly used as an artistic means of expression. It is only when reason is in command that inspiration can provide something. I do not believe that playing is just magic."

These, probably, are not exactly the words I used with my friend Ludwig. It is not that reason should be in command. It is at the basis of inspiration, which becomes, as one might say, a sort of exaltation of what has first been ordained and fixed by the intelligence. I am, of course, talking about musical interpretation. In fact, I have always thought that inspiration and work stimulate each other.

What about vibrato?

When used in a string instrument, the *vibrato* has an expressive function which you might compare to that of the voice in singing, but it remains obvious that *vibrato* in itself cannot be expressive, because that depends on how it is applied. The *vibrato* is a means of expressing sensitivity, but it is not a proof of it.

A modern composer said that "he works with joy". Could you say the same?

This is a claim which it would be very difficult to make as an instrumentalist. With the composer there may be the joy of working, a joy which will probably be mixed with the bitter pangs of the work coming from the recesses of the soul. Nevertheless, with him, the hours can pass very happily so that he loses all sense of time. The instrumentalist—at least I feel that way—does count the hours! And he does realise the torment of each minute. Some passages he has to repeat today, he will have to repeat again tomorrow. One has a conviction that one never gets near the goal in view.[1]

The colourful impression most people have of virtuosi was contradicted by Enesco when he said: "Poor devils! They are just like convicts (condemned to hard labour), martyrs . . . sometimes saints."

How true! When he goes to bed after a concert he sees his performance like a nightmare . . . of what it has been . . . of what it *could* have been.

Does this happen to you?

And how! Every time and always! Once I get to bed, I go through the whole thing in my mind and I see again, with perfect exactitude, everything which went off the rails, and I go through every single note. I cannot get to sleep until I have made this examination, exacting and painful.

And this may happen after the public has called you back a dozen times?

That side of success is only a thing of the moment, soon forgotten by the artist.

During some conversations Enesco had on the radio with Bernard Gavoty, he said that "on the one hand the impeccability which is expected from a virtuoso nowadays, and on the other the longing he has to evade the mechanical slavery, create a real conflict for the performer".

This is very true, and it has its origin principally in gramophone recording. Making a disc, where at least an external perfection is required, is conducive to mechanical performance. At a concert per-

---

[1] *In 1952 a barrister from Bombay sent a eulogistic letter to Casals in which he said, "For me you represent amongst performers what Bach and Beethoven represent amongst composers." Casals answered him: "I can only tell you, in all humility, that I have spent all my life working towards the ideal every artist should have. But I can also say that I am a long way from reaching the summit of the ideal, although I shall pursue it to my dying day."*

formance a slight hesitation or mistake may pass unnoticed, or in any case the general musicality of the performance can make up for it. There are some aspects in a performance—such as a slight mistake humanely understood—which should be considered of secondary importance, or, at least, ought not to become an agonising obsession; but the fact is that when making a gramophone record where every little detail is registered, the imposition on the artist is a real servitude and, what is worse, a dangerous servitude in regard to his inspiration or his musical feeling. We are now surrounded by mechanism everywhere.

The question of accelerating the tempi . . .

This is a serious and subtle problem. The question of *tempo* can be decided through the sense of measuring time in space, a sense which I believe I possess. This is a gift which does not belong to every artist and it is difficult for those without it to realise how the lack of it can make trouble in their performances. Yesterday afternoon, for example, a violoncellist came to see me. He had a masterly technique and a lot of feeling, and yet he had not got this sense of time in space. While he was playing the *Allemande* of one of the Bach Suites, he did not realise that in the succession of chords which form a cadence, these chords come too late one after the other, with the result that this "widening" made one lose the notion of the original *tempo*, and, in this case, he was not doing the repeats! (If he had been the result would have been fatal.) But nowadays artists who possess this sense of *tempo* risk losing it or, at least, forgetting it because of the modern tendency to play too fast. There are many reasons for this: the improvement of instruments and the technical achievement of performers, and so on. The modern tendency is to accelerate as much as possible all the quick *tempi* in order to achieve a success which is not very valuable. This inclination is spreading everywhere. A week ago, as I entered the drawing-room of a friend in Perpignan, I heard a gramophone record of the *Scherzo* from Mendelssohn's *A Midsummer Night's Dream*, and as I noticed the technical perfection and the speed of it, I thought it was an American orchestra. But at the end, as I realised it was played by a European orchestra of high repute, I had confirmation of what I consider to be a bad tendency: the systematic acceleration of *tempi*. This tendency seems to me very dangerous and as far as I am concerned I shall do all I can to counteract it.

Prokoviev wrote: "Some hundred and fifty years ago our ancestors were devoted to the gay pastorals of Rameau and Mozart; in the XIXth century everyone preferred slow and grave rhythms. Today we ask from music and from everything else speed, energy and movement."

This is true, and it is the reason why inspiration is so often lacking nowadays: somehow we must make an impression, even by artificial means. Systematic speed is artificial, and what is so regrettable today is the fact that these artificial methods should also deform the works of the great masters.

How do you come to know the real tempo?

There is no set rule: the words *allegro, adagio,* and so on are only "indications". The musical instinct of the performer must discover the *tempo* implied by printed words.

Your concern with precise tempo *gave rise to a controversy after you had conducted the Brahms'* Variations On a Theme of Haydn *in London.*

Yes, I did conduct this work. The controversy you allude to was on the subject of the 7th variation, marked 6/8 *Vivace,* which most conductors beat in two. Brahms, as well as Schumann, thought of these time signatures as meaning quite different things, and in 6/8 each note of the triplets has an effect which does not exist if you beat it in two. It is in the 6/8 time that this variation should be played. My rendering of it started discussion in the Press and in musical circles which lasted all the week. The whole thing became a sort of scandal until, on the following Sunday, *The Observer* wrote, "I was thankful to hear this variation played in its proper *tempo* for the first time, in fact as Brahms himself performed it."

To come back to the subject we discussed in the chapter on Bach and Handel, what do you think of this "historical fidelity", the respectful interpretation according to the customs of the period in which the work belonged?

Any historical knowledge is interesting and valuable, but the performer must deal with the music he is to play on its own merits. The artist of today cannot know or imagine with any certainty how a work was played in some remote period; anyone trying to pursue this way of "historical fidelity" risks becoming a crank, or being cramped by tiresome constrictions, and either possibility is contrary to the personal and actual conception required in any performance worthy of the name. We cannot revive feelings that are buried in the past. We don't know if we play better or less well than people did formerly. My opinion is that we play better because of the improvements in instruments, and also because we have benefited by the precious examples of the past. Haven't we got positive evidence that we know more and understand better than our ancestors how to play, for instance, Bach and Mozart?

In the Cahiers de Conversation *of Beethoven, we read that a friend said to him, "Yesterday they massacred your* Fifth Symphony." *It looks as if these crimes were the order of the day then as well as now.*

Neither the "purists" nor the "archaeologists" convince me. How do you imagine the orchestra sounded in the days of Mozart and Beethoven when all the wind instruments were "out of tune", as I explained to you before? And how much did the orchestral players of those days care for proper intonation? And that's only one thing. You all know that one of the duties of the leading violinist of those days was to drag the rest of the orchestra along. And that is exactly what happened: the leader was always heard very slightly ahead of the other instruments. That was considered normal; today we laugh about it. If only we had some gramophone records of how Beethoven Symphonies were played in those days! Many illusions would be destroyed. The great masters may have made do with the material at their disposal, but that does not mean they had no wish to improve or augment their orchestras. We read in one of Mozart's letters to his sister of his enthusiasm on hearing one of his compositions played by forty fiddles! Musical geniuses of all periods have always shown that they saw the necessity of enlarging and improving all the means of performance. And here is another point to consider: a masterpiece is something which is an actuality at all times. It is just the opposite to a fossil, since it continues to move us—thanks to its greatness and richness; we people of today should approach it with our own sensitiveness and conception of beauty.

Times have changed . . .

That is true, but I have an irresistible desire to blend together the different periods in a general perspective, so convinced am I that humanly and spiritually there is something common to all music.

So when a contemporary pianist says, "It is imperative now (having settled the question of tempo) *to put ourselves in the mind of the composer when he conceived his work." . . .*

That is obvious, as it is equally obvious that each artist must find his own way of "putting himself in the mind of the composer".

People say that when you study a work you read it first and sing the principal themes, after which you play the whole thing on the piano. Only when you have gathered some of its meaning do you take the 'cello and bow.

Yes. It is necessary for the musician to have technical mastery as well as a general conception of the work, and to know how to apply them to the particular work he studies. Nevertheless, during·this study and performance, he must guard against being a slave of technical possibilities, however good he is, and avoid anything which might lead to routine and monotony.

What do you think of Gieseking's method which he has inherited from his master Leimer? He never allowed him to use his instrument before he had completely assimilated the work in his head.

Hearing inwardly may give one a complete knowledge of the work. But I think it is not enough for an artist to learn music only through his eyes: he needs to experience sound physically. Although sound by itself will not change your idea of the work, the transmission of sound to the ear communicates a sort of exaltation which is beneficial and fruitful. When experiencing sound, I find that its richness helps me to create my performance in a way unlike simply reading from a score. The proof of this is that the artist finds something new in each performance, thus going further than he had decided when studying it visually!

Diran Alexanian says of you, "When he plays, each note is a prophecy or a recollection; this magician induces in us the presentiment of what is to come, as well as the remembrance of what has been."[1]

That is what I imagine form should be in the real meaning of the word. That is what musical interpretation requires: nothing should be isolated, each note is like a link in a chain—important in itself and also as a connection between what has been and what will be.

There are some artists who only feel inspired by reading or performing a piece when, at a given time, they recollect a landscape, or remember reading something which has helped them to penetrate the musical sense of the work in question.

That seems natural to me. When my pupils play, I sometimes ask them: what do you feel, what do you see? An artist has imagination and fantasy, and when he gives himself to music he ought to feel and see things, however vague and indefinite the vision.

What about his preoccupation with technical difficulties?

It all depends on his technical potentialities, and on the work he

[1] *Traité théorique et pratique du violoncelle.* (Editions Mathot, Paris.)

has done to overcome his difficulties. In any case, preoccupation with the instrument ought not to interfere with the performance or be noticed by the listener.

"*The problem of interpretation,*" says Furtwängler, "*is not one of technical difficulties. One must realise that formerly when we naïvely admired 'technique', it was a very different thing from what it is today. It was not the technique of a Bach or a Mozart (later, that of a Paganini or a Liszt) which struck the listeners of their day. Every time, it was their personality which found expression through the appropriate technique and exactly fitted their message.*"

This is so obvious that the fact that we should have to discuss it is a reflection of the confusion we are in nowadays.

"*Casals,*" said Alexanian, "*does not leave anything to chance. Everything he does is intended, thought out, selected from amongst all the different procedures which would lead to almost identical results. And perhaps it is this simple word: "almost" which should hold our attention . . . Casals has what he believes everyone should possess—control of all his thoughts, of all intentions, even those secondary ones which prevent complacency with approximate results. What he wants is full realisation, and until he has found it, he makes himself a docile and persevering servant of his reason.*"

It is only natural to try not to leave anything to chance. At no time do I want to go astray; each moment I must know where I am, in order to maintain a proper connection between all the different elements and not to lose the right proportions. I don't see why everyone should not do the same, or how any performer who is conscious of his responsibility could be satisfied with the "nearly" or the "approximate".

One day, last summer, sitting in this room waiting for the post to come, I heard you rehearsing a Beethoven Sonata you were supposed to record in Switzerland with Serkin. You stopped very often and annotated the parts. Considering you have played this work hundreds of times during the past fifty years, I could not help admiring your application.

Ah . . . you see, the reason is that, in a way, I always have to begin again. It is necessary to keep watch over habits, usual methods and careless confidence, any of which may endanger the spiritual state which is interpretation. We must try to work in such a way that for each performance our receptivity should be as free as it was when we first studied the work.

Is it true that in the course of time you have played certain passages in more than fifty different ways?

I have not counted them, but it is very likely. It is as I told you: however much we vary our playing in the course of our discoveries, we can never exhaust the multiplicity of nuances and subtleties which make the charm of music. And besides, how can we expect to produce a vital performance if we don't re-create the work every time? Every year the leaves of the trees reappear with the spring, but they are different every time.

People say that one of your most surprising faculties is the capacity you have for listening.

While I play I can hear the minutest details of my performance; I control them and my memory registers them. Isn't this the privilege and the torture of all performers?

Do you listen with a very strict sense of criticism?

Absolutely strict: I play, I listen, I judge myself.

You once told me that your contribution to music had consisted mostly in recalling the importance of its elementary and fundamental aspects.

Certainly. That is what I mean when I say that we know a lot of things but we forget the ABC. My aim has always been to revalue everything to do with music by the most natural means. This is an easy task for those who are able to see clearly the mutations of musical performance. The interpretation of a work is a series of expressions very like the series of vocal nuances and varied gestures which add to the expression of the spoken word: a little suspense, a question mark here and there, and so on.

Many people have noticed your insistence on the prime importance of intonation in performance.

Intonation must be the proof of the sensitiveness of an instrumentalist. Neglecting it is not acceptable for a serious performer and it lowers his standard, however good a musician he may be. It is curious to realise that this concern with good intonation is relatively recent among instrumentalists. When I was young I was stupefied to hear great players like Sarasate and Thompson play out of tune with the greatest ease in the world. In fact, having read many books on the classical period, I have never seen any reference to instrumental intonation, which makes me think that they did not attach much importance to it. And yet I can hardly believe that a composer like Mozart would not have felt the necessity of it. A great genius is always ahead of his time.

Would you tell me why you use the term "expressive" intonation?[1]

Intonation, as it is conceived today, has such sensitiveness and subtlety that the intonation of note must affect the listener, quite apart from any stimulating accent. The necessity of observing it is understood and observed by all good instrumentalists. In our day, the public would not accept a good soloist if he did not play in tune. Singers are taught "tempered" intonation, but I have noticed that the most gifted and the most artistic ones realise the importance and the subtlety of perfect intonation. The principle I am speaking of is of varied character in its application to string instruments. I make an exception for double-stopped playing: in this case one must compromise between expressive intonation and the "tempered" one.

Is there a marked difference?

I can give a demonstration which would astonish many people: for example I can prove with my system that there is a greater distance between a D♭ and a C♯ than there is in a semitone like C-D♭ or C♯-D♮.

It is a pity that such an essential part of performance as this real intonation should be, is still so neglected by some teachers. The other day when I was giving a young pupil his first lesson, I asked him how he had been taught; he said he had been taught intonation from the tempered piano. So you see what work he will have to do to correct this!

How do you reconcile "tempered" instruments with expressive intonation?

That is a kind of conflict which is, to me, more apparent than real. In those orchestras which possess great technical perfection and employ some first-class soloists (who practise this subtlety of semitones) the conflict does not arise, which proves that the "fusion"

[1] (*Here is a confused quotation of Alexanian, trying to explain what he thinks Casals means by "expressive intonation", but it does not really explain the point. Casals actually means that diatonic semitones are smaller than chromatic ones, and therefore it becomes a question of a sharper note being nearer the next note above it (such as F♯ to G) than to the semitone below it (such as G to G♭).*) (Note of translator.)

"In matters of intonation Casals does not concern himself with the comma, a distinction imposed by mathematical calculation between any given degree of the scale and its enharmonic equivalent. His insistence on the true quality of sharps and flats has a solid basis. He hardly recognizes sevenths or leading notes unless their specific harmonic tendencies draw them right away from the inertia of tempered pitch to the point where they are almost identical with their goal. This is what Casals calls *la justesse expressive*. And it is a thing which no musician can ever forget after hearing it in Casals' playing."

(*Alexanian.*)

between the "tempered" instruments and expressive intonation is perfectly possible.

You told me of the painful impression you get on hearing very good performers who are satisfied with the approximate intonation.

Yes, if an instrumentalist misses some difficult part of a passage, that does not influence my judgment, but I must say that I cannot forgive an approximate intonation in a so-called artistic performance. I want to feel that the performer has a constant care for perfect intonation which reflects his musical sensitiveness.

It must be very difficult to acquire perfect intonation for a student of a string instrument?

Of course it is, and I feel convinced that it should be dealt with at the beginning of his studies. Either because of insufficient listening power or through having contracted the habit of compromise, which is "tempered" intonation, the student will need to undergo a "cure" for his aural sense. Only yesterday I had the joy of seeing a pupil of mine, after long explanations and demonstrations, beginning to realise how much better he could hear the exact sound. The effects of any neglect of this kind at the beginning of studies (which is very frequent) can affect a player through the whole of his career, however gifted he may be.

I have read that your sense of distances is so accurate that you were able to play the Haydn Concerto when you had such a bad cold that you were quite unable to hear yourself play.

That happened to me more than once.

Shortly before the Prades Festival of 1952, you received a letter from Alexander Schneider in which he said, "When we arrive this year, I wonder if you will have put new strings on your 'cello?"

I have a great affection for my strings and it costs me a lot to change them. They always sound best just before they break. My friends seem to enjoy this attachment. . . . I keep my strings on as long as possible, and if one breaks before a concert it worries me a lot because I have to do a lot of preparation in order to get used to the characteristics of a new string.

And what happens if they break during a concert?

That has happened to me and it is far from being funny—but one must know how to control oneself. I must say that an audience is always sympathetic when this happens.

You have introduced many reforms in 'cello technique.

These modifications, which I applied when I was still very young, were always suggested to me through the necessities of the moment (but I never had any preconceived ideas of making innovations). Some of these technical ideas of mine are already widespread, but it does not mean that, at first, they did not shock many players of the old school.[1] One of these modifications consisted of using the extension of the fingers in a general way; this makes the playing easier and avoids a lot of shifts which are often detrimental to the music played.

Some people think that you have an exceptional hand which allows you to do these fingerings.

No, I have not an exceptional hand, but it is a flexible one which allows me these great extensions of fingers I told you of. If one's hands are too small it would be better to give up playing the 'cello. But with a normal hand a 'cellist should be able to include this extension of fingers in his technical equipment. These extensions should be practised in such a way that the maximum result can be attained with the least possible contraction of the muscles. In each case I choose the fingering which seems the simplest and the safest. I used to employ these extensions on a large scale but I have given up some of the more tiring ones in favour of the nearly natural fingering. We never gain anything by trying to do things against nature. Neither is it necessary to do so, since it is sufficient to know how to use the means nature has put at our disposal.

I have heard you insist on the necessity of taking every chance of relaxing muscular tensions.

That is very important. Playing the 'cello is so difficult and requires such a tension of the left hand that it becomes necessary to do certain exercises to maintain its flexibility in preparation for a performance. One of the things I teach my pupils is to know how and at what moment they can relax the hand and the arm. Even in the course of a rapid passage it is possible to find the right moment to relax. (This may happen within the tenth of a second.) It becomes a fundamental necessity in performance and if one does not take it into account there comes a time when one cannot relax (it is like being unable to breathe) and exhaustion sets in. This fatigue of the hand and arm mostly comes from the tension of the muscles produced through emotion and "stagefright". However, the will of the performer must overcome this

[1] *Casals receives many letters from 'cellists who show their appreciation and gratitude: here is an extract from a recent one written by a 'cellist in Cleveland:* "I know now that if my interpretations are successful I owe it all to you: you have changed the old way of playing the 'cello through your musicianship, the finger extensions (new fingering) and the suppression of unnecessary *glissandos*."

obstacle, and to this end the conscious practising of relaxation will prove very beneficial to complete control during a concert.

What about physical exhaustion?

Alas! I have known it more than once. It comes from too much work and general weariness. If one is forced to play in such a state it becomes a real martyrdom. One just feels empty and unable to give anything.

In spite of your long years of playing in public, I believe you have always been nervous before a concert?

Think of the number of great performers I have met in my long career—they all suffered from stage-fright, with some rare exceptions. (Fritz Kreisler, for instance, used to say he felt perfectly "at home" on the platform.) But can you imagine that I have not known any artist as tormented as I am with nerves? The thought of a public concert always gives me a nightmare.

Even now?

Yes, even now.

If I am not mistaken, when we talked of relaxation, you had your ideas confirmed by Coué's method. It was through auto-suggestion?

No, I was not interested in the auto-suggestion part of Coué's method, but in the fact that it taught one to relax completely different parts of the body, which is a thing many people could not do even if they wanted to. If you pay attention you can notice that when we think we are in a complete state of relaxation, we can generally find some part of the body that could be relaxed more. And don't you believe it is easy to do unless we have been through long exercises, which are exactly what we want, to keep up the suppleness of the arm and the fingers.

Do I understand that the necessary impulse to produce these flexible movements must come from the centre of the body?

This is, I believe, a theory entirely my own—at least no one ever talked to me about it, not even Monasterio. Only this impulse, coming from the centre of the body instead of each extremity, will group the different movements in a unified whole, producing better results and less fatigue. This impulse, coming from what I call the centre of the body, is rather like an image of what I feel at the time, not an easy thing to identify or to name.

This constant search for flexibility may partly explain the fact that at the age of seventy-seven you can still astonish those who listen to you performing works as exhausting as the Bach Suites?

It may have had a beneficial influence on me, and if at at my age I am able to continue playing the 'cello it is probably due to the muscular and nervous equilibrium which my organism fortunately possesses.

But don't you think that this precious equilibrium is partly due to some mental factor also? When you take your 'cello it looks as if some transformation came over you. Do you think you would keep the same balance and suppleness if you took on some manual work?

Very probably, if such work interested me a lot. But I am an absolute dud at doing any odd jobs or anything of that kind. Oddly enough my father and my two brothers were past masters at anything practical. The only "manual work" I understand is to play the 'cello or any other instrument. For instance, when two little boys came to see me the other day to show me the flageolets their parents had bought for them at the fair, I immediately seized one and played some well-known tunes for their benefit.

There is another question I want to put to you: everyone has always noticed how you make an entry: the very first note you play. . . .

Bravo! What you ask me is a very important and subtle question. It is not given to everyone to know how to play the first note of a work. When I hear my pupils play the first bar of a score, I often stop them and say, "No, this is not like a beginning." And yet it is not particularly a question of technique, but of sensitiveness, which is very difficult, if not impossible, to define or analyse.

I would say that your way of playing requires a great variety in the accents, and its superabundance of nuances would explain the wealth of colours on your palette.

The performer must first decide on the character of the piece he plays. Normally, nuances and accents will be different with each performer; either they are right or not: there is no rule in existence to settle these questions. Nevertheless the beauty and expressive value of a performance demands from the player an endless wealth of nuances in every part of the work he plays. Accentuation does not mean uniform intensity. Nothing that was uniform could move us. In fact it is the *diminuendo* following a *forte* accent which gives it its value, and what will give a *piano* indication a lively feeling is to bring slight variations of intensity into it. What happens in painting? When the artist wishes to make a colour stand out, he tones down the ones around it: in the same way with music, an accentuated note will stand out and keep its value, not so much because of its special intensity but principally because of the shade which succeeds it. These remarks find a parallel in a law of nature: *Let us shout very loud and observe the endless diminuendo which follows*. The performance of music cannot exclude this most natural reality.

On the whole, musical accents should be placed according to the character of the work in each of its sections. To know how to grade them according to their importance will on the one hand establish their relation with each other, and on the other, with the bulk of the work, thus unifying them into an organic whole.

My conception of musical accentuation offers some analogy with the use of the spoken word, that is to say with the endless inflections we use in our voices so that the words find their real meaning.

In the early years of my journeys through Europe and America, I heard that people were wondering "what is special about Casals?" I feel sure that the special things they thought I had came from the fusion of the principles I have been talking of.[1] When they are more widespread and applied to the orchestra, they will give it new and more rational expressive possibilities.

What was the origin of these principles?

When I was very young my instinct led me to observe and realise the amount of subtleties and nuances contained in music; later on I was able to make comparisons and analogies between my observations and the natural reality—so rich, so varied and so marvellously expressive of the spoken word. I can still remember the surprise of my teacher, Monasterio, when I talked to him about my ideas.

You barred the habit of constantly using the bow in all its length, didn't you?

Yes, I opposed any method which advocated such a course—I find that whenever something seems to go against music it is reflected in an ugly and inelegant gesture; even in my childhood I felt awkward whenever I watched violinists or violoncellists using the whole bow all the time. It seemed useless to me. The bow, being an element of performance, should be used according to the music one plays. It is quite natural to use it in all its length for long notes just as it is to use only part of it for shorter notes. The right hand should have the power to use whichever part of the bow is appropriate to the musical meaning of each note.

Both in the French School of playing and in the Belgian one

---

[1] *A critic has written saying it was very difficult to talk of "Casals as a musician" because "everything he does seems so natural that there is nothing to say!"*

(which have influenced each other), there has been a leading pre-occupation with what they call *l'archet à la corde*, which has become such an obsession that, in many cases, it went against the requirements of the language of music. This has led to an abuse of strength on the string and has resulted in a lowering of the musical interest through the impression of monotony it produces. My conception of interpretation prescribes a great variety of colours in loud as well as in soft passages. The range of expression goes from the softest *pianissimo* to the loudest *fortissimo*; besides, as I told you before, even a *fortissimo* will not sound like one, unless we add a *diminuendo*, which is precisely what will make the accent sound important.

Therefore you can understand why I oppose the principle of *l'archet à la corde* as anti-musical conducive to monotony and contrary to the economy of energy which a performance demands. Thanks to my pupils and followers, my views are already widespread and fairly well understood.

In order to acquire the maximum of suppleness in the handling of the bow, the first thing and the most elementary is to hold it properly. One sees such curious things: only the other day as I was giving the first lesson to a new pupil, I noticed that he was holding his bow with all the fingers pointing to the right, which produced an unnecessary contortion of the wrist, bound to be tiring in the end. The bow must rest on the first joint and should press on the point of articulation of the first and second joint. In that position the hand is placed naturally and the wrist is free.

At one time you had a piece of cork round the nut of your bow, and one noticed the number of 'cellists who adopted it—in the belief they had discovered your "secret".

However supple one keeps one's right hand, the thumb is bound to exert a considerable pressure. I began to have cramp, and I thought it was due to the drawing of the fingers too near to the thumb (which also happens to writers). That was why I had this piece of cork fixed on the bow, and I was amused to see how some other 'cellists imitated me without any physical reason for it. But that was a long time ago and fortunately the cramp went and with it the piece of cork!

Diran Alexanian speaks of "the eternal logic of Casals, always based on the reasoning which leads to evidence!" Ludwig noticed that in the course of conversation you often used the French word raison. Was this what was meant by the person who described your work as "controlled inspiration"?

Alexanian (who is an exceptional person) and myself have exchanged views for years on the question of 'cello and performance; these talks with him have always been most stimulating. He talks about my "eternal logic". But is this logic not guided and nourished by intuition?

In order to answer your question, I must explain that when I was young standards of interpretation were in a state of confusion. I felt it was necessary for me to bring my personal contribution into performance, without losing a sense of responsibility. I tried to bring order and normality into my playing.

All that must have required self-discipline.

Naturally!

But do you think discipline and spontaneity can work together?

In every branch of art, as well as in music, the work of preparation ruled by discipline should finally disappear, so that the elegance and freshness of the form should strike us as being spontaneous.

Could one say that Ysaye and Paderewski still belonged to a romantic age?

Possibly!

On the other hand, a critic has said that he finds in your mind the classic and the romantic.

I don't know, it is possible! You know that I don't care very much for this sort of classification.

In the days of Liszt, Chopin and Schumann, when romanticism was at its height, do you think your interpretations would have been appreciated as much as they are now?

If I had lived then, maybe I would not have been the same as I am now, and very probably my musical conceptions would also have been different.

I mentioned Paderewski just now: a critic, Marc Pincherlé, says that he was "inconsistency personified" but, more than anyone, could give in his best moments the highest impression of real creation!

Paderewski belonged to the period of confusion I was talking about. In his performance there were sublime moments, and at other times he would produce what I would describe as "musical whims" wrongly applied.

And Busoni?

Busoni was a very great artist with whom I played on many

occasions. I had such sympathy and admiration for him that, even when I did not agree with him, I always respected and accepted his convictions—I could not say the same about Paderewski. There was an astonishing aspect revealed in some of Busoni's performances; perhaps a spirit of contradiction, or more likely a deliberate purpose of deforming what he felt. For instance, he played the César Franck *Prelude, Choral et Fugue* in a diabolical way, a composition so full of mystical elevation. Knowing Busoni as I did, I could see that he was working against himself and was deliberately distorting the work.

Have you played with Arthur Rubinstein?

Yes, and he was very young then, perhaps eighteen, and hardly known as a pianist.

Which pianists do you admire most?

There are so many remarkable ones, but I think Rudolf Serkin stands apart for his profound and extraordinary musicianship.

A name to be remembered is Eugène Istomin, a young American of Russian parents. When I first heard him at the Bach Festival in Prades he was only twenty-five, but he made a great impression on me. I had not met such a mature artist of that age, and I would include him among the greatest pianists.

Amongst the contemporary 'cellists, I know you have a great regard for Feuerman and Piatigorsky!

Yes, what a great artist Feuerman was! His early death was a great loss to music.

What do you think of Pincherlé's opinion of present-day violinists? "Amongst the younger of the international champions (including Menuhin, so prodigiously gifted in many ways), I cannot see the appearance of any personality as generous and deeply original as that of Joachim, Ysaye or Kreisler."

I don't think Joachim was conspicuous for his originality (at least, the Joachim I heard). His performances aimed so much at being classical that they became rather cold.

I had the impression that he was afraid of exceeding certain limits, and consequently did not let himself go. Every time I heard him play alone or with his quartet, he made me feel that he did not always produce what there was in the music he played. But, mind you, Joachim had, obviously, a great personality, and his performances always commanded respect and sometimes attained great heights. And after this "classicism" we had the overflowing imagination of Ysaye's genius.

Another great artist who has influenced the younger generation of violinists by his personality is Fritz Kreisler. A few years later came Georges Enesco, a great interpreter for whom my admiration was limitless. And Jacques Thibaud, a star from Heaven, whom I consider as a natural product of the French School (although he was later influenced by his elders, Ysaye and Kreisler).

Following in chronological order we find Jascha Heifetz, an incredible violinist whose expression may sometimes sound excessive, but is so perfectly harmonious with the rest that it gives his playing impressive brilliance.

And we must not forget the two great names of Joseph Szigeti and Yehudi Menuhin.

Young Isaac Stern has, in my opinion, happily acquired the best characteristic of his illustrious predecessors, and he has done it in a way which has created a natural and harmonious whole.

Do you think there is progress in the domain of interpretation?

I think there is—and I sometimes wonder what artists like Liszt or Anton Rubinstein were really like, and what effect they would have on us if we heard them today.

In the days of our grandfathers (or even fathers) we were much struck by virtuosity, but, today, general standards of technique have so improved that we are not impressed by it any more, unless there is real musical thought behind it.

Have you had your superb Bergonzi 'cello a long time?

About fifty years—I call it a Bergonzi-Goffriller, because it is one of the most beautiful instruments made by Mateo Goffriller, a Tyrolese who settled in Cremona. I have never found a violoncello which suited my hands better. It takes a few years to get used to an instrument, to master its possibilities and to know its limitations.

Before you had this 'cello, did you play on the Gagliano which Queen Maria Cristina gave you?

Yes!

How is it that you never played on a Stradivarius?

I have never been tempted by a Stradivarius. These superb instruments have too much personality in my opinion; if I play on one, I cannot forget that I have a Stradivarius in my hands, and it disturbs me considerably. I said to a friend one day, talking of these instruments, "Their Majesties mind very much how one plays on them!"

All the same, you very nearly bought one of them!

It is true—a very long time ago. I was once fascinated by a Stradivarius 'cello belonging to Mr. Mendelssohn and considered the best one in existence. I made him an offer, but he did not accept it. Now I am glad he did not, for the reasons I have given you, and also because it was too big for me. It would have had to be shortened, which might have spoiled it. Mr. Mendelssohn emigrated to America when the Nazi persecution was on. He had a tragic end, but his 'cello is now in the hands of a well-known violin dealer in New York.

The Spanish Royal family had a quartet of Stradivarius instruments which had been specially made for them, and it had a second violoncello equally splendid. I am certain that if I had asked her, the Queen would have been pleased to lend me this second instrument. Some time after the change of *régime* in Spain, the republican authorities expressly put this instrument at my disposal. I felt very grateful, but decided to decline the offer. However, at that time I went to visit the Royal Palace in Madrid, and made arrangements for the instruments to be well looked after and preserved from deterioration.

I can remember a period when your Goffriller was being repaired and you played on a modern instrument!

Yes! The excellent violin-master of Mirecourt, Mr. Laberte, made an exact copy of my Goffriller for me. This instrument, although completely new, had some wonderful qualities.

One day, while I was rehearsing a concerto with Ysaye conducting the orchestra, he asked me, "Is it a Strad?" I did not say anything but just smiled. But when I explained what it was, Ysaye could not get over it.

Unfortunately, when I took this instrument to America for a tour, the different climate was so harmful that it lost a great deal of its magnificent tone.

This seems to be a proof that modern instruments ought not to be underestimated, as they generally are.

On this subject I can tell you about a very curious fact. My friend, Auguste Mangeot, the Director of the *Monde Musical* in Paris (and the founder of the *École Normale de Musique*), had often discussed with me the difficulty for students and young musicians of acquiring old Italian instruments, and the quite unjustified contempt people have for new instruments. We decided to "have a trial" (it was about 1910). We organised a competition which took place at the *Salle des Agriculteurs* in Paris. There were forty 'celli, some of them by Stradivarius and other well-known makers. I played on them all, except for three or four which were played by a 'cellist called Levenson. We had given a number to each instrument and a list to each listener. While I played the hall was kept in darkness, and when the lights were put on the listeners wrote down their impression of the last number. Do you know which instrument got the highest praise? A 'cello made by the maker Paul Kaul from Nantes. (This instrument had been brought to me by Paul Kaul and his associate a few months previously, when they asked me to play it.)

Another competition took place two or three years later, and it was for violins this time. Curiously enough, it was an instrument made by the same Paul Kaul which won the competition.

Your patience with pupils is well known, but I see that you also have to give them a lesson in modesty on occasion!

Most of the 'cellists who come to see me and wish me to hear them ask if they may play a Bach Suite. "Play whatever you like," I say, "even a Waltz. By the way you handle your instrument, I shall see straightaway how you stand."

Young musicians complain of their difficulties in making a start.

These difficulties have always existed. I advise my pupils and any young musicians to resist the temptation to give recitals in the big capitals. They would spend all they have earned through years of work, as well as what they have not yet earned. Anyone who has real talent gets recognition sooner or later.

Also, nowadays, there are international competitions.

Perfectly true! In my young days they did not exist. However, when I read the results of these competitions, I cannot help thinking of the numerous and bitter deceptions they may occasion. As a matter of fact I don't envy those who sit on the jury for these competitions. I remember only too well what happened to me in Paris once. Fauré, who was then Director of the Conservatoire, asked me if I would write the sight-reading piece for the 'cello competition. I agreed to do it, but at the same time I warned him that my piece would only take into account the standard I imagined should be that of a laureate of the Conservatoire of the French capital. Fauré agreed and said "Do what you think is right."

The day of the *concours* the hall was absolutely filled with the students, their families and their friends. Now what happened was that not one of the candidates could read the piece I had written. This started a terrific scandal, and I had to be let out through a special door, escorted by a few friends! This is what it costs to be honest!

When you hear some of your performances recorded on gramophone records, are you satisfied?

Not always. I very often do not recognise my tone. To my mind, once the playing has gone through a machine it loses the vitality the artist has put into it. Maybe it is bound to happen!

And yet the technique of recording is improving all the time.

That may be, but I still prefer the recordings of some thirty years ago. The tone is not so bright but more faithful.

I should like to hear what has been done with the recordings of the Bach Suites I made in 1937 and 1939, which have been adapted to long-playing records. It took me over a year to prepare these. I should be interested to see if the slow movements are not spoiled by mechanical factors, and if the personality of the performer comes through. As a rule, I prefer to hear the records I have made played faster. In the case of my records of the Bach Suites I like to hear them a tone, even a tone and a half, sharper. The difference of keys does not worry me at all.

Are you still decided against writing a treatise on 'cello playing?

Yes! I have spent my life meditating on the instrument and the works written for it, and, no doubt, I could say endless things on the subject. The performance of a few notes perfectly placed requires an analysis which would occupy pages of writing. So think of the length of a book which would deal with all these matters in detail!

And yet, this is not the principal reason; just as with the written signs of music, printed words cannot transcribe the meaning of music. How could one communicate the richness and the life of a single phrase by writing about it? And the hundreds of varieties in dynamics that are contained in a whole work? I don't think it is possible. Besides, what is written remains frozen, petrified, whereas my technique is always on the move. And since technique for me is a means and not an end, it naturally follows the lines of my own experiments and evolution.

What about gramophone records, which would register some of your lessons, not only with words but also with 'cello playing as you do?

That would be much more interesting. One American firm did approach me about it, but I did not see clearly what this firm had in mind, and I abandoned the idea.

From what you have told me, and what you have said, it follows that you are not thinking of publishing your editions of 'cello works? Not even the Bach Suites, for which you probably have received dozens of offers?

No! There will not be any edition of mine, of either the Bach Suites or the Beethoven Sonatas, although I have been asked by quantities of publishers to do it. (For the Suites I use the facsimile edition of Anna-Magdalene, Bach's copy.)

My way of performing a work does not last longer than the actual playing of it: that is to say, I don't know, and cannot know beforehand, if I shall not introduce modifications when playing it afresh. What would happen then when those who listen to me realise I am not observing the indications I wrote myself, and which they may have observed literally? This is what I was saying previously—my technical means develop side by side with my personal conceptions, and I don't see how I can communicate these unless I do it with my 'cello in my hands and—by chance—bringing some new contribution to each performance. I don't agree with those who, preparing some new edition, in order to justify their work, cram it with their personal additions. It creates such confusion; there are already too many editions, and mine would only add to the general confusion. The only thing that matters is the personal way of performing the notes and values we have in front of us, and there is no edition which can do that for us.

Alexanian says that you have established "a complete code of instrumental logic which can be continued and developed by anyone who will seriously study the violoncello".

Of course, the study of 'cello-playing cannot stop at the stage to which I brought it. What would you say of a tree which only came out one spring? For a tree to be fertile, its boughs must grow every year.

Much better than any treatises or editions, my pupils, all those who have had direct contact with me, will carry on my method and my conceptions. They will transmit and develop them. With musical interpretation, as in any other artistic activity, there cannot be any definite boundaries.

X

Before and During Exile

Is it a long time since you went to play in Russia for the last time?
Yes. I have often spoken to you about my great friend Siloti, who
was the beloved disciple of Liszt. His wife came from a great Russian
family. His father-in-law had founded the Museum of Modern Art
in Moscow and made a gift of it to the city. Siloti lived in St. Petersburg. He devoted all his talent and work to the cause of popular
education, and by so doing raised the mental standards of the people.
He and a few friends subsidised the running of an important orchestra,
which gave concerts for the students and the workers. He led a simple
life, free from ostentation. He lived for his art and for the people. The
most eminent Russian musicians met at his house. Then came the
October Revolution, when everything was taken from him and he
was subjected to all the usual inquisitions and interrogations. He became ill; as a living-place for his wife and five children he was given the
kitchen of his own house and a small adjacent room. The rest of his
house was occupied by young men of the new *régime* where they led a
life of debauchery. In order to survive, Siloti and his family had to do
the most impossible and degrading things. The only valuable they
managed to hide was a necklace. And it was thanks to the value of this
that after two or three years of martyrdom they managed to escape to
Finland.

I was very worried about them, since I did not receive any news.
But one day, when I was in Barcelona, there was a letter from Antwerp
from Siloti saying "We are here." I went off immediately, and when I
met them at Antwerp I could hardly recognise them; they looked like
ghosts. Since that day I have never wanted to go back to Russia. I do
realise that in a revolution certain excesses cannot, unfortunately, be
avoided, but I don't accept that, under the pretext of forming a new
social order, these leaders think they can persecute blindly the very
people who have *practised* fraternity with the workers and the people.

*One can read in Dostoievsky's The Brothers Karamazov the often
quoted question, "Would you sacrifice the child who is in front of you to
follow a revolutionary doctrine?"*

No, never! The end does not justify the means. I have protested and always shall protest against inhuman means.

And a few years later we had the Nazis who began persecuting people. . . .

Ah . . . when I saw that Einstein, Thomas Mann, Bruno Walter and so many illustrious personalities of science and the arts had to expatriate themselves, some persecuted because of their race,[1] others because of their ideas, I thought it was my duty to protest, and I declared I would not go back to Germany until intellectual and artistic liberties were restored. When, later on, Mussolini imitated the Nazis, I adopted the same attitude towards Italy.

The only weapons I possess are the 'cello and the conductor's baton. They are not very deadly, but I have no others, and do not wish to have any. In the circumstances I used what I had to protest against what I considered was disgraceful and ignominious.

However, the German public had a great veneration for you.

For me, it was very painful to leave them, but I thought that by taking this attitude I was more faithful to Bach and Beethoven, and all they stood for, than to the people who through weakness or fanaticism soiled the honour of a great country.

This attitude, and the one you took later, have raised a lot of comment on the subject of the relation between art and politics.

I am not a politician. I never have been and do not pretend to be one. I am simply an artist. But the question is whether art is to be a pastime, a toy for men to play with, or if it should have a deep and human meaning. Politics do not belong to an artist but, to my mind, he is under an obligation to take sides, whatever sacrifice it means, if human dignity becomes involved. Besides, the word politics, if not used in good faith, can cover up much confusion. It may mean the ordinary legislation of each nation, in which I have no right to interfere unless it concerns my own country. But the politics we spoke of concern the governments which betrayed the general rights of human nature. In this case moral principles are involved which prevail above all frontiers; all men of good will should fight against the violation of these principles.

Since the affaire Dreyfus *the goodwill of men seems to have declined, and for some time now we have been in a period called the "time of contempt". You are a glorious "survival".*

But is it possible that moral principles (which are not the same

[1] *"Casals is the only Aryan artist who has made a definite stand against the new barbarians."* (Emil Ludwig.)

thing as political formulas) should become unfashionable? If a persecution was unjust fifty years ago, would it not be so today? The great
victory of our civilisation is that it gives us a guarantee against being
persecuted for our ideas or feelings; also that the power which rules us
instead of being absolute and irresponsible, will be elected and controlled
by the people without exception. If this conquest is lost (and we have
sad instances of it) we see the appearance of barbarous despots, and the
fear and trembling of the subordinates. When it gets to that state my
conscience forces me to protest.

The artist in his ivory tower?

It would be too easy, under the pretext of artistic neutrality, to
retire into it, instead of fighting injustice. I have shown to you my
conception of all art, which should elevate and not degrade us. Considering that an artist is a man, he cannot as a man withdraw from his
solidarity with his fellow-creatures.

When I see innocent blood spilled and the tears of the victims of
injustice, it becomes more important to me than my music and all my
'cello recitals!

In the course of the first and terrible phase of the Spanish tragedy,
I got so indignant one day that I did not hesitate to risk my life to save
a man who was persecuted. I was at Sant Salvador practising the 'cello.
Two armed men entered my room and said, "We have been told that
Mr. X is here." (He was a business man from Barcelona who spent the
summer in a house next to mine.) "He is not here," I said. They went
off. A moment later they returned with poor Mr. X, whom they had
arrested, and who already feared the worst; his wife was at his side
crying. "We know you have a telephone and we want to telephone to
Vendrell to get them to send a cart." (Those famous carts they used for
carrying condemned people to be shot.)

I faced them and said: "I shall do the telephoning, not you. Why
did you arrest this man? You can do what you like but you will not
take Mr. X away, do you hear?" They had revolvers and guns. I had
nothing: but the tone of my voice made them understand that I meant
what I said. They had a moment of hesitation which was decisive. They
muttered, "We had orders from the Mayor of Vendrell." I took the
telephone and talked to the man who was supposed to be the mayor.
My words were of such a kind that he got frightened and said: "These
men have made a mistake. I told them to go somewhere else." The tone
of his voice belied his words. I communicated his answer to the men
and told them they could go and that Mr. X would stay. As they went

through the door they gave me a look of hatred and threatened me as well.

It shows that you had taken a stand.

Yes. For me and most of the Spanish intellectuals it was a question of principle: the main responsibility for the civil war fell on those who tried to abolish by force a legitimate Government (which had been elected by popular votes a few months before). And when their *pronunciamento* failed, they tried to secure the help of Fascist Italy and Nazi Germany. In all civilised countries one should accept the decision of the people, and those who are not satisfied should wait for the next elections.

The Barcelona University bestowed on you the title of Doctor honoris causa *in rather strange circumstances.*

Very strange, when you think that the authorities of the Academy signed the diploma the day before Franco's Army came into Barcelona! That was the last meeting of the Catalonia University. Italian aircraft were flying over the town all the time, evacuation had already started, and yet, at a time as painful and critical as it was, my country thought of paying me such a moving tribute. I shall never forget it.

When the civil war ended, did you decide to live in Prades immediately?

No. I had been away a little while, playing at concerts, and when the war ended I was in Paris, ill with all the symptoms of nervous depression. I was staying with an old pupil and was kept all day in complete darkness, as I could not bear any light. I felt broken and worn out. The news I got from home was terrible: oppression had begun in Catalonia; thousands of refugees were shut up in concentration camps in the South of France; my house in Sant Salvador was occupied and ransacked by the Franco troops; my brother Lluis was maltreated in Vendrell because he was my brother. . . . His situation obsessed me. He had such a fine character. During an epidemic of cholera at Vendrell he had done some wonderful acts of devotion without telling anybody. A friend from Barcelona came to see me in Paris. He was the first person who told me about Prades, where he had been a resident. He said it was a pretty little town at the foot of the Canigou, where almost everyone talks Catalan. This got me out of my torpor. I left Paris and went to Perpignan, where I met my friend Pichot. We visited many places on the coast as I am very fond of the sea. This was in the autumn of 1939: everything was already closed and I did not fancy any of the places I saw. Then I decided to go and live in Prades.

Did you enjoy your stay?

As soon as I got there the Catalan landscape acted on me like a sedative.

You had some hard work in front of you?

As soon as I felt better I gave myself up to the task of relieving my unfortunate compatriots who were living in the camps. Some Catalan friends, exiled in Prades also, helped me to organise everything with the greatest enthusiasm. I took a room in an hotel where we set up a regular office to centralise all the gifts, the purchases, the demands and distribution. We had lorries loaded with food and garments going to the camps. I wrote to friends for funds and we were glad of any gifts.

You visited the camps pretty often?

Yes, specially those at Argeles, Rivesalte, Vernet, Septfonds and some others. These camps were frightful, not because of deliberate cruelty but simply because of the improvisation and confusion which prevailed when they were established. The unfortunate people who were shut up there lacked the most elementary commodities. I realised that my visits brought some consolation to those who had lost contact with the world outside and who were lamentably demoralised, hopeless and abandoned. I tried to send small gifts to all those who asked me, and wrote little notes of encouragement. In those days I wrote thousands of letters and postcards.

The Second World War had started. Did you expect any danger?

Yes, I did. And my friends abroad even more. I received so many letters from American friends advising me to leave Europe and come to them.

To be exiled in America, sheltered from all danger, and also able to make a fortune with playing . . .

No, I could not do that. My duty was to stay with my compatriots who, like myself, had been hunted from their country, and try to comfort them with my presence. Also, since I had taken a stand against totalitarians, I had a moral obligation to stay when the war started which was supposed to rid Europe of totalitarianism—at least that is what I then believed would happen.

When the French defeat came in June 1940, you must have found yourself in a difficult position.

Very. At that time I thought all was lost in Europe. Also the rumour was spreading that the Spanish Army, taking advantage of the French retreat as the Italians had done, would cross the Pyrenees. Some refugee friends and I hired two cars to go to Bordeaux, in the hope of sailing to England from there. Before leaving I had burnt all the compromising papers I had, to save my correspondents from pursuit. (How I regretted the destruction of thousands of letters I had received from the camps. They formed a human document of such extraordinary interest.) When we reached Bordeaux we heard that the ship we hoped to sail in had been sunk by the German Air Force the day before. We tried other ships but it was all impossible, and we had to return to Prades, which we reached after a very difficult journey as all the roads were filled with refugees. There was such a panic at the time that when we got back to our hotel at Prades, in the middle of the night, no one would open the door, and it was only because the tobacconist opposite heard us and let us in that we did not spend the night outside. After that I went to live in the *Villa Colette* for a few years.

I went on with the work of helping my compatriots in the camps. Some of them had been transformed into what they called *Compagnies de Travailleurs*, which was a modern version of organised slavery. But with the news of the wonderful *résistance anglaise* we got more confident in the final issue of the conflict. Like millions of people, we anxiously listened every night to the radio from London. Things were difficult and food was seriously restricted.

Did you continue to give concerts during these years?

Before and after June 1940 I went to Switzerland in order to get the necessary funds to live on. When the French armistice was signed I thought I ought to help the French, who were going through a very difficult time, and gave concerts for charity in the free zone, Lyons, Marseilles, Perpignan; but after the Allied landing in North Africa the whole of France was occupied. I would not leave Prades, and with the German troops everywhere I thought silence was the only possible attitude.

Did the Germans worry you?

Once some agents of the Gestapo came to the *Villa Colette* and went through every bit of paper I had, and when they retired said: "Be careful. If our suspicions are confirmed we will arrest you."

The atmosphere became more and more intolerable; one day from my room window I saw three German officers coming through the gate and I thought we were for it. They came in, behaved extremely well, and said, after a military salute, "We are great admirers of yours and we have come to greet you and find out how you are." They sat down and started a conversation which lasted over two hours. "So you

are the Casals our fathers and grandfathers told us about?" "I am."
After a series of praises they came to the usual question: "And why
don't you go and play in Germany?" "For the same reason I do not go
and play in Spain." "We think you are mistaken. Hitler is a great man,
who protects artists and the arts." "That is your opinion; I have mine."
"Wouldn't you like to come and play in Berlin again? Hitler himself
will come and hear you, and if you like we'll put a railway carriage at
your disposal." "No, thank you." I guessed they wanted me to play
to them, but I was determined I would not do it. So when they asked
me to take my 'cello, I told them I had had rheumatic pains in the
shoulder for some days, and could not play. They insisted and said,
"Just a few notes." I refused. They saw my instrument and plucked the
strings. I felt disturbed at the thought that perhaps these hands had
spilled blood or were tainted. "Is this the 'cello you played on in
Germany?" "Very often." The Commandant sat at the piano and
started a Bach aria to get me going . . . it was useless.

"We cannot go away without a souvenir from you." I understood
their chief would ask them for proof of their visit; I signed a photograph on which I wrote: "In remembrance of your visit to Prades."
As they went, and I looked out of the window, they asked me if they
could take a photograph (another proof). I did not see them again.
But I had not played for them.

*After the Allied landing in Normandy, the situation must have been even
more tense.*

Yes. A young man who was engaged to the daughter of a friend of
mine, and who had joined the "French Militia" so that he would not
be sent to Germany, told me he had seen my name on a list of people
who were to be arrested, and heard the local chief say "When the
time comes, Casals will see what is in store for him." This young man
had the courage to stand up to him and said it was infamous and that
he would lodge a protest in front of anyone concerned.

For some reason we were left at liberty after the landing took place.
During those days every hour seemed like a hundred years. There was
a moment of great danger: the *Maquis* operating in the Pyrenees came
to Prades and attacked the house where the Gestapo were operating.
One German got killed and many were wounded. What would be the
reprisals? We could have been shot. Fortunately the Mayor of Prades
went to the military commander and told him all the responsibility for
the attack should be his. Nothing happened, and shortly afterwards
the moment we had been waiting for arrived. The German troops

evacuated the town. Hope became a reality. Our exile (at least so we thought) was nearing its end.

Two weeks later the young man of the Militia, of whom I have spoken, was on trial at Perpignan with three others. I was summoned as a witness after I had written to the President of the Tribunal to explain what he had done for me. The atmosphere of the court was thick with excitement and hatred for this Militia. I was feeling sick with fear for the life of the young man. I stuck to what I had said in my letter. Out of the four accused, three were given the death penalty and executed; the fourth, my young friend, was given thirty years' solitary confinement, but he only stayed in prison two or three years and was released.

You probably saved his life.

He, first, had probably saved mine. In any case, in those horrible days it was a small comfort to have been able to save one human life.

XI

Hope Frustrated

After the liberation you must have felt you were morally free to start playing again. I know you then received quantities of invitations. Everywhere they thought of you as a great artist who had resisted the seductions as well as the threats of Hitler.

After my voluntary banishment during those years, I started playing abroad again in the hope that I should soon be able to go back to my country as a free citizen. I went to England twice, to Switzerland, and also gave concerts in Paris and other French towns. Unfortunately the duration of this tour was much shorter than I had anticipated.

When you were in Switzerland you received a visit from Don Juan de Bourbon, the pretender to the Spanish throne?

Yes, I was at Staad, and Don Juan's secretary rang me up to say that Don Juan wished to see me. When we began to talk, this grandson of Queen Maria Cristina told me how often his father and grandmother had spoken to him about me. He was very affectionate.

Did he talk to you about Spanish politics?

He asked me what I thought of the Spanish situation and I gave him my sincere opinion. I said that I would not be a party to either a republic or a monarchy, but I would accept the *régime* freely chosen by my country. My adherence to this *régime* would depend on what it did, not on its label.

"I like people who talk to me in this way," he replied. And he added that, out of all the people he had spoken to on the subject recently, those he liked best for their sincerity were two Catalans: a refugee priest in Switzerland and myself.

I also told him that he would have to justify himself to the Spanish people for having offered to support the military revolt when the civil war began. "At that time," he said, "I did not think I could act otherwise."

Did you talk about Catalonia?

Of course. Don Juan said how proud he was to bear, amongst so

219

many titles, that of Count of Barcelona. "My ideal," he said, "is to settle the affairs of Catalonia as the good Catalans wish it."

What was your impression of the Pretender?

He seemed full of sincerity and goodwill. He agreed that a national plebiscite should decide the form of the future *régime* of Spain, and he added that he did not feel inclined to accept any direct offer made by the dictator (Franco). But later on, Don Juan changed his mind: now he does not contemplate a national plebiscite to find out what the Spanish people want; also he has agreed that his eldest son should be brought up in Spain under the auspices of the dictatorial government. So it looks as if Don Juan just obeyed the law of the dictator, and he is not the only one: the governments of most democratic nations are now doing the same.

Furtwängler also came to see you in Switzerland.

Yes. It was just before the collapse of the Nazi *régime*, when Furtwängler lived in Switzerland as a refugee. I did not pretend, and never will, to judge anybody, but neither did I wish to be used as a moral security. Each one to his conscience: such is my principle. Holding out to me a bundle of papers, Furtwängler told me he had protected some Jews, and so on. "It is quite unnecessary for you to give me any explanation," I said, "as I cannot interfere with anything one way or the other." "But I am a musician," he said, "and I want to make music." "Be patient," I said, "and consider yourself lucky that Switzerland has welcomed you."

You know how I admire Furtwängler as a musician and in what terms I talk to you about him. But, personally, I think that the higher the value of an artist, the more responsibility he has for all his actions.

At the time we speak of, I found myself in Paris for a banquet given in my honour at the Ministry of National Education. There I got into an awkward position: when I entered the drawing-room I noticed certain musicians who I knew had not behaved with any dignity or patriotism during the German occupation. I wondered what was the purpose of this banquet. When we reached the dessert I noticed the Secretary was making a sign to the Minister who was sitting next to me. "Do you mean to make a speech now?" I asked. "Of course." "Well, I must ask you not to do it because, if you do, I shall have to answer you, and I would feel obliged to say certain things which would be very disagreeable."

How things have changed in a few years.

They have. But I have not changed and I shall go on thinking that moral principles should prevail today as yesterday, for artists as well as for any mortal being.[1]

When you played in Paris again on November 13th, 1945, it was seven years since you had played there, and when you came away from the Salle Pleyel the Director said to you that he had never had such a demonstration in his Hall before! But if my memory is right, the first concert you played at after the war was in London, in June of the same year?

Yes. I went to London filled with hope and also full of admiration for the heroism and toughness the English had shown during the war, specially in the most difficult moments, when they were alone against Hitler's aggression. When I arrived in England I addressed a tribute to English musicians and the British people, which was published in some musical periodical.

(This message was published by the London Philharmonic Post *in July 1945.)*

"I am very happy to be given the chance to tell not only my colleagues but the English public how I followed with the greatest anxiety all that happened here during these six terrible years. In my Pyrenean retreat I was preoccupied from one hour to another by all the ups and downs you went through in this great country of yours, and I did not attach more importance to the numerous and stirring appeals from political and military chiefs to continue the fight, than to the admirable activities of your first symphonic orchestra and your soloists during these trying days. I know how you travelled from town to town during air raids, keeping alive the performances of great music, and I also realise how through these years of anguish millions of new listeners came to hear the works of the great masters.

"I feel sure that history will keep a record of what England did to keep burning the flame of civilisation during the horrors of war, and I am glad I lived to see that such things are still possible. I was already old when this war began, and I am older still now, but I would like to say that these years were very intense ones for me."

[1] *In 1945, when Casals was presented with the Cross of Grand Officier de la Légion d'Honneur, M. Georges Bidault, who was then Minister for Foreign Affairs in the provisional Government of the French Republic, said:* "You are one of the consciences of our time."

And the memorable concert at the Albert Hall?[1]

I shall never forget the reception I had from the London public.[2]

Yes, this welcome back was very moving, but even more was the demonstration outside when you came out and thousands of people were shouting deliriously.

The enthusiasm of all these people, who had just written one of the most glorious pages in history, moved me so much that I could only say "God Bless You" to them.

I believe you also had a chance to talk to the Catalans through the microphone of the B.B.C.

I had been away from my native land for seven years; now it is more than double that time.

When I arrived at the B.B.C. studio and began to think that after this long tragedy my compatriots would hear my voice, I found it very difficult to hold back my tears—I had to pull myself together to be able to read the pages I had written. Here is a fragment of this message in Catalan. "As I speak to you from the heart of London, my thoughts fly to you all who are listening and those who are on our beloved Catalan soil. When the magic of the waves will carry to you the sound of our old melody *El Cant dels Ocells*, I should like it to convey to you also an echo of the nostalgia felt by all those who are far away from our Land. May this feeling we share, and of which we are proud, make us work together—including those who perhaps hesitated at one time —united as brothers in the same faith, with the hope of a future period of peace, when Catalonia will again be Catalonia."

During these two concert tours you played in Edinburgh, Nottingham, Sheffield, Brighton, Cambridge, Liverpool, Chester, Reading and Chelsea.

[1] "At the age of seventy we find the great Casals perfectly capable of starting the life of a virtuoso with the energy and the ideals of a young man. When he appeared on the platform (the familiar figure and modest attitude, quite bald, not very much taller than the 'cello he was holding), finding his way through the stands of the B.B.C. orchestra, the crowd which filled the Albert Hall stood up to give a vociferous welcome to the man whose name will survive not only because of his artistic prestige but also on account of his symbolising the highest human virtues and resistance against tyranny. . . . He played the Schumann and the Elgar Concertos and, from the first notes, it was clear that he had not lost any of his 'magic'. Casals has succeeded in symbolising the spirit of resistance amongst musicians. The greatness of the artist can only be compared with the greatness of the man. Americans and English wanted to have the honour of bringing him to London by air. In the end the B.E.A. did not allow him to pay for his flight, and the Customs did not inspect his luggage." (*From a London daily paper.*)

[2] *I shall never forget the way Casals played the* Sarabande in C Minor *of Bach as an encore at that concert, which I attended.* (Note of translator, A.M.)

Everywhere the same demonstrations were made by official and private people. It is sufficient to read the English papers of the time to realise what a reception you had in England, and yet when you returned you took a step without precedent in the history of music. The renunciation you undertook must have been the most painful decision of your life! Could you explain to me the reasons which were at the origin of your decision?

As I told you before, I went to England full of hope. I really thought that I was nearing the end of my exile, since the victory of the Allied Nations was logically bound to put an end to the Franco *régime*. But my deception soon began. I read the papers and I talked to some important personalities and I realised that neither in the Government (the Labour Party was then in office) or in the Conservative Party was there any indication that they would decide to get Franco removed. On the contrary, the news and articles published in the Press were rather favourable to the Dictator.

What was going to become of the solemn promises of Churchill to uproot fascism wherever it was? I talked with Ministers, with highly placed Civil Servants, with newspaper editors. I went to the House of Commons many times and insisted on England with the other victorious Nations adhering to the ideas and principles for the defence of which millions of men had given their lives.

Doubts grew in my mind. I could feel my hopes being frustrated. In the middle of all the acclamations and receptions I was constantly thinking of my compatriots, with whom I am jointly responsible. The Spanish people were waiting to be given a chance to say freely what they thought. The best amongst the intellectuals of my country, who had been in exile for years, hoped, as I did, that the victory of the Allied Nations over totalitarian *régimes* meant for them and for thousands and thousands of "refugees" a prompt return to their country. For them there would only be deception at the hands of the victorious powers. In the circumstances, did I have a right to be privileged amongst so many unfortunate people? How could I honestly receive applause and fees from the democratic nations who were ready to abandon us? No, my duty was to protest against this ignominy. The deceit of friends is even more cruel than the attacks of the enemy. All I could do was to retire into silence and seclusion, keeping up my attitude of protest until a just reparation would be granted to my people, who have as much right as others to lead a civilised existence.

After a concert at Reading, I felt I could not go on. I refused to attend a reception given in my honour by the old Association of Musicians in London. It was my first act of renunciation—others followed. Oxford and Cambridge were going to invest me with the honorary titles of the Universities, but I wrote to my friend, Dr. Joseph Trueta of Oxford and my other friend, Roberto Gerhard of Cambridge, and said I would postpone my decision about receiving these honours as long as the attitude of England towards Spain had not changed. I remember giving a last concert in Liverpool.

I cancelled all my engagements in England for the following spring and prepared my return to Prades.

Sir Stafford Cripps sent me a request to come and see him. I answered "No, you would speak about politics and I about morals— we would not understand each other."

I believe you went to Buckingham Palace.

Yes, it was the day before I left London. I had told my dear friend, Myra Hess, that I wished to convey my ideas to the highest quarter. She arranged an interview, and for an hour I talked to the late King George VI's Secretary.

I set forth the Spanish case as clearly as I could, and what I thought was the moral duty of England and of the other Allied Nations—to re-establish a *régime* of freedom and tolerance in Spain. I reminded him that the responsibility was with the Democratic Nations for following the fatal policy of so-called "non-Intervention" adopted during the Spanish Civil War. The Spanish people, I added, would not understand that since the aggressors had been vanquished, they would not be given the chance to become again the masters of their own destiny. The Secretary bowed his head and said he would transmit my report to the King and that my visit had not been in vain.

Next day I left England. When I got back to Prades I found a letter from Myra Hess in which she said that the Secretary had informed the King of my visit and that, immediately, the Queen had sent a messenger to the Piccadilly Hotel asking me to come again to the Palace. Unfortunately, I had gone already!

Having returned to Prades, I thought my protest against the injustice done to my country would have repercussions. The following year, in 1946, I played at some Charity Concerts I had promised to do, the last one in Montpellier, but I declared I would not accept any invitation or engagement from anywhere, as long as a free *régime*, based on the freedom and the will of the people, was not re-established in Spain.

So I closed my own doors. It was the most painful sacrifice an artist could impose on himself.

After Casals had made his decision known, hundreds of letters came from everywhere. Some of the most moving ones would be interesting to reproduce here, if it were not for the added work it entails. Many of those who wrote, while approving of his moral attitude, begged him to reconsider his decision, and to take up his artistic activities again.

"I cannot do it," *said Casals.* "I cannot go back to the countries where I should have to reproach their Governments for the injustice they committed. However worthy might be the intentions of the authorities and the audiences, I could not forget the sad realities of my native land. At least I can now sleep with a clear conscience since I know I have done my duty. If I had not done so, the nights would be constant torture to me."

At that time Casals received some fabulous proposals. Already in 1939, when he wanted to stay in Europe in spite of the threatening war, he had received a blank cheque, on which he was supposed to fill in the figure for a tour of the United States, if he would like to go. He thanked them for their intention and the trust they showed, but he returned the cheque. Amongst the proposals he received there was one of two hundred thousand dollars for concerts in America. They all proved fruitless. In spite of the sacrifice it meant, each proposal was answered in the negative—they have continued during the last seven years, and have not yet ended.

And what does Casals do? People wonder! He leads a very laborious life far from the great cities. The tasks of an instrumentalist and of a composer would already be sufficient to occupy a man like him. Also, there are the pupils. Young 'cellists from America, Japan, France and Mexico, from England or China, Germany or Greece, have all come to find their master in his Pyrenean retreat.

And there are visitors! People of all kinds and conditions knock at the door of the little house now called El Cant dels Ocells, and when they go through the garden gate, accompanied by the barking of "Follett", the faithful dog of the master, they know that the great man is simplicity itself. Of course, there are numerous musicians amongst the callers, from the most well known to the young pupil from a Swiss Conservatoire, who has come by hitch-hiking, and hesitates a long time before knocking at the door.

Also, there are the letters to be answered; they come by the hundreds, from compatriots or not, and Casals spends three or four hours a day dealing with them, very happy when he realises that someone has been helped in their misfortune.

And so the months and the years go by for the artist who has become a recluse. Then came 1950, a celebration year for the second centenary of Bach's birth; and since Casals had decided to shut himself up in Prades, the musicians and music lovers from all over the world joined him there to celebrate together the immortal glory of the great Cantor, an event without precedent in the history of music.

XII

The Prades Festivals

Could you tell us how these Festivals originated?

Yes, at the start are some of my good American friends and, first of all, Alexander Schneider. Already, before 1950 when the first Festival took place, I had received a cable in which many of the intellectuals living in America, headed by Albert Einstein, said they considered it essential for me to come to America. Then many personal requests came: Mrs. Sprague Coolidge, Stokowski and Ormandy, who wrote individually as well as for the musicians of their orchestras.[1]

I refused. Alexander Schneider wrote to say he was coming to Prades to offer me all I could wish in order to give a series of concerts in his country. He arrived, and we spent a few days together making music and talking at great length. He had come with the definite idea of convincing me, and he named some astronomical fees. "It is not a question of money," I said, "it is purely a moral question."

When he realised that I definitely refused the offer, Schneider ventured to say: "You cannot condemn your art to silence. Since you don't wish to leave Prades, would you allow us to come here, a group of musicians, and give concerts with you? It so happens that next year is the bicentenary of Bach's birth, and it would be a fitting occasion to do it." I thought it over for a bit and felt that what he was offering me was in line with my attitude. So I accepted the offer and thanked Schneider for the very touching consideration he and his friends showed me.

The description of Prades in the Larousse Dictionary is as follows: "Prades (Latin Prata), Chef-lieu d'arrondissement des Pyrenees

[1] *In 1948 Casals received from America a complete edition of Bach's works published from the photo-lithographed reproduction of the Bach-Gesellschaft edition. On the inside of the first volume one can read the following dedication: "To Pablo Casals. From a few of his friends, colleagues and fervent followers who wish to present this modest token of their affection, veneration, admiration and gratitude. Signed by Ernst Bloch, Arturo Toscanini, Paul Hindemith, Bruno Walter, Jascha Heifetz, Arthur Rubinstein, Wanda Landowska, Arthur Schnabel, Rudolf Serkin, Serge Kousevitzky, Dimitri Mitropoulos, Gregor Piatigorsky, Alexander Schneider, etc."*

Orientales, 41 kilometres from Perpignan, on the Tét, in the fertile plain of the Conflent at the foot of the Canigou (one of the high peaks of the Pyrenees range); 4,170 inhabitants."

It is in this small town that the Festival has taken place in the last four years, and where the following artists have appeared: Serkin, Stern, Szigeti, Myra Hess, Clara Haskil, William Primrose, Marcel Dupré, Alex Schneider, Milton Katims, Horzowski, Istomin, Marini, Grumiaux, Maria Slader, Tortelier, Tabuteau, Wummer, Mannes, William Kapell, Jennie Tourel, Yvonne Lefebure, Joseph Fuchs, Cahuzac, Doda Conrad, Paul Baumgartner, Milton Thomas, Bernard Goldberg, etc.

The audiences have been made up of amateurs and professionals from all European countries and from both Americas, and also of Chinese, Japanese, Hindus, Turks, Israelis, Australians, Syrians, Javanese, South Africans. There is an atmosphere of fervour at these concerts, the fervour Casals had in his youth and which made him transform a café into a concert hall, and a concert hall into a temple.

The first Festival in 1950, dedicated to Bach, was rehearsed for about six weeks, and in the course of thirteen concerts the six Brandenburg Concerti were played and conducted by Casals, the Six Suites for Solo 'Cello were played by him, and also the Clavier and Violin Concerti. He was seventy-three then and he never neglected a minute of rehearsal on account of his age.

The concerts took place in the parish church of the little town and began on June 2nd, in the evening. There was a tremendous audience but no applause for three weeks, until after the last Cantata, when the Bishops of Saint Flour and of Perpignan gave the signal to applaud and it lasted over twenty minutes!

The 1951 Festival took place in the great courtyard of the Palace of the Majorca and Perpignan Kings, in Perpignan. But in 1952 and 1953 they took place in the marvellous abbey of St. Michel de Cuxa, two kilometres outside Prades, and those who had the privilege of being there will never forget it. The splendour of the building, dating from the Xth century, made an unforgettable setting for such music.

XIII

Grandeur and Solitude

Although Casals' exile continues invitations keep on arriving and, as has been said before, the refusals give him a painful feeling of renunciation. Fairly recently he had to decline the invitation to conduct a concert in Liège on the occasion of the transfer of Ysaye's heart to the Liège Conservatoire; also to conduct the St. Matthew Passion *in Zürich; then a concert in Paris to celebrate the centenary of François Arago; he was asked to take part in the B.B.C.'s London commemoration of Dvořák's centenary, to conduct a festival "like the Prades one" at Hollywood, to conduct the London Symphony Orchestra for its golden jubilee, to give a concert at the Château de Versailles at the invitation of the President Albert Sarrault.*

When he was asked to go to Liège for the Ysaye ceremony his first reaction was to accept, but after, he had to decline. "No, I cannot! There should not be an exception in my attitude, otherwise the situation would become impossible. Oh dear, how painful it is to have to say 'No' sometimes!"

If Casals had not chosen the "Voice of Silence" the concerts he could give now would constitute an apotheosis. If he appeared on a platform now this little old man who, fifty years ago, was already considered one of the greatest artists in the world, would raise the frenzied enthusiasm of his audiences, and it may be that no other artist would have known, now or in the past, such a glorious twilight.

However, inside the four walls of this little room (which we described in the Preface) there is another glory, a silent one which every day awaits our great musician—that of a man who, without thinking of the "transcendent immortality of the artist" of which Renan speaks, spends his time in helping, comforting and encouraging the unfortunates who come to him.

We have already referred to the time it takes him to deal with his correspondence (in 1951 when he came back from Switzerland, where he had been for a month and a half, the Prades postman handed to him a packet containing 665 letters!). Of course, a number of these letters come from well-known people, but hundreds are from unfortunates who ask for help, advice or a favour. If one could see, as I have, the patience and the perseverance of Casals when it is a question of helping even an unknown person, and his joy when he can give a favourable reply!

During the 1953 Festival an eminent musician advised him to postpone reading his letters (they were piling up on the table). "You are very tired." "It is true," *said Casals,* "but there may be someone in distress who cries for help and has pinned his faint hopes on me. That is more important than all the Festivals, I think." *One day he confided in me alone and said,* "I receive such proofs of affection, and in this room how often I shed tears with a letter in my hand."

Another day Casals would say: "Important people and delegates often come to ask me to join some governing body or political group. I have always refused and I don't intend to depart from the line I have taken. Alone, I possess a moral independence which I would not have if I acted differently. I am not a politician; as I have said, and I shall always repeat, I am an artist who wishes to keep faith with human principles."

Here we are in the little room. Someone knocks at the door downstairs. It is an American girl. "I came to Europe to see you," *she said to Casals.* "After, I shall go to Africa to see Dr. Schweitzer. Then I shall return to the United States."

Two Benedictine brothers from Montserrat spent a few days in Prades and discussed musical matters with Casals for a long time. Later he received a letter from them saying that when they got back "all Montserrat gathered together and everyone, from the Father Superior to the young choir boys, enquired after you". "In Montserrat," *said Casals,* "they never ceased to sing my compositions even in the darkest days."

In 1952 Casals received from Belgium an album filled with signatures from people waiting to testify their admiration on the occasion of his seventy-fifth birthday (which took place on December 29th, 1951). On the first page there was a very affectionate message from Queen Elisabeth. Her daughter, the ex-Queen Marie-José of Italy, came to Prades soon after the end of the 1951 Festival, when Casals and Serkin played a Beethoven Sonata for her. Soon after this she wrote to Casals saying "Have courage, dear friend. I also know what exile means."

In 1952, also, Casals received an album with hundreds of signatures from Japanese music-lovers. There was only one photograph of a concert given in Tokio (the men on one side and the women on the other), with the discs of the Prades Bach Festival. The pages of the album were classified by towns in Japan. At the top of one page was the name "Hiroshima". Underneath there were untidy signatures, obviously from little children. At the bottom there was an inscription in Japanese and English which said, "We were born after the time of the Hiroshima atom bomb and already we are admirers of your great art."

We have already mentioned that in September 1951 Casals went to Zürich to conduct a concert on the occasion of his seventy-fifth birthday. Some hundred and twenty 'cellists from all countries took part in the concert. One had never seen such a number of 'cellists in an orchestra before! Tickets were sold out two days after the announcement, and some people paid as much as ten times their value to the retailers who had bought them as a speculation.

We had also mentioned that Schweitzer, who was staying at Gunsbach, at the time, came to the Zürich concert. One of the items on the programme, played by all the 'cellists, was Les Rois Mages, *a fragment of Casals' unpublished composition* Oratorio del Pessebre. *Dr. Schweitzer told Casals that what he had just heard belonged to the great music of all time.*

There is a photograph hanging on the wall, in which we see the hermit of Lambarene and the hermit of Prades looking very pensive. "This photograph was taken at Zürich at the time of this concert?" "Yes: after the concert we went to a reception where Schweitzer took me apart, and said he wanted to speak to me, and it was during this conversation that my great friend said 'It is better to create than to protest!' 'And why not do both,' I answered. 'The Prades Festivals have the double character of creation and protest, and further, protest can be the most arduous creation and the most exacting.' 'In any case,' said Schweitzer, 'I accept everything you do since I know the moral motives which inspire you.' I explained to him the real reasons of my protest, and then we both remained silent, deep in thought, and without our noticing it someone must have taken this photograph of us which I treasure particularly."

In the summer of 1952 Casals went to Zermatt to give lectures on the interpretation of Bach. The profits of these lectures and those of the preceding concert in Zürich were used for the construction of a Spanish Pavilion at the

Pestalozzi Institute of Switzerland. Casals was looking forward to the pleasure of talking with the Alpine guides. "What men they are and what devotion they practise." *They gave him a tremendous welcome and conferred on him the title of* First honorary guide of Zermatt. *Here is the text of the official diploma which they presented to him:* "Homage to Pablo Casals". *(Casals thanked them by giving them a private recital.)* "*In the year 1952 the Corporation of the Zermatt guides, through its President, has conferred on Pablo Casals the title of* Honorary Guide of Zermatt. *Through this distinction it wishes to prove its gratitude to a Master of universal reputation, who has given to this little place a special lustre by holding this musical course. Pablo Casals has thus shown to all artists the inspiration to be found in our mountains. He has been the guide* par excellence, *who leads to the highest summits. We are proud to add him to our membership.*" *The artists who attended this music course were from Switzerland, America, Germany, England, Italy, Greece, Japan, Mexico, Argentine, etc. Here is a letter written by an Italian 'cellist, which he sent to Casals, and which shows that the atmosphere of the course was better than any description of it:* "Days go by, the spark which you have lit seems gradually to take hold of all our ideas, feelings and work. Everything seems a pleasure, everything is alive. What we thought had nearly achieved a definite shape has acquired new meaning; the humblest problems of the 'cello from general principles to the smallest details of this performance. With an instrument like the 'cello, or with a prayer, or by any other means, beauty can be evoked. This conviction, this faith, must be continually with us, even if, as it sometimes happens, a feeling of solitude and shortcoming takes hold of us, and if, when we play, we almost get to hate the sound of our instrument. You have given us the strength to fight against this solitude—you have given us the joy of a Victory, a joy which we had lost and has been born again."*

In December 1953 Mr. Roger Nordman, General Secretary of the Chaîne du Bonheur Internationale, *wrote to Casals to ask his participation in his work for charity.* "In the name of the Broadcasting organisations of Switzerland, France, Italy, Germany, Austria, Belgium, Holland, Trieste and Saarbrücken, we ask you to do us the great honour of playing for four or five minutes and making an appeal for children, in Catalan, to the millions of Europeans who will be listening to you."*

The broadcasting of this Chaîne du Bonheur Internationale, *which is given in Lausanne every year before Christmas, is the only one re-transmitted simultaneously by a group of European stations. Casals accepted the invitation after he had made sure that Spanish children would get their share of gifts.*

The technical service of the French Radio came to Prades on Sunday, December 20th, to record Casals' appeal and his performance of Bach's Pastorale *for Organ and the Carol from the Catalan Folk-tune* El Cant dels Ocells.

From his little room, on the evening of December 22nd, Casals listened to the broadcast. As the last notes of the Catalan carol faded out he heard the announcers one after the other: "This is Lausanne. The bells of our City will now be rung to thank you, Pablo Casals. . . . This is Rome, the bells of our City will now be rung to thank you, Pablo Casals. . . . This is Paris. . . . This is Vienna. . . . This is Brussels. . . . This is Hamburg. . . ."

The American writer, Max Eastman, has said of Pablo Casals: "No other man has been able to combine in this way musical genius with moral stature. This stature received a touching tribute that evening."

Sometimes Casals will say to an intimate friend, "I will show you my treasures." *He then opens a large and beautiful box, inlaid with ivory, which once belonged to Franciso Pizarro, the conqueror of Peru. First he brings out a small piece of parchment with a few notes traced on the stave.* "From Beethoven, with his own hand," *he says.* "The very first sketch of the beginning of the IX Symphony, a gift from my friend U. Bodmer of Zürich. One does not find these notes in the Symphony, we all know. Nevertheless it sets out the primary idea of an immortal work." *Then he brings out an autographed letter of Beethoven, the manuscript of a Mozart quartet, one of a Brahms quartet, and so on.* "All these," *he said,* "and all the musical treasures, pictures and documents I have at Sant Salvador, as well as my house, I shall present to my country."

Casals enjoys remarkable health, and is astonishingly vigorous for his age, but we have not forgotten what he said one day when he didn't feel well. "I am now prepared for everything! Nothing that happens will surprise me. The pursuit of music and love for my neighbours have been inseparable with me, and if the first has given me the purest and most exalted joys, the second has brought me peace of mind, even in the saddest moments of my life. I am every day more convinced that the mainspring of any important human enterprise must be moral strength and generosity."

INDEX